WELCOME

ABOVE: Mustang ace Major Urban Drew flew the P-51D nicknamed *Detroit Miss* with the 375th Fighter Squadron. Creative Commons Martin Čížek via Wikipedia

The story of the North American P-51 Mustang is like no other in the history of military aviation. Historians and aviation enthusiasts agree that the Mustang is the most celebrated fighter aircraft of World War Two. Its combat record remains one of courage, sacrifice, and of victory as embodied in the saga of the intrepid men who flew it. Welcome! In these pages, the P-51 comes alive. Incredible stories of men and missions offer a compelling read.

During the course of World War Two, Mustang pilots were credited with the destruction of nearly 5,000 German, Italian and Japanese aircraft, while 2,520 were lost to enemy action, accidents, or other damage. The P-51, therefore, stands as one of the finest combat aircraft ever flown and may arguably claim its place among the war winning weapons of the conflict.

At the height of World War Two, US President Harry S Truman had authorised a US Senate War Investigating Committee, and its 1944 conclusion as to the value of the P-51 Mustang was succinct, stating that it was 'the most aerodynamically perfect pursuit plane in existence'.

Few could argue that point.

The Mustang was first an example of American ingenuity and dedication to the task. James H 'Dutch' Kindelberger, the president of North American Aviation, promised a high performance fighter-bomber and reconnaissance aircraft for his British customers, and though the company had never produced a fighter before, his design team, led by Edgar Schmued and Lee Atwood, delivered – in an astonishing 117 days.

When Rolls-Royce test pilot Ronald Harker flew the Mustang for the first time, he understood its superb qualities in the fighter-bomber and reconnaissance roles, but also realised that the new airframe's full potential had yet to be realised. When he suggested that the two-stage supercharged Merlin 60 series engine would make the Mustang a formidable high-altitude fighter, the result was transcendent.

The P-51's progress came about through the marriage of Allied ingenuity and example of co-operation, an American airframe with British engine that would be licence-built by the US Packard Motor Car Company of Detroit, Michigan. Sources also indicate that the two-stage supercharger had its origins in France, extending the vital bridge of co-operation.

The Merlin-powered Mustang's performance was dazzling during assessment and later, where it counted most, in combat. The P-51 performed its assigned tasks with spirit and efficiency, first with the Royal Air Force and then with American air forces around the globe. The turning point in the air war in Europe occurred when the Mustang's great range with external

LEFT: General Jimmy Doolittle, commanding the US Eighth Air Force, unleashed the offensive prowess of the P-51 Mustang fighter. Public Domain

drop tanks allowed fighters to escort heavy bombers of the US Eighth Air Force on long distance raids against targets deep inside Germany, defending against the vaunted fighter pilots of the Nazi Luftwaffe intent on shredding the bomber formations.

Then, when General Jimmy Doolittle took command of the Eighth Air Force and introduced a new fighter tactic, the Mustang, and its fellow US fighter types, the Lockheed P-38 Lightning and Republic P-47 Thunderbolt, joined by the intrepid pilots of the RAF and their superb Supermarine Spitfire, had become the executioners of the Luftwaffe. In particular, the Mustang pilots were ordered to sweep beyond the heavy bomber formations. Doolittle saw the fighter as an offensive weapon, unleashing his most formidable greyhounds of the sky, and the Mustang became a hunter-killer.

The P-51 racked up an impressive score against the Germans, and the enemy was defeated through attrition. There simply were not enough experienced Luftwaffe pilots to contest air supremacy over Europe. From start to finish, the P-51 Mustang was innovative, a machine that matched the mettle of the men who flew it. Welcome to this tribute to an iconic military aircraft.

LEFT: Caught in gun camera footage, a German Focke Wulf Fw-190 fighter breaks apart under the machine-gun fire of a US fighter plane. Public Domain

MAIN COVER IMAGE: A P-51D Mustang presented in the colours of the *Frances Dell* as flown by Lieutenant Clark Clemons of the 84th Fighter Squadron during World War Two. Darren Harbar Photography

CONTENTS

Mustang pilots of the 359th Fighter Group arrive on the runway as they prepare for an escort mission. Public Domain

Gun camera footage from an American Mustang catches a German pilot baling out of his stricken Focke Wulf Fw-190 fighter in January 1945. Public Domain

Lieutenant Thomas V Thain stands before his P-51D Mustang nicknamed *Sweet and Lovely* at RAF Duxford in 1944. Public Domain

This North American P-51B nicknamed *Shoo Shoo Baby* was lost in a mid-air collision with another Mustang in February 1945. Public Domain

A P-51 Mustang flies during an air show and exhibits the sleek airframe and raw power that made it famous. Creative Commons John Bauld via Wikipedia

Two P-51A Mustangs of 1st Air Commando fly in the China-Burma-India theatre. Public Domain

ISBN: 978 1 80282 846 7
Editor: Mike Haskew
Senior editor, specials: Roger Mortimer
Email: roger.mortimer@keypublishing.com
Cover Design: Steve Donovan
Design: SJmagic DESIGN SERVICES, India
Advertising Sales Manager: Brodie Baxter
Email: brodie.baxter@keypublishing.com
Tel: 01780 755131
Advertising Production: Becky Antoniades
Email: Rebecca.antoniades@keypublishing.com

SUBSCRIPTION/MAIL ORDER
Key Publishing Ltd, PO Box 300, Stamford, Lincs, PE9 1NA
Tel: 01780 480404
Subscriptions email: subs@keypublishing.com

Mail Order email: orders@keypublishing.com
Website: www.keypublishing.com/shop

PUBLISHING
Group CEO and Publisher: Adrian Cox
Published by
Key Publishing Ltd, PO Box 100, Stamford, Lincs, PE9 1XQ
Tel: 01780 755131 Website: www.keypublishing.com

PRINTING
Precision Colour Printing Ltd, Haldane, Halesfield 1, Telford, Shropshire. TF7 4QQ

DISTRIBUTION
Seymour Distribution Ltd, 2 Poultry Avenue, London, EC1A 9PU
Enquiries Line: 02074 294000.

FIGHTER CONCEPT

From the time that the era of manned flight began in the early 20th century, it was no great leap to find its application in a new dimension of warfare. Astonishingly, in less than half a century, the aircraft evolved from crude contraptions of wood and wire clawing aloft at the whim of the prevailing winds to the metal machines that streaked across the skies in apparent defiance of physical limitations.

Advances in technology have, on a historical basis, often found their way into the waging of war, but it may well be argued that none had such an impact on the conventional aspects of battle than the introduction of the aircraft. By the outbreak of World War Two in 1939, the world's great powers had acknowledged the influence of air power on the outcome of a conflict. They had seen the progress of the air battle from one of opponents pointing pistols and rifles at one another while conducting reconnaissance missions during World War One to one of deadly, earnest business.

Weapons were fitted to aircraft and then a natural progression followed. Machine guns, some even firing forwards through a propeller in synchronisation, made

the aircraft a deadly weapon. And in the crucible of war, the fighter plane was born. Its raison d'etre evolved right alongside. Control of the air became a critical element in the successful prosecution of battle on the ground and at sea, while it also ushered in the haunting spectre of great armadas of heavy bombers laying waste the cities and industrial infrastructure of enemies. Truthfully, one observer admitted that in the 1930s, the threat of heavy strategic bombing was viewed largely with the same trepidation as that of a modern nuclear exchange.

The fighter plane, therefore, would be instrumental in the outcome of any conflict – in victory or defeat. The power that controlled the air also dictated the successful implementation of strategic bombing, as well as tactical ground attack against enemy troop concentrations, supply convoys, strongpoints, and even armoured vehicles. The fighter that reigned supreme paved the way for these other aspects of warfare to play out, and air superiority became a prerequisite to other operations, even though there were hard lessons to be learned regarding bomber survivability.

A generation after the open cockpit, wood, canvas, and wire fighter planes of World War One had introduced civilisation to the concept of aerial warfare, the fighter planes of World War Two became legendary. Enclosed cockpits, heavy armament, and sheer speed made the fighters, both Allied and Axis, efficient killing machines. And quite probably the very best of those driven by piston engines was the North American P-51 Mustang. Sleek, agile, and speedy, the Mustang served in all theatres of World War Two and most significantly wrested mastery of the skies over Europe from the Nazi Luftwaffe.

The Mustang and its skilled pilots played a key role in escorting heavy bombers of the US Army Air Forces on raids deep into the heart of the Third Reich, while also engaging German fighter pilots in single combat. The P-51 proved itself a war winner, introduced at the critical moment in the air campaign. On the cusp of the Jet Age, the Mustang's performance set it apart in translating the foremost mission of the fighter plane – air superiority – from theory into practice.

JAMES H 'DUTCH' KINDELBERGER

When James H 'Dutch' Kindelberger put the reputation of North American Aviation on the line with the commitment to a new fighter design that would become the P-51 Mustang, the most successful fighter aircraft of World War Two, he was no stranger to risk taking.

Kindelberger became the chief executive of North American in 1934. At the time, it had only one order for a single passenger aircraft on its books. After joining the manufacturing division, he quickly rose to take charge of the company and energised its development efforts. After learning that the US Army Air Corps was looking for a new trainer, he capitalised on North America's capabilities to deliver in just three months the prototype of the BT-9, from design to construction and test flight, leading to a $1m contract to produce the aircraft that became the famed T-6 Texan.

A self-made man and aviation legend, Kindelberger had been in the business since 1920. Born in Wheeling, West Virginia, on May 8, 1895, he was the son of a steelworker. He dropped out of high school in the 10th grade to go to work as an apprentice in his father's occupation but continued his education through correspondence courses. During World War One, he enlisted in the US Army and learned to fly. He then served with the fledgling Aviation Section of the Army Signal Corps, primarily as a flight instructor at Park Field in Memphis, Tennessee. He became a friend of future military air power titans Henry 'Hap' Arnold and Billy Mitchell.

Arnold went on to become a five-star general and led American air forces during World War Two. Mitchell became a lightning rod with his advocacy of air power between the world wars. He was court martialled for his stance but was later vindicated as aerial warfare became a dominating aspect of the 1939-1945 conflict. Kindelberger, meanwhile, received his high school diploma through an equivalency examination and studied engineering at the Carnegie Institute of Technology in Pittsburgh, Pennsylvania.

Dutch's big break in the aviation industry came in 1920 when he was hired by the Glenn L Martin Company in Cleveland, Ohio, as its chief draftsman and assistant chief engineer. Five years later, he left Martin to accept a position with the Douglas Aircraft Company in California and worked directly with its head, Donald Douglas, who recognised the young engineer's talent.

Kindelberger advanced rapidly at Douglas and was heavily involved in the design of the MB-2 bomber, which Mitchell used in a famous demonstration of bombing capability in the sinking of an obsolete battleship in the 1920s. After working

as chief draftsman and assistant chief engineer, Kindelberger rose to vice-president of engineering at Douglas by 1928 and became a key contributor to the development of the DC-1 and DC-2 transport aircraft, forerunners of the famous DC-3 that became a huge success. The military version of the DC-3 became a legend as the C47 Skytrain during World War Two.

During his nine years with Douglas and particularly as the DC series was developed, Kindelberger forged a lifelong friendship with fellow engineer J L 'Lee' Atwood. When an opportunity with General Aviation, soon to be renamed North American Aviation, came along in 1934, Donald Douglas wished both Kindelberger and Atwood well as they took positions with the company. Kindelberger became North American president and general manager, while Atwood took over as chief engineer.

Likelihood of war

In the autumn of 1940, as the probability of American entry into World War Two increased, President Franklin D Roosevelt called upon the US aviation industry to produce 50,000 military planes annually. It was a staggering number. When Donald Douglas called a meeting of fellow aircraft producers in Santa Monica, California, a consensus »

LEFT: Donald Douglas founded his famous aircraft company in 1921 and promoted Dutch Kindelberger. Creative Commons Los Angeles Times via Wikipedia

FAR LEFT: James H. 'Dutch' Kindelberger led North American Aviation for 28 years. No Restrictions via Wikipedia

LEFT: John Leland 'Lee' Atwood was an outstanding aeronautical engineer and close associate of Dutch Kindelberger. No Restrictions via Wikipedia

was achieved to work together in the interest of the nation and the Allied cause. With the formation of the Aircraft War Production Council, Kindelberger was made president on the recommendation of none other than Douglas.

In the spirit of co-operation during extraordinary times, Dutch worked with his old friend General Arnold and helped to keep raw materials available in sufficient quantities, while also sharing information on production efficiencies with companies that would ordinarily have been direct competitors. His experience was key in assisting Ford Motor Company to transition from manufacturing automobiles to aircraft and in bringing the famed Willow Run factory outside Detroit, Michigan, online to produce the Consolidate B-24 Liberator heavy bomber.

The saga of the P-51 Mustang's development unfolded in due course, with Great Britain at war with Nazi Germany and heavily dependent on American industrial might for the supplies and materiel necessary to fight the Third Reich.

Another major North American Aviation contribution to the Allied victory in World War Two was the design and development of the twin-engine B-25 Mitchell medium bomber. More than 9,800 were built during the war years, and Kindelberger named the bomber in honour of his friend Billy Mitchell. He also worked closely with Lieutenant Colonel and future General James H 'Jimmy' Doolittle to prepare a squadron of B-25s, land-based bombers, for take-off from an aircraft carrier.

Doolittle's squadron of B-25s then executed an audacious raid on the Japanese capital of Tokyo on April 18, 1942, taking off from the pitching deck of the aircraft carrier USS *Hornet*. The Doolittle Raid sealed the place of the B-25 and North American Aviation in the annals of aerial warfare.

During World War Two, North American Aviation produced a total of 42,000 aircraft for the Allies. Remarkably, the company manufactured trainers, bombers, and fighters virtually at the same time. This feat was largely accomplished through techniques of mass production and efficiencies developed by Kindelberger himself.

As chairman of the board and chief executive officer of North American by 1948, he had always understood that hard work was essential to success. He once famously quipped: "You cannot pull a rabbit out of the hat unless you carefully put a rabbit in the hat beforehand!"

Kindelberger led the company in the development of the F-86 Sabre, the premier US fighter aircraft of the Korean War era. He further advocated advances in technology and engineering as the company ventured from propeller-driven aircraft to jet and rocket propulsion as well. He was at the forefront of the development of the famous hypersonic, rocket-powered X-15, and North American became a primary contractor for the burgeoning US space programme.

When Kindelberger retired from daily operations at North American in 1960, he was succeeded by his long-time associate Atwood as chief executive but retained the title of board chairman. When he died two years later of congestive heart failure aged 67, Dutch Kindelberger had spent 46 years in the aviation industry. He had led North American Aviation for 28 years, and the company survives today as a division of the Boeing Company.

In recognition of his achievements, Kindelberger was inducted into the National Aviation Hall of Fame in 1972 and the International Aerospace Hall of Fame in 1977. He was featured in the Public Broadcasting System 2006 documentary 'Pioneers in Aviation: The Race to the Moon'. His contribution to the aviation industry was immeasurable, and certainly among the greatest was his pledge to develop the aircraft that became the legendary P-51 Mustang during the most difficult days of World War Two.

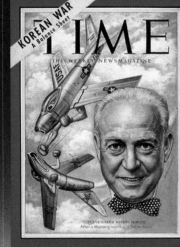

MUSTANG DESIGN AND SPECIFICATIONS

The North American P-51 Mustang fighter, the most famous combat aircraft in the history of the US Air Force and its predecessors, was the product of an ally's prescience as war threatened to engulf Europe for the second time in the first half of the 20th century.

In 1938, the British military establishment was under no illusions as to the intent of Nazi Germany, even after Prime Minister Neville Chamberlain returned from a summit at Munich waving a single signature page and proclaiming: 'Peace in our time'. Fully comprehending that Britain's own production of military aircraft would not be sufficient to successfully fight another major war with Germany, military men, diplomats, and industrialists established the British Air Purchasing Commission.

The commission's overtures met with success, and a contract for 1,740 Curtiss P-40 Tomahawk fighters was concluded along with completed negotiations with North American Aviation of Inglewood, California, for 200 T-6 Texan trainers, known to the British as the Harvard. Soon enough, Britain was at war with Nazi Germany, and the British commission returned to its New York offices in early 1940. By then, it was apparent that Curtiss could not deliver the full complement of P-40s until late in that year. The situation, however, was urgent. New fighter planes were needed immediately.

When the British remembered they had made an earlier deal with

ABOVE: The prototype NA-73 led to the production model on the P-51 Mustang fighter. Public Domain

LEFT: This P-51D Mustang is the last original aircraft of the 352nd Fighter Group known to exist. Public Domain

North American and were pleased with the results, they approached the company's president, James H 'Dutch' Kindelberger, with the proposition that North American produce P-40s under licence from Curtiss. Kindelberger was taken aback by the overture, but North American representatives spent some time in early 1940 discussing British specifications. After some thought, Kindelberger approached his chief designer, Edgar Schmued, in March of that year.

When the president posed the question of licensed P-40 production to Schmued, the response was direct. "Well, Dutch," Schmued offered, "don't let us build an obsolete plane. Let's build a new one. We can design and build a better one."

Kindelberger went back to the British, confident in the ability of his design team. Some accounts purport that a rough drawing of a completely new fighter was already in his hands. It was the first North American attempt to design a »

LEFT: This restored P-51C is shown in the markings of the 332nd Fighter Group, the famous Red Tails. Creative Commons Max Haynes via Wikipedia

high-performance fighter plane, but Kindelberger promised that a flyable prototype would be developed rapidly. The British issued a letter of intent on April 10, 1940, and offered eight months for its delivery, but Kindelberger told his design team it had 120 days. On May 29, 1940, the contract for 320 planes, designated the NA-73, was signed.

Single caveat

The British did insist on one caveat. They wanted North American to purchase the wind tunnel data on the latest Curtiss updated fighter, the XP-46. John Leland 'Lee' Atwood, vice-president of North American, went to Curtiss to secure the information and paid $56,000 for it. The final design of the NA-73 resembled the look of the XP-46, but North American officials declined to credit the Curtiss aircraft with any substantial influence. The NA-73 was already expected to outperform the XP-46, which had a top speed of 355mph at 12,000ft.

Schmued and North American chief engineer Ray Rice led a herculean effort that brought the prototype from concept to reality in four months. The design team worked day and night, and some observers noted that the determined group went home 'early' only on Sundays – and that was at 6pm.

The investment of 78,000 man-hours and 102 days of labour produced the NA-73X without an engine. Three weeks later, the Allison V-1710-39 powerplant arrived. It was the same Allison engine that powered the P-40, but unexpected modifications had to be made – and fast. A new motor mount compatible with the engine's electrical system was hastily constructed.

The prototype design was completed in roughly 117 days, and on October 26, 1940, the NA-73 took to the air for the first time. Contract test pilot Vance Breese made the historic flight, and several others that followed. After about three hours at the controls, Breese gave a favourable report on the plane's characteristics and performance. The British also liked what they saw, increasing their initial order by 300 planes. North American later changed its designation to the XP-51, and on December 9, 1940, the British Air Purchasing Commission addressed a letter to North American advising that they had officially named the NA-73 the Mustang.

On November 20, 1940, test pilot Paul Balfour strapped into the cockpit of the prototype, apparently exhibiting something of a nonchalant approach that morning and choosing to forego the standard pre-flight check procedures. Shortly after take-off, the Allison engine failed. Without power, Balfour attempted vainly to reach the airfield. Realising that he would come up short, the pilot put the landing gear down and crunched into a freshly ploughed field. As the main wheels dug into the soft ground, the plane flipped completely over. Balfour walked away from the crash, but the aircraft was extensively damaged. Repairs were begun immediately, but the plane did not take to the sky again until January 13, 1941.

Inquiries as to the problem with the Allison engine indicated that Balfour, in his haste, had possibly omitted a change in fuel selector and cut off the fuel supply, but there is ample evidence that the plane was not fully fuelled by ground crewmen, leaving one of its tanks virtually empty. The ground crew may have failed to fuel the tanks as instructed, and Balfour may have selected the near-empty tank. Regardless, he was transferred to the testing programme for the B-25 Mitchell medium bomber after the incident. He was killed in the North American test flight of a modified Mitchell on November 10, 1951. Another possible explanation was a design flaw, which placed the air intake scoop too far behind the aircraft's nose, which tended to cut off airflow at high angles,

causing the engine to shut down. This problem was corrected later when North American engineers moved the scoop as far forward as possible.

Several innovations

Although it shared the Allison engine with the P-40 and other aircraft types, the NA-73 was built to include several innovations such as a minimal fuselage cross-section, tightly cowled engine, and low-profile canopy. Each of these would reduce drag, but more remarkable features would enhance that reduction even further.

The NA-73 would be constructed with the new laminar flow wing. Conventional wings of the day included the thickest cross-section roughly one-fifth of the way across the wing from its leading edge with most of the camber on top. The

new laminar flow wing relocated the maximum thickness well aft, with almost the same camber on the bottom and top. The result was a 20 per cent reduction in drag.

The design of the radiator was also modified to a position beneath the rear of the fuselage for the smallest cross-section possible. Atwood, an expert engineer, was instrumental in the repositioning, which achieved excellent cooling while virtually eliminating drag.

Further speed enhancement was achieved through maximising the so-called 'Meredith Effect', which took advantage of the heated air exiting the radiator for additional propulsion.

The British designated the first production model the Mustang I, and the initial aircraft with serial number AG345 was flown by pilot Bob Chilton on April 23, 1941. He took the plane up several times during the next month. He also piloted the second production aircraft, and by late summer, the Mustang was ready to deliver to Britain. In

Edgar Schmued

October 1941, the first Mustangs were offloaded from ships at Liverpool, and further evaluations confirmed a fine performance at low to medium altitudes. By the end of the year, 138 Mustangs had been delivered to the RAF, and its pilots offered positive appraisals of the new aircraft. The Mustang flew under the auspices of the RAF Army Co-operation Command, and soon 14 squadrons were operating the plane in a reconnaissance role with ground support and fighter capabilities.

The US Army approved the design for export but required that two planes remain with it for evaluation. An order was subsequently placed for 150 planes to fulfil a commitment to the Royal Air Force through the Lend Lease programme, but the USAAF was slow to consider the Mustang for its own use.

The first official US Army Air Forces order for 310 P-51A models was not placed until June 1942, but room in the annual budget for that year allowed funding of a new dive bomber, and an order had been placed for 500 A-36s, the ground attack and dive bomber variant, in April of that year. The circumstance surrounding the slow walk of the P-51A was probably since commitments had already been made to continuing procurement of the P-40 and agreements to purchase the Republic P-47 Thunderbolt and the Lockheed P-38 Lightning fighters. However, the situation changed with the Japanese attack on Pearl Harbor on December 7, 1941, and US entry into World War Two as a need arose for greater numbers of fighter aircraft in the Pacific.

Meanwhile, North American had geared up for production.

Kindelberger had visited German manufacturing facilities belonging to Messerschmitt and Heinkel in 1938 and studied their methods for the best production tips he could distil. He also had some ideas of his own, and the mixture of these yielded superb results. Numbers steadily climbed to more than 850 Mustangs per month at peak levels, and more than 15,000 were built in all types between 1940 and the end of World War Two.

Capable fighter

The P-51A, designated the Mustang II by the British, was a capable fighter aircraft, and 50 were delivered to the British by the end of 1942. However, the performance of the Allison engine was greatly diminished at altitudes above 20,000ft. In a stroke of genius, though, the P-51 airframe was paired with the two-stage supercharged Rolls-Royce Merlin engine. The results produced the most outstanding high-altitude fighter of the war. And finally, the USAAF establishment realised that it had the aircraft that could fulfil the requirements of a high-altitude escort for heavy bomber formations that were previously being decimated by Luftwaffe fighters during raids over Nazi-occupied Europe. With external fuel drop tanks, the range of later models extended beyond 1,600 miles.

General Henry 'Hap' Arnold, a long-time advocate of the maxim that the 'bombers will always get through' had relied on the heavily armed Boeing B-17 Flying Fortress and Consolidated B-24 Liberator formations being able to defend themselves against marauding German Messerschmitt Me-109 and Focke Wulf Fw-190 fighters »

While the P-51B became an outstanding performer, the aircraft did present challenges in flight. It was difficult to take off with a full load of fuel and somewhat unstable in flight until the rear fuselage fuel tank was emptied. More troubling, its four wing-mounted .50-calibre machine guns were prone to jamming due to mounting at an angle that was unsuitable for the wing's thickness. Visibility to the rear and below was sub-optimal as well. Pilots also called for more robust firepower. In comparison, the P-47s then in service carried eight .50-calibre machine guns.

In response to these issues, the P-51D was developed. The razorback canopy was eliminated as the type incorporated a new bubble canopy like the Malcolm hood that had been developed by the RAF and installed in its Mustang IIIs. The P-51D was up-gunned with six .50-calibre Browning machine guns. These were installed in a modified wing section that could accommodate the guns in a fully upright position, solving the problem with jamming. This model became the most highly produced of the Mustang family, with more than 8,000 rolling off North American assembly lines. A few of these were allotted to the RAF and designated the Mustang IV.

Luftwaffe menace

The P-51D became a menace to Luftwaffe aircraft, the manoeuvrability and firepower of the earlier Mustangs enhanced even further with this latest variant. Its top speed was 440mph with the Packard 1650 powerplant – slightly slower than the P-51B – with a service ceiling of 41,900ft, range of 1,650 miles with external drop tanks, and rate of climb of 3,200ft per minute. Its length was 32ft, 3in, height 13ft, 4½in, and wingspan 37ft. The aircraft weighed 7,365lb empty and 9,200lb fully loaded. In addition to its six .50-calibre machine guns, the P-51D

and drop their payloads on military and industrial targets all the way to Germany and back. However, with mounting losses in the USAAF bombing campaign by the autumn of 1943, he was compelled to admit: "It may be said that we could have had the long-range P-51 in Europe rather sooner than we did. That we did not have it sooner than we did was the Air Force's own fault."

Indeed, Arnold and the bomber faction of the USAAF bore a great deal

of the responsibility for a later arrival of the P-51 in theatre. And many American bomber crews may well have paid for that delay with their lives.

The dazzling Merlin-powered Mustang, known to Americans as the P-51B and the British as the Mustang III, exhibited an increase in airspeed of 51mph to an electrifying 441mph. Prior to the first test flights, the USAAF was aware of the startling capabilities of the fighter and ordered 2,200 of them. The P-51B, powered by the Packard V-1650 engine, a licence-built version of the Merlin, arrived in Europe to begin equipping American fighter squadrons in September 1943.

As production requirements ramped up, North American moved its B-25 assembly lines to a Kansas facility and increased P-51B Mustang production at Inglewood. At the same time, a factory was built in Dallas, Texas, producing the P-51C when it came online. The P-51B and P-51C aircraft were identical, the change in letter designation made only to denote the fighter's origin. For further identification, Inglewood P-51Bs were given the suffix NA, and the P-51Cs built in Dallas were given the suffix NT.

A P-51B Mustang of the US 355th Fighter Group escorts B-17 bombers of the 381st Bomb Group in 1944. Public Domain

could carry up to 1,000lb of bombs or a complement of 127mm HVAR rockets attached to hard points under each wing.

The later P-51K was virtually identical to the P-51D. Its only variance was due to differences in the propeller and canopy shape inherent with multiple suppliers. A dorsal fin was added to the vertical stabiliser in the P-51D to correct stability concerns that persisted, probably due to the increased weight of the model.

Late in World War Two, the lighter P-51H was in production, but few of these entered service before the end of the conflict. The P-51H was the final production version of the Mustang and intended for deployment during the expected invasion of Japan, an operation

that was shelved for good with the dropping of the atomic bombs on Hiroshima and Nagasaki in August 1945.

The P-51 Mustang had truly changed the dynamics of the air war in Europe, performing in the tactical fighter bomber and photo reconnaissance roles, proving an excellent dogfighter, and providing the high-altitude escort so sorely needed on long bomber missions against the Third Reich. Quite arguably the best propeller-driven fighter aircraft of World War Two, its pilots claimed to have shot down nearly 5,000 enemy aircraft.

As Clarence 'Bud' Anderson, a Mustang ace with 16¼ aerial victories to his credit, once assessed: "I felt like me and that Mustang could take on anything Germany had."

ALLISON ENGINE

The V-1710 was the first engine produced solely by the Allison Division of General Motors Corporation and the only V-12 liquid-cooled production engine made in the United States during World War Two. Development of the V-1710 began in the late 1920s, and its first run occurred in 1930.

Meeting the military specification of 1,000hp in 1937 for a new 150-hour test, the engine generated 2,800rpm, displaced 1,710cu in and weighed 1,340lb. The US Army Air Corps initially specified that the V-1710 should be a single-stage supercharged engine, relying on the fact that a turbosupercharger then under development might be used if higher altitude capability was required. Its C variant, with its propeller shaft extended 12in, was the first in a 'long nose' series that provided the foundation for subsequent improved and higher-powered examples of the engine.

During World War Two, the V-1710 powered several American-built aircraft including the Bell P-39 Airacobra and P-63 Kingcobra, the Lockheed P-38 Lightning, the Curtiss P-40 Tomahawk, the North American A-36 Apache, and preliminary versions of the North American P-51 Mustang. Around 70,000 Allison V-1710 engines were produced by the end of the war in 1945.

As the enhanced performance of the two-stage supercharger became more apparent during combat conditions, Allison made some alterations to the base V-1710, its two-stage supercharger powering the Bell P-63. However, several features already incorporated in the two-stage Rolls-Royce Merlin engine were not present in the early Allison, and those Allison engines installed in the F-82 Twin Mustang needed many hours of maintenance for each single hour of flight. Still, improvements to the engine were continual throughout the war, with the V-1710-143/145(G6R/L) generating 2,300hp and the subsequent V-1710-127, the final wartime variant, producing 2,900hp at lower altitudes and 1,550hp at 29,000ft.

Still, issues were inherent with the Allison engine and the installed turbosupercharger, forcing aircraft designers to often choose between the maintenance issues with the turbosupercharger or the lack of high-altitude capabilities in the basic engine configuration. The twin-engine P-38 Lightning was eventually the only fighter that entered combat during World War Two with the turbo-supercharged Allison.

Subsequently, Allison did attach an auxiliary supercharger to its production engine in 1943, beginning with the V-1710-45, but the P-51 had already been fitted with the Merlin 61 powerplant.

A quartet of P-51D Mustangs from the US 339th Fighter Group soars above RAF Fowlmere. Public Domain

The Allison V-1710 engine powered numerous American aircraft during World War Two. Creative Commons Smithsonian via Wikipedia

RAF ASSESSMENT AND DEPLOYMENT

The Royal Air Force was the first to deploy the Mustang in combat. The initial Mustang Mk Is to enter service with the RAF were delivered to No 26 Squadron based at RAF Gatwick in February 1942. The Mk 1 was heavily armed with two .50-calibre Browning machine guns in the nose just below and aft of the spinner and two .30-calibre machine guns in each wing. A US Army Air Forces modification dropped the .50-calibre machine guns and added four long-barrelled Hispano Mk II 20mm cannon. Mustangs entering RAF service with this configuration were designated the Mk Ia.

The RAF intended the Mk I for low-altitude ground attack missions, along with photo reconnaissance (a modification referred to as the F-6 by the Americans), so there were no immediate concerns regarding high-altitude performance. The Mustangs initially came under the control of RAF Army Co-operation Command rather than Fighter Command due to their anticipated functions, which would limit dogfighting and pursuit encounters with the Luftwaffe. From the initial deployment, a total of 14 squadrons of the Army Co-operation Command were equipped with the new fighter. The original Allison engine was more than adequate for the original intended functions. Through the spring of 1942, reports from RAF pilots were positive as to the Mk I's performance below 15,000ft.

The first Mustang Mk I flight over Nazi-occupied France took place on May 10, 1942, and on July 27, a flight of 16 Mk Is made the first long-range reconnaissance mission while flying over Germany itself. They therefore

became the first Allied fighter/reconnaissance aircraft to penetrate German airspace while flying to and from airfields in Britain. Another reconnaissance mission over Germany occurred in October 1942, when a Mustang pilot photographed the Dortmund-Ems Canal.

On August 19, 1942, the first major Mustang combat missions were flown in support of Operation Jubilee, the tragic raid on the French coastal town of Dieppe. During the action, Flying Officer Hollis Hills, an American in service with the Royal Canadian Air Force, was credited with the first Mustang aerial kill, a Focke Wulf Fw-190. In October, RAF Mk Is escorted 22 Vickers Wellington bombers on a daylight raid into Germany as well.

Some controversy surrounded the Hills air victory as Luftwaffe records do not clearly indicate the presence of Fw-190 fighters in the vicinity of his encounter and there was no corroborating German record of a loss on that day. However, the plane might well have been damaged seriously. Evidence also exists but cannot confirm the loss of two German aircraft to RAF Mustangs prior to the Hills claim. Nevertheless, Hills no doubt hit a German fighter hard that day over Dieppe and set an early mark that foreshadowed the future of the Mustang as a prodigious fighter in aerial combat as well as the reconnaissance and ground attack roles.

LEFT: This
Mustang III of No
112 Squadron RAF
was photographed
in Italy late in
World War Two.
Creative Commons
Richard Sullivan
via Wikipedia

top scoring RAF ace in the type during the conflict.

Squadron Leader James MacLachlan scored 16 aerial victories flying the Fairey Battle, Hawker Hurricane, Supermarine Spitfire, and the Mustang Ia. He survived being shot down over the island of Malta by a German Me-109 pilot. He was severely wounded and lost an arm. Returning to the air in April 1943, he familiarised himself with the Mustang and shot down three enemy aircraft, sharing another kill with a fellow pilot, while flying some missions apparently without authorisation.

On July 18, 1943, MacLachlan's Mustang was either hit by ground fire or experienced mechanical problems as he crossed the coast of France near Dieppe. Flight Lieutenant Geoffrey Page watched as MacLachlan's plane pitched up abruptly and then saw him pull back the canopy in preparation to bail out. The Mustang then levelled off, and MacLachlan decided to stay with the plane, crashing through a field and careening into a nearby orchard. He was severely injured with a fractured skull and taken prisoner by the Germans. He lingered on until July 31 and died in a German hospital at the age of 24. MacLachlan was a recipient of the Distinguished Service Order, and the day before his death, he was awarded a second bar to his Distinguished Flying Cross.

No 414 Squadron RCAF pilots proved proficient in the Mustang after transitioning from the Supermarine Spitfire, and during the war they shot down 29 enemy aircraft, damaged 11, shot up 76 rail locomotives, and sank 12 vessels of various description on waterways across occupied Europe.

During World War Two, hundreds of Mustangs were built by North American Aviation and supplied to the RAF through the Lend Lease programme. Among the types and quantity constructed were Mustang Mk I 620, Mustang Mk III 852 and Mustang Mk IV 876. The Mustang remained in RAF service after World War Two, and the last of its type were removed from active roles in 1947.

LEFT: A Mustang
Mk Ia of No 35
Wing RAF flies
over the French
countryside in
November 1943.
Public Domain

BELOW: The gun
camera of Flying
Officer J Butler's
Mustang III, No
65 Squadron RAF,
records his kill
against a German
Fw-190 that has
attacked an Avro
Lancaster heavy
bomber in 1944.
Public Domain

Upgraded contract

In June 1942, a contract was placed for 1,200 Mustang Mk IIs (known in the USAAF as the P-51A) with an improved Allison engine and armament consisting of four wing-mounted Browning .50-calibre machine guns. Later orders were placed for the P-51B and P-51C, produced at the North American Aviation facilities in Inglewood, California, and Dallas, Texas, beginning in the summer of 1943. These incorporated the Rolls-Royce Merlin engine licence-built in the United States by the Packard Motor Car Company in Detroit, Michigan, and designated the V-1650. RAF units converted these in late 1943 and early 1944, and the RAF designated them as the Mustang Mk III. The P-51D, armed with six wing-mounted .50-calibre machines guns, was designated the Mustang Mk IV. The introduction of the Rolls-Royce Merlin engine that turned the Mustang into the premier propeller-driven fighter and high-altitude escort of World War Two was undertaken in the spring of 1942 at the suggestion of Rolls-Royce test pilot Ronald Harker.

RAF Mustangs flew extensively as reconnaissance and ground attack aircraft from 1942, and Mustang Mk I and Mk Ia pilots participated in low-level strafing attacks against targets of opportunity. These hazardous missions were called rhubarbs, and though the Mustangs were more susceptible to ground fire at lower altitude, they were quite successful. During the first 18 months of these sorties, eight Mustangs were lost, but more than 400 railroad locomotives and river traffic such as supply barges were heavily damaged or destroyed outright. As the war progressed, Mustang pilots specifically targeted for destruction the launch sites for the V-1 Buzz Bomb, a pulsejet flying bomb and forerunner of the modern cruise missile that carried a 1,870lb warhead and terrorised London and other British cities as well as major cities in Western Europe such as the port of Antwerp, Belgium.

During World War Two, 13 RAF pilots became aces flying the Mustang, while 26 others destroyed five or more of the V-1s in flight. Some 27 RAF aces scored at least some of their victories while flying the Mustang after transitioning from the Republic P-47 Thunderbolt fighter. Flight Lieutenant Maurice Pinches of No 122 Squadron shot down nine German planes while flying the Mustang and became the

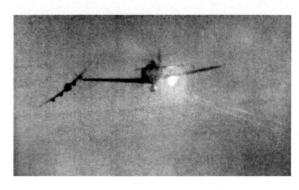

A-36 INVADER

Fiscal constraints prevented the conclusion of a contract for a new fighter in 1942, but unallocated funding remained available for a new ground attack aircraft. The foresight of two officers, General Oliver P Echols, responsible for development and procurement of aircraft for the USAAF, and Colonel Benjamin Kelsey, fighter projects officer, kept the basic P-51 in production with modifications for use as a dive bomber. Eventually, 500 A-36s, originally designated the NA-97, were constructed, and the Invader, sometimes called the Apache, was deployed in North Africa, the

On December 30, 1944, Lieutenant Michael Russo led a flight of a dozen A-36 Invader dive bombers in a ground attack mission near Rome, as troops of the Allied Fifth and Eighth Armies slogged their way toward the Eternal City, capital of Fascist Italy, and other objectives on the Italian mainland.

Russo's aircraft was the dive bomber and ground attack variant of the famed P-51 Mustang fighter, and though its primary role was in tactical ground support, the A-36 was a capable air-to-air adversary in experienced hands. Russo had already shot down three German planes, a formidable Focke Wulf Fw-190 off the Salerno beachhead, a light Fieseler Fi-156 Storch observation plane, and a Junkers Ju-52 transport.

On this day, Russo, and his charges from the 522nd Fighter Bomber Squadron, 27th Fighter Bomber Group, completed their mission but were jumped by at least 16 Messerschmitt Me-109 fighters at an

altitude of around 4,500ft. Lieutenant Russo pitched into the attackers and shot down two of them, achieving his fourth and fifth aerial victories of World War Two and gaining ace status. According to most sources, Russo was the only A-36 ace of the war. The air combat had taken place at low altitude, which allowed his A-36's Allison engine to operate at optimal efficiency. The P-51s that became famous in the skies over Europe were fitted with the two-stage supercharged Rolls-Royce Merlin engine, necessary for dogfighting at high altitude.

The A-36 was quite similar in construction to the early P-51s, particularly the P-51A and the Mark I, as it was known in the British Royal Air Force. The first Mustangs had been introduced to regular service with the RAF in the long-range reconnaissance and ground attack roles. While the British introduced the Mark I in the spring of 1942 to supplement their available Curtiss P-40 attack planes, North American Aviation, the P-51 manufacturer, sought a contract with the US Army Air Forces (USAAF) to produce the aircraft as a fighter.

Mediterranean theatre, and the China-Burma-India theatre during World War Two. The type's service life was relatively limited. By 1944, the robust Republic P-47 Thunderbolt fighter was an inevitable replacement for the Invader, as were newer types of P-51s equipped with bomb racks and rocket launch rails that allowed them to serve efficiently in the ground attack role.

The A-36 was distinguishable from its P-51 counterpart by the addition of rectangular, hydraulically operated, cast aluminium dive brakes that controlled air speed at critical times during the act of dive bombing. These were located above and below the aft section of each wing. Although the liquid-cooled Allison V-1710 engine had a limited operational ceiling, its 1,325hp at an altitude of 3,000ft and maximum speed of 365mph were quite adequate for the dive bomber and ground attack roles, while the model could defend itself in a dogfight at lower altitude as well.

Primary element

In its primary element, the A-36 would be placed in a near vertical

dive from an altitude of roughly 12,000ft to 14,000ft. The bomb release would occur between 2,000ft and 4,000ft, while the dive brakes were deployed and limited the air speed to around 390mph. Early combat operations revealed a tendency of the aircraft to roll slightly with the extension of the brakes after entering the dive due to variances in hydraulic pressure. However, skilled pilots learned to deal with such phenomena after gaining experience in the A-36.

North American Aviation engineers modified the P-51 further with the addition of bomb racks and sturdier wings and other airframe points expected to absorb greater stress during dive bombing. The A-36A was armed with two .50-calibre machine guns in the nose and four wing-mounted .50-calibre machine guns for air defence and strafing ground targets. Capable of carrying up to 1,000lb of bombs, the external hard points were also useful in holding 75-gallon external drop tanks that extended the plane's operating range. The initial A-36A was completed at the North American assembly plant in Inglewood, California, in September 1942. Test flights began within days at Eglin Field, Florida, and production brought the first deliveries to the USAAF in a remarkably short period of time.

The first A-36s were delivered to the 27th Bombardment Group and the 86th Bombardment Group of the Twelfth Air Force (both later renamed as fighter bomber groups) in North Africa. The 27th was operating out of Ras el Ma in French Morocco with a complement of Douglas A-20 Havoc light bombers as well. The 86th arrived in March 1943. On June 6, 1943, the A-36s of the 27th Bombardment Group flew their first combat sorties, hitting Pantelleria Island in the Strait of Sicily. During one mission, the Invaders duelled with German Me-109s, and one of the enemy planes was shot down. It was credited to the entire group of 27th pilots then in the vicinity.

After Allied troops occupied Pantelleria Island, it served as the base for the A-36s operating in support of the invasion of Sicily in July and during subsequent operations on the Italian mainland. In the late summer of 1943, two squadrons of A-36s reached an airfield at Dinjan, India, along with a squadron of P-51As. These were slated to perform reconnaissance and ground support missions, but the pilots were wary of the nimble Japanese fighters they faced, particularly the highly manoeuvrable Nakajima Ki-43 Oscar.

Nevertheless, the A-36 was a fine dive-bombing platform, and Captain Charles E Dills of the 522nd Fighter Bomber Squadron, who flew 39 of his 94 combat missions in the A-36,

praised the aircraft. "The plane was designed to be a low-altitude attack plane," he observed, "and it did its job very well. When strafing, we would go into enemy territory at 200ft or 300ft. At this altitude, we had the element of surprise. We would be there, give the targets a burst from the machine guns, and be gone before they could even pick up their guns. We looked for targets of opportunity – anything that looked like enemy war stuff. We did not bomb civilian farmhouses, unless there was a reason to believe that the enemy was using them as observation posts. In those cases, we were given specific targets to attack."

Dills continued: "When dive bombing, we would go in much higher, probably 14,000ft. German gunners had a problem in that the computers on their 88mm guns had to try to predict where the plane was going to be in 15 or 20 seconds, and when we dived straight down to the target, the 88mm guns could not be elevated to 90 degrees. So, they couldn't aim at us until we pulled out. At that point, we were travelling at over 400mph. All we had to do was change our course or elevation very slightly every 15 seconds or so."

The A-36 proved itself as a versatile aircraft, although it was supplanted by other combat types within a relatively short time. As a fighter, it earned the respect of the enemy as its pilots accounted for 84 Axis aircraft during World War Two.

ABOVE LEFT: This example of the A-36A, deployed with the 86th Fighter Bomber Group, was lost to German flak over Italy in January 1944. Public Domain

ABOVE RIGHT: North American A-36 Invader dive bombers fly in formation. The A-36 was the attack variant of the P-51 Mustang. Public Domain

BELOW: This modern A-36A dive bomber resides at the National Museum of the United States Air Force in Dayton, Ohio. Public Domain

ALLISON TO MERLIN

RIGHT: Lieutenant Colonel Thomas Hitchcock was an American World War One fighter pilot, outstanding polo player, and advocate for the Merlin-powered Mustang. *Public Domain*

FAR RIGHT: Lieutenant Colonel Thomas Hitchcock worked to persuade the US Army Air Forces establishment to evaluate the Mustang powered by the Rolls-Royce Merlin engine. *Public Domain*

When the call came into RAF Hucknall that morning, the response from Rolls-Royce test pilot Ronald Harker was affirmative. The Air Fighting Development Unit at Duxford had offered an opportunity to fly a newly acquired aircraft of American manufacture. The plane was named the Mustang I, and it was a hybrid built in the US by North American Aviation to British specifications for a low-altitude ground support and reconnaissance aircraft.

Harker took the Mustang up on the morning of April 30, 1942. In short order, he put the aircraft through its paces, appreciating its exceptional characteristics. He noted its resemblance to the German Messerschmitt Me-109 fighter, praised its fuel capacity which was three times that of the current Supermarine Spitfire Mark in service, approved of its heavy armament, and discovered a remarkably manoeuvrable airframe that exhibited excellent aerodynamics and handling below 15,000ft to 20,000ft.

By the spring of 1942, Harker was approaching his 33rd birthday. A veteran test pilot, he had worked with Rolls-Royce as a teenager, learned to fly after being laid off when the company was in the throes of the Great Depression, and returned in 1934. He became the first test pilot for Rolls-Royce and evaluated numerous types of RAF aircraft. He was heavily involved in bringing the first Hawker Hurricane squadron, No 111 based at RAF Northolt, to active status in 1938. He joined No 504 City of Nottingham Squadron, Royal Auxiliary Air Force, conveniently based at Hucknall where Rolls-Royce located its testing programme. With the outbreak of World War Two, Harker's squadron was placed on active status and ordered to France. Harker, however, was too valuable in the test pilot role and remained in that capacity at Hucknall, serving Rolls-Royce, the RAF, and the Allied cause admirably in the role.

Considering the fine attributes of the Mustang, Harker noted one opportunity that might well unlock its potential as a high-altitude fighter. The Allison engine then in use was a fine powerplant for the intended role of the Mustang, but Harker knew the characteristics of the two-stage, two-speed supercharged Rolls-Royce Merlin 60 series engines. He was captivated by what the heavier powerplant, in this case the Merlin 61, might do and even took measurements of the aircraft's engine compartment to see if it could fit.

Harker's initial overture on the subject received only a tepid response from the Air Ministry. Along with the RAF, the ministry was vexed by the appearance of a nasty surprise, the swift and agile German Focke Wulf Fw-190 fighter that was alarmingly faster than the Spitfire V. The Merlin engines then being manufactured were steered toward the new Spitfire IX variant to deal with the Fw-190. Harker refused to give up and was advised by Ray Dorey, chief of the flight test group based at Hucknall, to go straight to the top of the Air Ministry. Without hesitation, Harker petitioned Air Chief Marshal Sir Wilfrid Freeman, air member for production and research, for permission to try the promising experiment. Persistence paid off.

Doubts unfounded

Although there were doubters within the Air Ministry and the RAF, in August 1942, five Mustang Is were allotted for the installation of the new Merlin 65 engine, and the hybrid was designated the Mustang X. Captain R T Shepherd, head test pilot for Rolls-Royce, took the Mustang X into the air for the first time on October 13, and trials continued into December. The performance of the plane was outstanding. It was considerably faster than other contemporary fighters, and the higher the altitude the faster it flew, graduating from around 400moph at 10,000ft to an astonishing 450mph or more at 35,000ft, 100mph faster than the Allison engine at peak

BELOW: The Mustang X paired the North American airframe with the Rolls-Royce Merlin engine for the first time. *Public Domain*

performance. The Mustang X could dive faster and had a snappier roll rate than other planes as well. It was later determined that with the addition of auxiliary fuel drop tanks and the installation of another fuel tank behind the cockpit, the range of the fighter could be extended from 450 miles to 1,650 miles or more.

Apparently, there was little convincing left for Harker – and now Shepherd – to do. And somewhere along the way, Harker did receive a handsome financial reward in recognition, a weekly pay increase of £1. He was later given the Order of the British Empire and the Air Efficiency Award.

Still, a formidable obstacle remained. Rolls-Royce was producing Merlin 60 series engines at capacity, and these were already committed to the Spitfire IX, as well as the de Havilland Mosquito light bomber and reconnaissance aircraft, and the Avro Lancaster four-engine bomber that was being developed from the disappointing Avro Manchester bomber powered by the Vulture engine. Harker had a hand in the evolution of the iconic Lancaster and assisted in the redesign and engineering of other RAF bombers to accept the Merlin. However, he is best remembered for his contribution to the success of the P-51. He died in New Zealand at the age of 90 on May 30, 1990, and will forever be known as the 'man who put the Merlin in the Mustang'.

The worries with the availability of the Merlin were solved with the involvement of Packard Motor Car Company of Detroit, Michigan, which was already licensed to build the Merlin in the United States and was producing a version of the engine, identified as the V-1650, with a single-stage supercharger for the Curtiss P-40 Warhawk (known to the RAF as the Kittyhawk). Meanwhile, Air Chief Marshal Freeman became a staunch advocate of the Mustang X and realised that the Americans would have to be involved to produce the Merlin-powered Mustang in a meaningful quantity. Freeman provided two of the Mustang X aircraft to the US Army Air Forces in Britain for further testing, but just as the Air Ministry had been sceptical at first, so was the American air establishment.

Lieutenant Colonel Thomas Hitchcock Jr was serving as an assistant air attaché in London during the trials of the Mustang X, and he was enthusiastic about the prospects of the type entering full-scale production in the United States. Hitchcock was a veteran aviator, a fighter pilot in World War One who had shot down three German planes before he was shot down himself and captured. In a daring escape, he leaped from a moving train and then walked more than 100 miles to safety in neutral Switzerland.

Between the wars, Hitchcock became one of the foremost polo players in the world. Well known in social circles, he was an investment banker and the model for the character Tom Buchanan in F Scott Fitzgerald's acclaimed novel 'The Great Gatsby'. At age 42, he was considered too old to serve in combat with the outbreak of World War Two, but his role in the future of the Mustang was indispensable.

Opposition erodes

Hitchcock's reports on the Mustang X were received coolly in Washington, DC, and he lamented: "Sired by the English out of an American mother, the Mustang has no parent at Wright Field to appreciate and push its good points." However, he had also apprised North American Aviation of the British trial results. Opposition eroded rapidly.

North American test pilot Bob Chilton flew the first of a pair of XP-78 fighters on November 30, 1942, **»**

LEFT: Air Chief Marshal Sir Wilfrid Freeman served with the Air Ministry and became an advocate for the Mustang and Merlin engine combination.
Public Domain

LEFT: A Mustang III sits on the field at RAF Hucknall in 1943. The model incorporated the Merlin engine.
Public Domain

BELOW: The field at RAF Hucknall, where Ronald Harker evaluated RAF aircraft for Rolls-Royce, is pictured in 2005.
Creative Commons Mick Garratt via Wikipedia

MUSTANG X

P-51B
GVG / PD / 1.0

MUSTANG III (P-51B) WITH MALCOLM HOOD

and the name of the plane was soon changed to the XP-51B. Chilton stayed aloft for 45 minutes in the airframe powered by the Packard-built V-1650-3 Merlin engine and noted an issue with the cooling system, which was clogging the radiator. The second XP-51B was refitted with a modified radiator and scoop design, which eliminated the problem.

Production of the P-51B got underway shortly after, and Hitchcock had predicted that it would be the best Allied fighter aircraft to enter combat in 1943, delivering new dimensions of air superiority and long-range escort for Boeing B-17 Flying Fortress and Consolidated B-24 Liberator heavy bombers on missions deep into Nazi Germany.

The high-performance Mustang arrived just as the US Eighth Air Force was preparing to revive its daylight bombing campaign over Germany. Losses of the big bombers had been staggering in the summer and autumn of 1943, compelling a temporary suspension of the campaign until a suitable escort could be found. The P-51B fitted the bill, and the subsequent deployment of the P-51D, with its armament increased from four

to six wing-mounted .50-calibre machine guns and a bubble canopy for better visibility, only enhanced the Mustang's lethality.

Hitchcock assumed the post of deputy chief of staff for 9th Air Support Command and maintained a close association with the Mustang. Despite the P-51's successes, reports were received that it sometimes became unstable in a steep dive, and issues had emerged with its external drop tanks. On April 18, 1944, Hitchcock took it upon himself to evaluate the concerns and piloted a Mustang on a test flight over Salisbury, Wiltshire. He was unable to pull out of a dive and was killed in the crash.

Prior to the tragedy, Hitchcock no doubt understood that the introduction of the P-51 powered by the Merlin engine was a turning point in the air war in Europe. During the bomber offensive known as Big Week in February 1944, it is estimated that Mustang fighter pilots shot down and killed 17 per cent of the total complement of experienced Luftwaffe pilots. Therefore, it may be concluded that the Allied air forces defeated the Germans in the skies over Europe by eliminating the enemy pilots in single combat. And the P-51 Mustang was the principal executioner.

Other startling statistics support this. Research has revealed that between January and April 1944, the Luftwaffe lost more than 1,000 pilots, many of them aces. Some 28 of the German pilots shot down and killed had been credited with 30 or more aerial victories, and eight of them had shot down more than 100 Allied planes each.

The Mustang and the Merlin had, therefore, turned the tide. In doing so, both become the stuff of legend.

ROLLS-ROYCE MERLIN ENGINE

Shrouded in mystery and tradition, the figure of Merlin was said to have worked magic as a key figure in the tales of King Arthur, and when the Rolls-Royce aircraft engine that bore the same name was paired with the P-51 Mustang fighter airframe the result was…magical.

In fact, Rolls-Royce named the Merlin engine after a small bird of prey resident to the Northern Hemisphere, but no matter. Those who know the story behind the development of perhaps the finest propeller-driven fighter plane of World War Two also know that the Merlin engine made the difference in its performance. Although the original Allison V-1710 was adequate at lower altitudes and had powered numerous other US designed and built military aircraft, it was not geared for high altitude performance.

The Merlin, with its eventual two-stage supercharger, could convince the powerplant that it was performing at its optimal altitude by forcing additional air into the engine and producing a greater power yield for the given engine displacement. Not only did the Merlin engine power the Mustang, but it was also the primary engine of the legendary Supermarine Spitfire and Hawker Hurricane fighters, the speedy de Havilland Mosquito twin-engine light bomber and reconnaissance

aircraft, the Handley Page Halifax four-engine heavy bomber, and the storied Avro Lancaster, the four-engine workhorse of RAF Bomber Command during the combined air offensive against the Third Reich in World War Two.

The first run of the fabled Merlin engine occurred on October 15, 1933. The four-stroke piston engine was originally known as the PV-12, and during its production life that stretched until 1950 nearly 150,000 examples in 50 variants were manufactured. The engine was built at Rolls-Royce facilities in Crewe, Glasgow, Derby, and Trafford Park, where the Ford Motor Company had a production plant. The Packard V-1650 version was built in the United States to augment the supply of Merlin engines due to high wartime demand. At the time of the innovative move with the Mustang, the British government and Packard Motor Car Company were already doing business. A contract had been signed in September 1940 to produce engines for the British war effort, and its sum was $130m, a tremendous investment at the time.

The Merlin was a liquid-cooled, 12-piston engine that displaced 1,650cu in, and the Air Ministry specifications for new, modern fighter planes issued in 1935 led to the Spitfire and Hurricane being developed around the PV-12, which

was renamed about 1936, roughly the time these planes entered production.

The first Packard-built Merlins were manufactured with a single-stage supercharger and were similar to the Merlin XX. Subsequent versions were based on the British-built Merlin 60 series with the two-stage supercharger developed by Rolls-Royce engineer and mathematician Stanley Hooker, and these were made famous in the Mustang with engines built by Packard and designated the V-1650-3. The 60 series engine first ran in March 1941 and was flight tested that summer.

The first conversion of the Mustang powered with the so-called 'high altitude' Merlin was a strictly British affair. It flew in the Mustang Mk X in October 1942 and was powered by the Merlin 61 engine. The first production Mustangs powered by the Merlin, the P-51B, rolled off North American Aircraft assembly lines and entered service in 1943.

LEFT: The Packard-built V-1650-7 was one in a series of licence-manufactured Merlin engines. GNU Free Documentation License Kogo via Wikipedia

BELOW: This Packard V-1650 engine resides in a museum in Munich, Germany. Creative Commons Arjun Sarup via Wikipedia

BOTTOM: This Packard V-1650 licence-built Merlin engine was salvaged from a crashed P-51 Mustang. Creative Commons happy days photos and art via Wikipedia

MUSTANGS AT DIEPPE

A lthough the P-51 Mustang, designated the Mustang Mk I by the British, had been in the air during various missions since the spring of 1942, the fighter/reconnaissance plane participated in its first major air engagement on August 19 of that year during the ill-fated Operation Jubilee, the heavy raid on the port city of Dieppe on the coast of Nazi-occupied France.

The raid was primarily executed by Canadian forces, along with British Commandos and a handful of US Army Rangers. In its execution, the ground phase encountered significant resistance, and the forces were withdrawn with heavy losses. In the air, one of the largest battles of World War Two unfolded. Air Marshal Trafford Leigh-Mallory co-ordinated the air support with the Royal Air Force, committing 74 squadrons to the effort, while the US Army Air Forces contributed six squadrons. Sixty-six of the RAF squadrons allotted were fighter units, and four of these flew the Mk I Mustang. No 26 and No 239 Squadrons RAF and No 400 and 414 Squadrons Royal Canadian Air Force (RCAF), components of No 35 Wing, were assigned a photo reconnaissance role as they were detailed from Army Co-operation Command.

On the morning of the raid, American Boeing B-17 Flying Fortress bombers struck the German airfield at Abbeville-Drucat with an escort of RAF Mk IX Supermarine Spitfire fighters. RAF Hawker Typhoon fighter bombers executed a feint

towards the city of Ostend, Belgium, and the Mustang squadrons flew outside the main area of ground activity on alert for potential German reinforcements on the roads from Le Havre, Yvetot, Rouen, and Amiens to Dieppe. Taking to the air from their bases at RAF Gatwick and RAF Croydon near London, the Mustangs radioed intelligence information to a headquarters ship off Dieppe and later

telephoned reports to Leigh-Mallory's office. They flew hazardous sorties until about noon that day.

The reconnaissance Mustang I had first flown over the coast of France near the village of Berck-sur-Mer on May 10, 1942, while the first long-range reconnaissance mission was undertaken on July 27, the Mustangs penetrating airspace over Germany. During the Dieppe action, Pilot Officer Hollis 'Holly' Hills of No 414 Squadron, RCAF, accompanied Flight Lieutenant Freddie Clarke on a reconnaissance mission between Dieppe and the town of Abbeville. While they scanned the terrain for the approach of any reinforcing enemy armour or infantry, a group of German Focke Wulf Fw-190 fighters suddenly appeared.

Hills remembered in a 1992 interview: "As we approached the French coast, the sky was full of fighters in one massive dogfight. A couple of miles short of landfall I spotted four Fw-190s off to our right at about 1,500ft. Their course and speed were going to put them directly overhead when we crossed the beach. I called a 'tally ho!' When Freddie turned right to intercept our recce road at Abbeville, we were put in an ideal position for the FWs to attack. I swung very wide, dusting the Abbeville chimney tops. That kept me beneath them.

"The lead Fw-190 hit Freddie's Mustang with the first burst. Glycol was streaming from the radiator but there was no fire. I was able to get

a long-range shot at the leader but had to break right when his number two had a go at me and made a big mistake of sliding to my left side ahead of me. It was an easy shot and I hit him hard. His engine caught fire, and soon after it started smoking and the canopy came off. I hit him again and he was a goner, falling off to the right into the trees."

Hell and corruption

Clarke, meanwhile, had no idea that he was in imminent danger until he felt the impact of the German's fire on the engine of his P-51. "The next thing I know is there is 'all hell and corruption' going by," he said in the same interview. "I'd been hit. The radiator was shot up, my instruments on either side of me were gone. The armour plating saved me. So, I jettisoned the hood hoping that it hadn't been jammed with the shots, and it wasn't. And I thought, they're right, it's nice – not windy in here at all!"

While Hills, an American from Pasadena, California, who had volunteered for Canadian service, enlisting at Toronto in September 1940, recorded the first confirmed air-to-air kill by a Mustang fighter, Clarke was forced to ditch in the English Channel as his Allison engine had haemorrhaged coolant. Turning towards the sea, Clarke hoped to settle into the water and survive the sinking of his fighter to the bottom. He lost all memory for a time, recalling that he was 10ft above the waves at an airspeed of 90 knots before being rendered unconscious. When he woke up, he was lying on the deck of a landing craft.

"I limped out to the water," Clarke recalled. "Just as I crossed the coast that prop seized. There I am down wind, across the trough. Everything's against you. Using my trim to keep my tail down, the last thing I remember is about 90mph on the clock, trying to get that tail down. I wanted the tail to hit first to kill the

speed before she flopped in because it would just go in if you hit the air scoop. I hit the gun sight, I think. They say a young Army guy hit the water with his arms going and got me out of the aircraft. I would give anything to have known who he was."

Clarke was among a group of wounded later transferred to the destroyer HMS *Calpe*, which was under regular attack by German aircraft for much of the day as its crew pursued rescue efforts. He was treated for his injuries and returned to the squadron.

"About 5am the next morning, my door burst open," Hills recalled. "I was grabbed in a bear hug by what smelled like a huge clump of seaweed. It was Freddie Clarke, rescued by the amphibious forces. His head sported a huge bandage covering the severe cuts he had received in the ditching. We had been warned that ditching a Mustang could be hazardous to your health."

In January 1943, Hills received Mention in Despatches for the Dieppe action, which read: "This officer accompanied his Flight Commander on two low reconnaissances over the approaches to the battle area. During the second of these, they were attacked by three FW190s. When Flying Officer Hills found he could not warn his Flight Commander, owing to a radio failure, he engaged the three enemy aircraft, shooting down one and driving off the other two, until the Flight Commander became aware of the situation."

Hills was recommended for the French Croix de Guerre a month later. He had already transferred to the US Navy, later to survive being shot down over the Pacific Ocean and received an American Distinguished Flying Cross for his service.

Flight Lieutenant Clarke returned to active duty and continued to fly missions over Nazi-occupied Europe until May 1943, when health issues took precedence. Clarke had experienced severe headaches and periodic blackouts. After 10 days of medical leave, he returned to No 414 Squadron and became its operations liaison officer, forbidden from flying future sorties. He remained with the unit through the campaigns on the continent in 1944-45 and was the last surviving member of the original squadron formed in August 1941. He died aged 88 in 2005.

Sources state that 11 Mustangs were lost in combat during Operation Jubilee, while the P-51 squadrons of the RAF and RCAF are credited with two Luftwaffe planes destroyed.

LEFT: An RAF Douglas Boston light bomber drops its payload during the Dieppe Raid, August 19, 1942.
Public Domain

LEFT: This Mustang Mk I fighter, flying over California, was one of the original 300 ordered by Britain in late 1940.
Public Domain

LEFT: The crew of the destroyer HMS *Calpe* rescued Flight Lieutenant Freddie Clarke after his Mustang Mk I was shot down over Dieppe.
Creative Commons Calpaeo via Wikipedia

USAAF BOMBER DOCTRINE

RIGHT: Italian officer Giulio Douhet influenced the doctrine of heavy bombing after World War One. Public Domain

Between the two world wars, the air command establishment of the US Army was enamoured with the concept of daylight precision bombing.

During World War One, the Italian officer and aviation advocate Giulio Douhet put forward the concept that future wars might be won from the air and said: "A slower, heavily armed plane, able to clear its way with its own armament, can always get the best of a faster pursuit plane. A unit of slower heavily armed planes is able to stand up to the fire of enemy pursuit planes and carry out its mission successfully."

In other words, Douhet believed that heavy bombers were capable of defending themselves against enemy fighter planes and delivering their bomb payloads against strategic targets, destroying the enemy's infrastructure and ability to wage war while also eroding the morale of its people. In support of that premise, British Prime Minister Stanley Baldwin addressed Parliament in 1932, delivering a speech titled: "A Fear of the Future."

Baldwin told his audience: "I think it is well also for the man in the street to realise that there is no power on earth that can protect him from being bombed." He also offered a phrase that reverberated across the ensuing years and came to epitomise the bombing doctrine of the US Army Air Forces in World War Two: "Whatever people may tell him, the bomber will always get through."

Although there were detractors, most high-ranking officers in the Army Air Corps and later Air

RIGHT: General Henry 'Hap' Arnold was a staunch supporter of daylight precision bombing. Public Domain

BELOW: The development of the Boeing B-17 Flying Fortress bomber was a cornerstone of US Army Air Corps bombing doctrine on the eve of World War Two. Creative Commons Airwolfhound via Wikipedia

Forces endorsed the idea that heavy bombers would rain destruction on enemy targets while capably defending themselves in the event of attack by hostile fighter planes. In the 1930s, strategic bombing became the focus of the US preparation for a future air war, and by 1940 with the development of the Boeing B-17 Flying Fortress and Consolidated B-24 Liberator heavy bombers, coupled with the state-of-the-art Norden bomb sight, daylight precision bombing of enemy infrastructure, including industrial capacity and military targets along with population centres, if necessary, became entrenched.

That year, Major General Henry 'Hap' Arnold, commander of the US Army Air Corps, declared: "The Air Corps is committed to a strategy of high-altitude precision bombing of military objectives." The general's statement came amid the teaching and implementation of such doctrine primarily as lectured to participants at the Air Corps Tactical School (ACTS) at Maxwell Field, Alabama. The concept of unescorted daylight precision bombing had developed in the 1930s at the ACTS, and by method the bombers were to concentrate on specific targets of high value rather than dropping ordnance across a wide area that might reduce effectiveness.

By the summer of 1941, President Franklin D Roosevelt had asked the Army War Plans Division to formulate a comprehensive production plan to defeat the enemies of the United States in the event of war. In concert with the Rainbow and ABC series of war plans, the former colour coded with respect to the nation involved – Germany was black – and the latter formed in co-operation with Canada and Great Britain, the Air Corps was allowed to compose an addendum to the production plan, an in-depth analysis of air requirements that generated staggering numbers of aircraft projected to sustain a strategic bombing programme. The four officers who produced the analysis, Lieutenant Colonel Kenneth

L Walker, Lieutenant Colonel Harold L George, Major Haywood S Hansel, and Major Laurence S Kuter, had all been instructors at ACTS at Maxwell Field, and all were proponents of daylight precision bombing. Their report AWPD-1, or Air War Plans Division – Plan 1, specified that more than 13,000 bombers and nearly 8,800 fighters would be required to defeat Germany, altogether the estimated total of aircraft topped 63,000.

Unproven method
Although the principal planners and those of other Air Corps departments

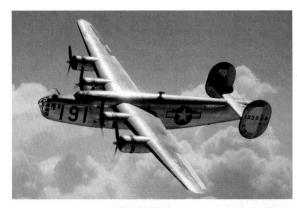

ABOVE: The Consolidated B-24 Liberator bomber was expected to play a key role in US daylight precision bombing raids in Europe.
Public Domain

RIGHT: General Ira C Eaker sold Prime Minister Winston Churchill on the idea of round-the-clock bombing.
Public Domain

who contributed had borrowed data from the Royal Air Force, which was then conducting its own nocturnal aerial bombing campaign against Nazi Germany, and had gleaned information on German industrial infrastructure from various sources, including blueprints of factories and other facilities from American banks that had financed their construction after World War One, the fact remained that daylight precision bombing was an untried and unproven method of warfare.

AWPD-1 and its follow-on AWPD-4 and AWPD-42 acknowledged that air superiority was the primary immediate goal. The cost of a sustained bomber offensive against the Nazis would perhaps be too high without achieving it, and the possibility existed that a successful air campaign might negate the need for a ground invasion of Nazi-occupied Europe. There was no question that air superiority had to be achieved for such an endeavour to succeed. Therefore, the destruction of the Luftwaffe and the factories that manufactured aircraft or supplied components became high priority intermediate targets.

"The degree of success attained by our sea and ground forces will be determined by the effective and timely employment of air superiority units and the successful conduct of

RIGHT: A heavily armed Boeing B-17 Flying Fortress bomber drops its payload while flying in formation.
Public Domain

strategical missions," read the plan. "No major military operation in any theatre will succeed without air superiority or at least air superiority disputed."

The plan also advocated the development of the escort fighter. None existed at the time the report was delivered. At the same time, it noted that heavily armed bombers, the B-17 was armed with 13 machine guns, flying at high speed and high altitude in a formation that allowed their armament to be mutually supportive with interlocking fields of fire, would be sufficient for the aircraft to deliver their destructive payloads and return to base with acceptable losses.

Meanwhile, both the bomber and fighter perspectives prevailing in the Army Air Corps on the eve of World War Two contributed to delayed innovation. The idea of the escort fighter was contrary to the notion that the fighter pilot was a hunter, an offensive airman. An officer on the air staff in 1941, future General Hoyt Vandenberg, commented that escort duty was 'incompatible with the mission of pursuit'.

When the US entered World War Two, Field Manual 1-15, Tactics and Techniques of Air Fighting, said bluntly that the role of the fighter escort was thoroughly defensive in nature. "Their firepower may be considered as replacing or augmenting the defensive firepower of the supported force," it read. "Their mission precludes their seeking to impose combat on other forces except as necessary to carry out their defensive role."

Such a perspective was symptomatic of the rigid positions many senior air staff officers held onto. Advances in fighter technology during the

interwar years had been substantial, but one study concluded that the need for the escort fighter had 'not been thoroughly demonstrated'.

In January 1943, President Roosevelt and British Prime Minister Winston Churchill met at Casablanca to discuss the course of the war. Churchill had been disappointed with the contribution of the American Eighth Air Force to the bombing campaign against Nazi-occupied Europe and was determined to convince Roosevelt to order the American forces to switch to nocturnal area bombing, alongside the RAF.

However, the US commitment to daylight precision bombing was so embedded that General Arnold, aware of the situation, urgently ordered General Ira C Eaker, commander of the Eighth Air Force, to Casablanca to head off the prime minister. Eaker met Churchill and successfully dissuaded the effort.

In doing so, Eaker presented Churchill with a single page memorandum supporting the rationale for daylight precision bombing, including the time and trouble of retraining air crews for nocturnal operations and the potential for accidents when too many planes were airborne at night. However, a single sentence really won Churchill over. Eaker wrote: "If the RAF continues night bombing and we bomb by day, we shall bomb them round the clock and the devil shall get no rest." The prime minister, of course, appreciated a well-turned comment.

In theory, the American ideal of successful daylight precision bombing might have appeared plausible, but in reality, there was the devil to pay. The drama was to play out in the skies over Europe.

AIR COMRADES
SPITFIRE, P-38, AND P-47

RIGHT: A graceful Supermarine Spitfire, hero aircraft of the Battle of Britain, flies above an air show in 2018. Creative Commons Airwolfhound via Wikipedia

The British Royal Air Force and the US Army Air Forces fought the Axis for mastery of the skies across Europe and in Asia and the Pacific during World War Two. The primary types that were deployed in fighter interceptor, escort, and ground support roles were the British Supermarine Spitfire, the Lockheed P-38 Lightning, the Republic P-47 Thunderbolt, and the North American P-51 Mustang, flying in all theatres of the conflict.

The Mustang appeared in its long-range bomber escort role after the other types had been performing the function in support of Allied bombing raids in Europe for some time, although limited by their range. The Mustang and other types were renowned as dogfighters as well. In addition to these, the Hawker Hurricane, Typhoon, and Tempest, the Curtiss P-40 Tomahawk, Grumman F4F Wildcat and F6F Hellcat, Vought F4U Corsair, Bell P-39 Airacobra, and others were iconic fighters of World War Two, either in the European or Pacific theatres or both.

The Supermarine Spitfire was the thoroughbred of the RAF and the first all-metal stressed-skin fighter to enter production in Britain. It was the only British fighter type produced throughout World War Two. Engineer Reginald Mitchell, dying of cancer at the time, designed the Spitfire to Air Ministry specification F.37/34, and after his death in 1937, colleague Joseph Smith stepped in as principal designer. The Spitfire prototype flew first on March 5, 1936, and production was started in 1938, ending a decade later with more than 20,000 completed in 24 different variants, or Marks. The Spitfire was recognisable with its elliptical wings, designed by Mitchell and other engineers to minimise drag, but also to accommodate folding

landing gear and the anticipated wing-mounted armament.

The Spitfire gained lasting fame during the Battle of Britain as the RAF thwarted German aspirations to control the skies above the English Channel and the British Isles in preparation for a seaborne invasion of Great Britain. In the event, the Spitfires took on German fighters while the Hurricanes attacked enemy bomber formations, and so many black-crossed planes were shot down that Hitler's Operation Sea Lion was cancelled. American pilots flew the Spitfire before their country entered World War Two, comprising the three famed Eagle Squadrons of the RAF. The US 4th Fighter Group also flew Spitfires until it was replaced with the P-47 Thunderbolt in March 1943 and later the P-51.

The Spitfire Mk V is representative of the performance of the fighter, which was progressively enhanced through the course of World War Two. The aircraft was powered by the Rolls-Royce Merlin 45 V-12 liquid-cooled piston engine generating 1,470hp with a top speed of 370mph and a range of 479 miles. Its armaments included a mixture of up to eight .303-calibre Browning machine guns and 20mm Hispano Mk II cannon, .50-calibre Browning machine guns, and even rockets. The Spitfire Mk IX was an urgent upgrade intended to counter the shock of the Luftwaffe's Fw-190 when it appeared in combat, enhanced with the Merlin 61 engine and other modifications.

BELOW: This restored Spitfire MkIIa is the only existing airworthy example of the type that fought in the Battle of Britain. Public Domain

BELOW RIGHT: A twin-engine Lockheed P-38 Lightning fighter roars across the sky. Creative Commons CindyN via Wikipedia

ABOVE: A modern P-47 Thunderbolt flies at an air show in Chino, California, in 2014. Creative Commons Tim Felce via Wikipedia

LEFT: A photo reconnaissance version of the P-38 Lightning, designated the F-5, and painted with recognition stripes for the D-Day invasion of Normandy, flies above the French countryside. Public Domain

Highly adaptable

Conceived as a short-range fighter interceptor, the Spitfire airframe proved successful in the role and highly adaptable during the war years. A carrier-based variant, the Seafire, was developed, and it was also used in a photo reconnaissance role.

The Lockheed P-38 Lightning was designed in response to a US Army Air Corps specification for a long-range interceptor and escort fighter with a top speed of 360mph and service ceiling of 20,000ft. It first flew in January 1939 and entered production the following year, ceasing in 1945 with more than 10,000 built.

The Lightning design was revolutionary with a twin boom fighter, its cockpit nacelle in the centre, and a pair of Allison V-1710 12-cylinder liquid-cooled engines providing 1,150hp each in the earliest version for a top speed of 414mph and a maximum range of 1,300 miles. The engine capacity was increased with successive variants during wartime production. The Lightning was also heavily armed with four .50-calibre nose-mounted Browning M2 machine guns and a 20mm Hispano M2 cannon in the L variant, along with options for 4.5in M10 rockets and up to 2,000lb of bombs.

The P-38 was distinctive with its twin-boom design and tricycle landing gear. Although it was slightly less manoeuvrable than contemporary single-engine fighters, it was a reliable and versatile combat platform, holding its own against enemy types in Europe and the Pacific and bringing its pilot back to base on one engine if the other became disabled. The P-38 earned the nickname of der Gabelschwanz Teufel, or Fork-tailed Devil, from its German adversaries, and on one memorable occasion, April 5, 1943, squadrons of 26 P-38s of the 82nd Fighter Group shot down 31 German fighters in a single day's combat.

The P-38 was flown in the Pacific by the highest-scoring American ace of all-time, Army Major Richard Bong, who shot down 40 Japanese aircraft. The Lightning was also the type flown by American fighter pilots who shot down Japanese Admiral Isoroku Yamamoto, commander of the Imperial Japanese Navy's Combined Fleet and architect of the Pearl Harbor attack of December 7, 1941, in a long-range interception mission in April 1943. In addition to interceptor, escort, and fighter bomber roles, the P-38 was also used as a photo reconnaissance aircraft.

Prior to US entry into World War Two, American military aviators and designers watched the progress of the air war in Europe with great interest. Engineer Alexander Kartveli, the primary designer of the P-47 Thunderbolt, had originally been working on lighter fighter airframes. However, he was redirected towards a more robust and heavy-duty aircraft that would be powered by the hefty Pratt & Whitney R2800 Double Wasp 18-cylinder radial engine.

The result of the Republic design team's reimagined work was dubbed the Lightning. Pilots who flew the plane in combat appreciated its rugged performance, particularly its ability to take punishment and stay in the air, bringing its pilot home. Many of them swore by the big fighter, nicknaming it 'The Jug' due to its resemblance to a milk bottle.

The P-47 weighed more than 9,000lb empty, considerably more than other contemporary fighters. Its wingspan was just short of 41in, and its length exceeded 36ft. The R2800 powerplant delivered progressively higher top speeds, well above 400mph, with successive variants. The first flight of the P-47 occurred on May 6, 1941, and the initial production variant, the P-47B, began rolling off assembly lines in the spring of 1942. The Lightning was produced through 1945, and over 15,600 were built in five major variants.

The P-47 was familiar in both a razorback canopy design and the later bubble top configuration. It proved to be adept in the escort and fighter-bomber ground support roles. Its heavy armament of eight wing-mounted Browning .50-calibre machine guns, could be augmented by a maximum of 2,500lb of bombs or rockets. Like other types, the P-47's range could be extended with the addition of external drop tanks. Its range on internal fuel tanks was limited to 575 miles.

Although the P-51 is credited with altering the course of the air war in Europe as the quintessential long-range Allied escort fighter of World War Two, the Spitfire, Lightning, Thunderbolt, and other aircraft types played significant roles in achieving the ultimate victory as well.

LEFT: A Republic P-47 Thunderbolt streaks away after strafing a ground target during the Allied advance in Western Europe. Public Domain

MUSTANG ENTERS COMBAT

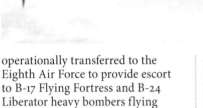

In the winter of 1943, the P-51B Mustang flew combat missions for the first time in World War Two, and the pilots of the 354th Fighter Group based at RAF Boxted are credited with the new aircraft type's baptism of fire.

Activated on November 15, 1942, at Hamilton Field, California, the 354th trained with the Bell P-39 Airacobra fighter, relocating to Tonopah Field, Nevada, Santa Rosa Field, California, and Portland-Columbia Airport, Oregon, initially under the command of Colonel Kenneth R Martin, a skilled tactician who extolled the virtues of the head-on attack in aerial combat. Martin was later involved in a mid-air collision over Nazi-occupied Europe and taken prisoner by the Germans.

In the autumn of 1943, the 354th Fighter Group boarded the transport HMS *Athlone Castle,* crossing the Atlantic to the port of Liverpool and arriving on November 1 en route to its initial base at Greenham Common. Crates carrying the new P-51B Mustang were transported along with the personnel, and as they were unloaded at the dock, the pilots and ground crewmen of the 353rd, 355th and 356th Fighter Squadrons first realised that they would be flying the new fighter.

Within days, the 354th had arrived at RAF Boxted, Colchester, Essex, and within a month the P-51s were active. On December 1, 1943, two

dozen P-51s of the 354th took off on their first combat mission, a fighter sweep over the Pas-de-Calais and Belgium led by Lieutenant Colonel Donald Blakeslee, commanding officer of the 4th Fighter Group and a veteran combat pilot, having flown with the RAF Eagle Squadrons and piloted the P-47 Thunderbolt fighter. With that experience, the 354th gained the nickname of the Pioneer Mustang Group.

Originally assigned to the Ninth Air Force, commanded by General Elwood R 'Pete' Quesada, which had relocated from North Africa and recently undergone reorganisation in its role of tactical air support, the 354th Fighter Group was soon operationally transferred to the Eighth Air Force to provide escort to B-17 Flying Fortress and B-24 Liberator heavy bombers flying missions into Nazi-occupied Europe and Germany.

During the air war in Europe, the 354th Fighter Group was credited with the destruction of 701 enemy aircraft. The group flew the P-51 for the bulk of its time in action during World War Two, flying the P-47 for a brief period from November 1944 to February 1945. It received the Presidential Unit Citation for performance through May 1944, having relocated to RAF Lashenden the previous month.

Successful pilots

Among the large number of successful fighter pilots in the 354th was Major James Howard, whose exploits on January 11, 1944, resulted in his award of the Medal of Honour as the only fighter pilot

ABOVE: A P-51B Mustang of the 356th Fighter Squadron is shown in flight in 1944. Public Domain

LEFT: Jack T Bradley, an ace of the 353rd Fighter Squadron, sits in the cockpit of his P-51D Mustang. Public Domain

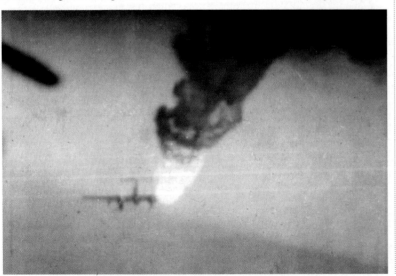

LEFT: A German Messerschmitt Me-410 fighter goes down under the guns of a 354th Fighter Group Mustang on December 17, 1944. Public Domain

in the European theatre to receive the decoration. Howard was flying escort for a formation of B-17s of the 401st Bomb Group and became separated from his 356th Squadron mates. Left alone, he did not hesitate to come to the aid of the bombers when he spotted a swarm of 30 German fighters headed toward them. Howard shot down three enemy aircraft and damaged several others in the twisting battle. When he ran out of ammunition, he bluffed numerous German pilots into evasive action with daring approaches. Finally, the Germans were driven off.

Glenn T Eagleston, the highest scoring pilot of the 354th Fighter Group, shot down 18½ enemy planes with two probables, and five more destroyed on the ground. He commanded the 353rd Fighter Squadron and shot down two communist MiG-15 fighters during the Korean War. Eagleston ended a 27-year career with the rank of colonel.

Other top pilots of the 354th included Major Don M Beerbower, the second highest scoring ace with 15 ½ air-to-air kills. Beerbower was killed in action on August 9, 1944, after downing a German fighter and then shooting up an enemy gun emplacement. His Mustang was hit by ground fire in the wings and fuselage and went into a near-vertical climb before stalling and plunging earthward. Beerbower jettisoned the canopy and bailed out but struck the tail of his plane and never opened his parachute. He was awarded a posthumous Distinguished Service Cross.

Colonel Jack T Bradley shot down 15 German planes, much of his combat activity recorded on gun camera footage. He also

commanded the 353rd Fighter Squadron. Shot down three times during the war, Major Kenneth Dahlberg flamed 14 German aircraft with the 353rd Squadron and was taken prisoner in February 1945. Captain Wallace N Emmer claimed 14 enemy planes but was shot down by flak and captured on August 9, 1944, the same day he was named commander of the 354th Fighter Squadron. Badly burned in the incident, he died in captivity on February 18, 1945. F Michael Rogers shot down 12 German planes while flying with the 353rd Fighter Squadron. He reached the rank of four star general and retired from the top post of US Air Force Logistics Command in 1978 after a 36-year career.

Second Lieutenant Wah Kau Kong lost his life on February 22, 1944, during a mission over Blomberg, Germany. Born in Honolulu, Hawaii, he was the first American fighter pilot of Chinese ancestry and was credited with 1½ aerial victories. During his 14th and final mission, the young pilot accompanied Jack Bradley in an attack against a German Me-410 fighter. As the enemy plane went down, Kong's Mustang was hit by fire and exploded in mid-air.

First Lieutenant Charles F Gumm of the 355th Fighter Squadron was the first Mustang pilot credited with shooting down an enemy aircraft in the European theatre. He was also the first 354th Fighter Group ace of the war. During a mission over Bremen, Germany, on December 16, 1943, Gumm shot down an Me-109 fighter and a Junkers Ju-88 twin-engine bomber. Flying his P-51D nicknamed *My Toni* for his wife and baby daughter residing in Spokane, Washington, he shot down an Me-110

ABOVE: A P-51B Mustang of the 354th Fighter Group sits at RAF Boxted in late 1943. Public Domain

LEFT: Lieutenant Wah Kau Kong was killed in action while flying with the 354th Fighter Group. Public Domain

fighter over Brunswick on February 21, his fifth confirmed kill.

On March 1, 1944, Lieutenant Gumm was making a routine flight from RAF Boxted to RAF Goxhill when, shortly after take-off, his P-51's engine lost power at an altitude of only 800ft. Civilians watched from the ground as the pilot struggled to maintain control of the plane rather than bailing out over a densely populated area around the village of Nayland. Gumm stayed with the plane, which crashed in an open field near the River Stour and high ground known as Court Knoll. Apparently, just before hitting the ground the plane's wing clipped a tree and the pilot was thrown from the cockpit and died on impact.

Undoubtedly, Lieutenant Gumm had saved civilian lives in making his heroic decision. He claimed 7½ victories prior to his untimely death at age 23. He received posthumous awards of the Distinguished Service Cross and the Silver Star. He was buried in his hometown of Spokane, and the people Nayland memorialised his sacrifice with a bench in the centre of town. In 2001, a new bench was dedicated, and brass plaques related to the event were relocated to a nearby churchyard.

The 354th Fighter Group rendered valuable service during World War Two in Europe and recorded historic firsts with the P-51 Mustang. Its legacy is one of heroism and dedication to duty.

LEFT: Lieutenant William B King of the 355th Fighter Squadron poses with his P-51B nicknamed *Georgia Peach* at an airfield in France. Public Domain

COLONEL DONALD BLAKESLEE

RIGHT: Don Blakeslee and the 4th Fighter Group flew the P-47 Thunderbolt fighter before transitioning to the P-51 Mustang.
Public Domain

For fighter pilots of the US Eighth Air Force, a tour of duty consisted of 250 hours of flying time. Colonel Don Blakeslee, commander of the 4th Fighter Group, was always leading from the front, and the story goes that one of his adjutants often doctored flight logs to make combat missions look like training flights. In doing this, it appeared officially that Blakeslee had more mission hours to fly, but he is thought to have spent more than 1,000 hours in the air against the Luftwaffe.

He would not have had it any other way. Finishing World War Two with 14½ aerial victories, Blakeslee became legendary for his leadership, ability to motivate the men who flew for him, and his skill in the air, although he admitted that he was not the best shot and often manoeuvred his fighter into point blank range before opening up on a German aircraft.

Blakeslee was among the first of the first. When young American pilots left the US for Canada and Great Britain to enlist as pilots to help the Royal Air Force fight the Luftwaffe before the United States had been drawn into World War Two, Blakeslee was one of the earliest to do so.

Born on September 11, 1917, in Fairport Harbor, Ohio, he became enamoured with flight after travelling to the National Air Races held at the airport in the city of Cleveland during the 1930s. He worked for the Diamond Alkali Company, scraping up money and saving to buy an aircraft of his own. He persuaded a friend to chip in, and the two became the owners of a Piper J-3 Cub monoplane, which they flew regularly from Willoughby Field in suburban Cleveland.

RIGHT: Don Blakeslee flew combat missions with the Republic F-84 Thunderjet during the Korean War. Public Domain

BELOW: Don Blakeslee lobbied for the 4th Fighter Group to receive the North American P-51 Mustang fighter.
Public Domain

Unfortunately, in 1940, Blakeslee's friend crashed the Piper Cub, ending the venture for the young men. After considering his options, Blakeslee realised that with World War Two underway in Europe, the best way to continue flying would be to volunteer his services. He had joined the US Army Reserve in 1938 and was honourably discharged in 1940, clearing the way to venture to Canada and enlist in the Royal Canadian Air Force (RCAF). He completed pilot training there and arrived in Britain on May 15, 1941, where he was assigned to No 401 Squadron RCAF stationed at RAF Biggin Hill.

During the difficult days of World War Two in the West, Pilot Officer Blakeslee flew fighter sorties over France in the Supermarine Spitfire. On November 18, 1941, he damaged a German Messerschmitt Me-109 fighter over Le Tourquet, and four days later he claimed his first air-to-air kill, an Me-109 shot down above Devres. After turning

for home, he spotted and damaged another Me-109. Several months passed before he scored again, downing two Focke Wulf Fw-190 fighters on April 28, 1942.

Qualities recognised

Blakeslee's leadership qualities had been recognised, and he was promoted to acting flight lieutenant that summer, receiving the British Distinguished Flying Cross on August 14. By that time, he had already been reassigned to No 133 Squadron RCAF, one of the fabled Eagle Squadrons comprising American volunteers flying for the Royal Air Force. His citation read in part: "This officer has completed many sorties over enemy territory. He has destroyed one, probably destroyed two and damaged several more hostile aircraft. He is a fine leader whose keenness has proved most inspiring."

Although he had shunned overtures to immediately join the Eagle Squadrons, quipping that they 'played sister in making their claims', Blakeslee was given the opportunity to serve as an instructor and joined No 133 Squadron as its commanding officer. The move allowed him to remain on combat duty, and he relished the idea. During the ill-fated Dieppe raid of August 1942, the squadron flew air cover, and he shot down an Fw-190. He claimed another Focke Wulf the next day and became one of the earliest American fighter aces of World War Two.

A month later, with the United States now in the war, the three Eagle Squadrons, Nos 71, 121, and 133, were assimilated into the US Army Air Forces (USAAF) as the 4th Fighter Group. Under Blakeslee's command, the 4th would go on to achieve legendary status, and his initial charges were the pilots of the newly organised 335th Fighter Squadron. One issue from the start, however, was the transition from the sleek Spitfire to the rugged, heavy Republic P-47 Thunderbolt. The burly P-47 handled differently but proved a worthy opponent for the Me-109s and Fw-190s it came up against.

Blakeslee personally accounted for the 4th Fighter Group's first kill in the Thunderbolt, shooting down an Fw-190 on April 15, 1943. He followed that up with another confirmed Focke Wulf shot down the next day. The commander flew with his pilots regularly, guiding them above Nazi-occupied France and over western Germany. He became adept at an early version of fighter director tactics, circling at a distance and vectoring his pilots onto enemy aircraft. Of course, he often joined in the hunt as well.

Elevated to command of the 4th Fighter Group in January 1944, Blakeslee acknowledged that the P-47 was a tough and effective fighter plane. However, word that the P-51 Mustang might be available circulated among the squadrons, and he lobbied vigorously for a transition

LEFT: Don Blakeslee stands at far right with Allied generals including SHAEF commander Dwight D Eisenhower and air officers Carl Spaatz and Jimmy Doolittle. Public Domain

BACK: Edwin Chickering, 357th; Hub Zemke, 56th; James Stone,78th; Blakeslee,56th Glen Duncan,353rd; Frank James,55th; Wm Cummings, 355th; Ed Malstrom, 356th; Avelin Tecon, 359th; J.L. Mason, 352nd; Barton Russell, 20th; Thomas Christian,361st. FRONT: Ed Anderson, 4th; Murray Woodbury, Bill Kepner, Jesse Auton, and Francis Griswold. Kepner, Ftr Comd, and other three wing commanders.

LEFT: Don Blakeslee stands, back row fourth from left, with fighter group officers of the Eighth Air Force in 1944. Public Domain

to the new long-range fighter. He had flown the Mustang for the first time in December 1943 and became sold on its characteristics. He assured his superior officers that a transition would not require lengthy training time, and many of the 4th Fighter Group pilots took to Mustang cockpits, flying combat missions with less than an hour to familiarise themselves with the new controls.

After telling his pilots that they would 'learn to fly them on the way to the target', Blakeslee led Mustangs on an escort mission over Berlin, riding shotgun for Boeing B-17 Flying Fortress and Consolidated B-24 Liberator bombers in the first large-scale Eighth Air Force raid on the Nazi capital. Blakeslee led the 4th Fighter Group during the long Operation Frantic missions to shuttle bombs and land in the Soviet Union, returning to England after flying nearly 1,500 miles round trip. Meanwhile, the 4th had become one of the leading fighter groups in Europe, its aggressive pilots shooting down more than 500 German planes by the spring of 1944 and accounting for

more than 1,000 total in the air and on the ground by the end of the war.

During his combat period, Blakeslee was the recipient of two US Distinguished Service Cross awards, the Legion of Merit, the Silver Star, and the Distinguished Flying Cross with silver and two bronze oak leaf clusters, among numerous other decorations. He remained in the US Air Force after World War Two and commanded the 27th Fighter Escort Group in South Korea and Japan during the Korean War. He flew several combat missions piloting the Republic F-84 Thunderjet fighter bomber during the conflict. Promoted to colonel in the spring of 1963, he served as director of operations for the Seventeenth Air Force and retired in 1965 after 28 years of military service. He died at the age of 90 on September 3, 2008, at his home in Miami, Florida.

Through the course of World War Two, Blakeslee commanded several of the greatest American fighter aces. He was a staunch advocate of the P-51 Mustang, and his leadership proved instrumental in its success.

LEFT: Colonel Don Blakeslee, a hero of the 4th Fighter Group and Mustang ace of World War Two, is shown in his later years. Public Domain

TACTICAL AIR SUPPORT

ABOVE: This P-51 Mustang fighter flew with the 382nd Fighter Squadron, 363rd Fighter Group.
Public Domain

Although the US Ninth Air Force had been operating for more than two years by the spring of 1944, its role during World War Two had evolved from being tasked to perform multiple functions in support of the British and later American forces fighting in North Africa and the Middle East while also conducting strategic bombing missions.

Experience in tactical air support in the Middle East, North Africa, and the Mediterranean led Allied leaders to conclude that such capability would be crucial to the success of

ground operations following the expected invasion of Nazi-occupied Europe. Therefore, in early 1943, preparations were made for the Ninth Air Force to transfer to Britain with orders to serve as the American tactical air force that would support the ground advance following the Normandy landings on June 6, 1944.

Under the command of General Lewis H Brereton, the IX Bomber, Service, and Fighter Commands arrived in England in the autumn of 1943. The first fighter group assigned to the Ninth Air Force was the 354th, which reached Britain in November,

stopping briefly at RAF Greenham Common and then moving on to RAF Boxted in Essex mid-month. The 354th Fighter Group was composed of the 353rd, 355th, and 356th Fighter Squadrons, equipped with the P-51B Mustang.

Although original plans had been to equip several Ninth Air Force fighter groups with the P-51, only the 363rd, which arrived at RAF Keevil in December 1943 and took on its Mustangs there, would join the 354th with the new North American Aircraft-produced fighter. Still, a total of 17 fighter groups were assigned to the IX Fighter Command in the first half of 1944.

Among the veteran Eighth Air Force fighter pilots temporarily assigned to the Ninth Air Force's IX Fighter Command to train its newly arrived pilots for combat, Lieutenant Colonel Don Blakeslee, most recently flying the Republic P-47 Thunderbolt, was impressed with the performance of the P-51. He led a group of pilots strongly recommending the assignment of all newly arriving P-51 fighter groups to the Eighth Air Force's VIII Fighter Command.

Blakeslee got his wish, and Mustang fighter groups were soon

RIGHT: This P-51B Mustang of the 354th Fighter Group was photographed in England in 1944.
Public Domain

being assigned to Eighth Air Force. Meanwhile, most of the fighter groups of Ninth Air Force flew the P-47 or the Lockheed P-38 Lightning. Ironically, the development of the Mustang as a high-altitude escort fighter for Eighth Air Force heavy bomber formations, had occurred after the initial request from the British Air Ministry for more low-altitude tactical fighter bombers. The introduction of the Rolls-Royce Merlin engine had thoroughly changed the P-51's role.

Even so, for several months the Ninth Air Force's bombers and fighters were technically under the operational control of the Eighth Air Force. The fighter groups flew escort missions for B-17 Flying Fortress and B-24 Liberator heavy bombers, striking strategic targets in Nazi-occupied Europe, and their pilots became proficient in air-to-air combat defending their big friends. At the same time, the escort missions took away opportunities for training in tactical air support, vital to the progress of Allied ground forces once they had come ashore in Normandy.

First mission

The 354th Fighter Group flew its first mission on December 1, 1943, as 28 P-51s conducted a fighter sweep over Northwestern France above St.

Omer and the Pas-de-Calais, then flying above Flanders and the village of Knokke, Belgium. Four days later, the 354th completed its first escort mission, accompanying bombers to the city of Amiens, France. On December 13, the 354th P-51s joined with P-38s of the 55th Fighter Group, escorting bombers on a 500-mile mission against the German port city of Kiel. During another escort mission to Kiel on January 5, 1944, the 354th pilots shot down 16 German

planes. Two weeks later, Major James Howard of the 356th Fighter Squadron took on 30 enemy fighters attacking a heavy bomber formation, shot down three German planes, damaged others, and chased off the rest, earning the Medal of Honor. The 363rd Fighter Group conducted its initial missions, primarily as fighter escort, in February 1944.

By mid-April, the 354th Fighter Group had relocated to RAF Lashenden and begun »

ABOVE: Many Ninth Air Force pilots trained on the Bell P-39 Airacobra before piloting the P-51 Mustang.
Public Domain

LEFT: The Ninth Air Force conducted tactical bombing raids with aircraft such as the Martin B-26 Marauder.
Public Domain

ABOVE: This Mustang flew with the 161st Tactical Reconnaissance Squadron after the redesignation of the 363rd Fighter Group. Public Domain

conducting a greater number of tactical fighter bomber missions along with the 363rd Fighter Group. Their Mustangs attacked railroads, bridges, supply concentrations, and gun emplacements, strafing with their .50-calibre machine guns and dropping 250lb or 500lb bombs from racks attached to each wing. Even as escort missions continued, the Mustang pilots were given the freedom to attack targets of opportunity on their return flights.

During the D-Day landings on June 6, 1944, the Ninth Air Force Mustangs escorted C-47 transport aircraft towing gliders loaded with troops for insertion into France near Cherbourg on the Cotentin Peninsula. Further missions were flown over the invasion beaches in Normandy and in direct support of the movement of infantry and armour inland. Although enemy aircraft were encountered less frequently by mid-1944, the 354th pilots shot down 68 German planes and lost 23 of their own while flying from RAF Lashenden.

Just two weeks after the invasion, the 354th Fighter Group relocated from Britain to an airfield near Circqueville, France. The 363rd moved to the continent as well, and while on patrol on August 13, a dozen of its P-51s attacked 25 German bombers, shooting down eight and scattering the rest.

In July, Lieutenant Jim Carl, just out of pilot training, joined the 356th Fighter Squadron in France. Swiftly, he was airborne and taking part in one of the hazardous tactical ground support missions that claimed several low-flying Mustangs. The pilots took off to attack targets of opportunity and shot up a German troop train loaded with soldiers and supplies headed for the front lines. Box cars erupted in smoke and flame, and the locomotive – riddled with .50-calibre bullets – spewed steam.

RIGHT: First Lieutenant Charles Gumm, first American pilot to shoot down a German plane and first ace of the 354th Fighter Group, poses with his ground crew. Public Domain

While the P-51s made multiple passes at the train, streaking low across the sky at more than 400mph, the Germans below fired machine guns and anti-aircraft guns from flatcars. Carl strafed the enemy train from locomotive to guard's van. A wheel was blown off one of the box cars and whizzed past his cockpit while tracer bullets pierced the air around him like needles. He flew so low that the expressions of terror and amazement were visible on the faces of the German troops, many of whom were killed, while others ran for whatever cover they could find.

During another mission, the P-51s of Carl's squadron were armed with bombs to hit enemy ground installations. As they began making their bomb runs, a fellow pilot yelled a warning, "Bogeys!" Dozens of German Messerschmitt Me-109 fighters swept down, and the Mustang pilots jettisoned their bombs, turning to fight. Two Mustangs were lost, one pilot was killed and another missing and presumed dead. But in exchange, the Americans shot down 24 Me-109s. Carl had been a

witness. After lining up on an enemy fighter, his guns jammed. He flew through the maelstrom and returned safely to base.

Pilots of the 363rd Fighter Group engaged in ground attack and escort missions after D-Day, shooting down 19 German aircraft but losing about that number of Mustangs – mostly to intense anti-aircraft fire – while conducting tactical ground support missions. In September 1944, its three squadrons, the 380th, 381st, and 382nd, were redesignated the 160th, 161st, and 162nd, and the group was reorganised as the 363rd Tactical Reconnaissance Group, gathering intelligence and assessing Allied bomb damage.

The Mustang pilots of the Ninth Air Force destroyed enemy armour and troop concentrations during the crucial stage of the Battle of the Bulge in December 1944 and flew through to the end of World War Two in Europe. In addition to their essential tactical support missions, the 354th Fighter Group destroyed 701 German planes in the air, the most of any US fighter groups in the European theatre.

RIGHT: The nose of this Me-110 night fighter is equipped with Lichtenstein radar apparatus.
Public Domain

The Fw-190 entered service in August 1941, and though the Allies were aware of its existence, its flight performance came as a nasty shock to pilots of the larger and less responsive Supermarine Spitfire V, then flown by the RAF. When an Fw-190A-3 accidentally touched down in England and was evaluated, its performance was even better than British engineers had expected. Substantially faster than any plane then in Allied service, it was more heavily armed and offered its pilot an excellent field of vision. While the Focke Wulf fighter never supplanted the Me-109 in terms of wartime deployment, it was rapidly deemed a worthy adversary in the air.

RIGHT: A pair of Messerschmitt Me-110 twin-engine fighters flies above Budapest, Hungary, in 1944.
Creative Commons Bundesarchiv Bild via Wikipedia

Improved characteristics

The later F-series carried rockets and other special armament configurations as a tank busting aircraft, while others were outfitted as two-seaters and even carried torpedoes in a rare anti-ship kit. The G-series included improved fighter-bomber and dive-bomber characteristics. However, by 1943 the attention of the Luftwaffe was firmly fixed on the defence of the Reich against air assault by waves of RAF

and USAAF bombers. A night fighter version was developed, but the bulk of the manufacturing resources were devoted to the Fw-190D series, dubbed by the RAF as the long-nosed or 'Dora' model.

The Fw-190D came in response to the high altitude at which American bombers flew by day, and its production ramped up as rapidly as possible by the autumn of 1944. Its supercharged Junker Jumo 213 engine and pressurised cockpit made it ideal for high-altitude interceptor missions. Swift and agile, the Fw-190D was flown by Kurt Tank himself, and it was said to have outrun a flight of P-51D Mustangs that surprised the engineer during a test flight.

During World War Two, the Fw-190 was a proven dogfighter, although the preponderance of the great Luftwaffe aces on both the Eastern and Western Fronts flew the Messerschmitt Me-109. The Focke Wulf fighter was, however, a prodigious hunter and killer of American four-engine heavy bombers. Its toll was tremendous, and several Luftwaffe pilots racked up confirmed kills against two dozen or more Boeing B-17 or Consolidated B-24 bomber formations, although the numbers fell off with the introduction of the P-51 in the long-range escort role.

Other well-known Luftwaffe fighters of World War Two appeared in the skies above the Reich to do battle with Allied fighters. The twin-engine Messerschmitt Me-110 was intended as a ground support aircraft and later as a fighter escort and attack aircraft against Allied bomber formations in day and night fighter configurations. While it was successful in the former role early in the war, it proved a disaster when it came up against the RAF Spitfires and Hurricanes during the Battle of Britain. Nicknamed the 'Destroyer', it was itself destroyed in great numbers, proven incapable of matching the manoeuvrability of the Allied fighters. The introduction of advanced Spitfire Marks and the American Lockheed P-38 Lightning, Republic P-47 Thunderbolt, and of course the P-51 Mustang led to the Me-110 being nicknamed 'Meat on the Table' by Allied fighter pilots.

The Messerschmitt Me-262 was a dazzling performer with air speeds that easily topped any other fighter in general production. However, it was introduced in too few numbers and too late in World War Two to allow the Luftwaffe to regain the initiative in the skies above Europe. The Me-262 was the shape of things to come. Along

with it, the rocket-powered Me-163 Komet was designed as a bomber interceptor with two 30mm MK 108 cannon mounted in each stubby wing.

The Me-163 was powered by a Walter HWK 509A-2 bi-propellant rocket burning hydrogen peroxide and hydrazine/methanol engine generating 3,750lb of thrust and a top speed of roughly 620mph. Although its fuel mixture was volatile, the aircraft itself was remarkably stable. However, it was able to stay aloft for only a short period of time. Introduced in 1944, only about 370 were built, and its combat record reveals up to 18 Allied bombers shot down for the loss of 10 Me-163s.

RIGHT: Caught in the gun camera footage of an American P-47 fighter, a German Me-163 rocket-powered fighter is about to be shot down.
Public Domain

4th FIGHTER GROUP

on April 1, 1943, and then to the P-51 Mustang on February 25, 1944, after Blakeslee lobbied for his squadrons to receive the P-51 as soon as possible. The 4th maintained an intense rivalry with the 56th Fighter Group, led by the famed ace Hubert 'Hub' Zemke and nicknamed Zemke's Wolfpack, during the air war in Europe. The 56th flew the Thunderbolt throughout the conflict.

During the war, the group was credited with the destruction of 1,016 enemy aircraft, the highest number of any US fighter group, and nearly 600 of these were shot down in aerial combat. It flew 416 operational missions, and 293 of these were with the P-51, including high-altitude escort for American heavy bombers, fighter sweeps strafing targets of opportunity, and escort sorties during Operation Frantic, the shuttle bombing missions from Britain to the Soviet Union and back.

The group was the first to use external fuel drop tanks that

ABOVE: Pilots of the 4th Fighter Group posed for this photo at RAF Debden in early 1944. They soon received the P-51 Mustang and went on to achieve outstanding results. Public Domain

RIGHT: This P-51 Mustang nicknamed *Man O' War* was photographed at an air show in 2012. Creative Commons Tomas Del Coro via Wikipedia

BELOW: Lieutenant Ralph 'Kid' Hofer sits in the cockpit of a P-47 Thunderbolt fighter. The ace was later killed in action. Public Domain

The fabled 4th Fighter Group of the US Army Air Forces (USAAF) flew the P-51 Mustang with the highest profile of any organised air unit in World War Two. And when the United States entered the conflict, many of its pilots were already combat veterans.

The 4th Fighter Group was constituted at RAF Debden on September 29, 1942, after elements relocated from RAF Bushey Hall. The 4th came into being as the first American fighter group activated within a theatre of war, and its lineage was from the proud Eagle Squadrons of the Royal Air Force. The Eagle Squadrons, Nos. 71, 121, and 133 RAF, had been formed in 1940 to incorporate volunteer American pilots who ventured to Britain to fight the Nazis before formal US involvement in the conflict.

The three Eagle Squadrons were assimilated into the USAAF as the 334th, 335h, and 336th Fighter Squadrons, and the first commander of the 4th Fighter Group was Colonel Edward W Anderson, who took charge in September 1942 as one of 10 officers who led the group during the war years. Its most famous commander was Colonel Donald Blakeslee, who displayed tremendous qualities of combat leadership and claimed 14½ aerial victories while logging flying hours well more than prescribed limits.

The 4th Fighter Group transferred from the Spitfire to the rugged Republic P-47 Thunderbolt fighter

extended the range of the Mustang, the first American fighter group to engage enemy aircraft over Paris, the first to penetrate German airspace, to engage German fighters and escort bombers over the Nazi capital of Berlin, and the first to destroy more than 300 enemy aircraft. The group received the Presidential Unit Citation for action between March 5 and April 24, 1944, during which its pilots destroyed 323 German planes, 189 in air-to-air dogfights and 134 on the ground. During its wartime deployment, 248 planes of all types were lost, 212 of them P-51s, 125 pilots were killed, and 105 became prisoners of war.

Legendary pilots

Some 81 of its pilots achieved ace status, and among them were some of the legends of the air war in Europe, including Major Don Gentile with 21.84 aerial victories, Major John T Godfrey with 16.33, and Lieutenant Colonel James A Goodson with 15.

The pilots flew their last combat mission on April 25, 1945, and after relocating to RAF Steeple Morden in July, they returned to the US, where the group was deactivated that November.

The combat record of the group remains impressive, and its pilots endured hours of harrowing air battles. Second Lieutenant Norman 'Doc' Achen, a pilot with the 334th Fighter Squadron, remembered one vivid encounter during a strafing run over Nazi-occupied France. "I had a perfect sight picture on the German staff car," he wrote in his book *Go With God*. "I squeezed off a long burst and watched the tracers go directly into the target. Three German soldiers leaped from the car into a lethal storm of 50-calibre gunfire. They began twitching and jerking in what seemed a macabre dance around the now burning vehicle – and then they lay dead on the ground. In those few moments I had become judge, jury, and executioner."

On August 15, 1944, Achen was shot down by German flak during a strafing run against a train and taken prisoner. After liberation, he volunteered for duty in the Pacific, but the war ended before he was deployed.

One of the most colourful aces of the 4th was Lieutenant Ralph Kidd Hofer (born Halbrook). Hofer was credited with the destruction of 15 German planes in the air and a like number on the ground. He received the Distinguished Flying

Cross with silver and bronze oakleaf clusters during his combat career and became the favourite son of Salem, Missouri, his hometown. His P-51B was emblazoned with the nickname *Salem Representative*, and the local newspaper, the *Salem News*, kept close watch on his exploits, while a correspondent in England for the *St. Louis Post-Dispatch* labelled him the 'Screwball Ace of the Air Forces'.

Hofer, a champion Golden Gloves boxer before the war, was known to break radio protocol from time to time and was regularly being reprimanded by 4th Fighter Group commander Blakeslee. The young pilot had joined the military on something of a whim. While on a trip to the West Coast to do some boxing, he found himself in Windsor, Ontario, and happened to walk past an enlistment location for the Royal Canadian Air Force (RCAF). When he was approached about enlisting, he simply said to himself: "Why not?" and changed his surname to Hofer on the application. He flew with the RCAF until transferring to the 334th Fighter Squadron in September 1943, and shot down an enemy fighter on his first mission.

The local Chamber of Commerce resolved to send a congratulatory letter to the hero with the signatures of 30 local business owners affixed. According to the *Salem News*, it read in part: "You are undoubtedly Salem's No 1 fighter, and we are quite proud to have Salem mentioned as your hometown in all the dispatches now appearing in the metropolitan newspapers containing stories of your destruction of Nazi planes. We have every confidence you will continue this fine work until you have set a new high record of your own – and we are pulling for you."

Just 22 years old, Hofer was not shy when the spotlight was shining on

ABOVE: Lieutenant Howard Hively of the 4th Fighter Group is greeted by his dog at RAF Debden just before the change from the P-47 to the P-51 fighter plane. Public Domain

LEFT: Colonel James A Goodson was a leading Mustang ace of the 4th Fighter Group. Public Domain

him, and after being shot down and returning to his base unharmed, he brought back a souvenir of a German helmet for his squadron leader. He told the press: "Nobody minds being a hero," and he gushed with a tale of one aerial encounter, telling a reporter: "I shot down one of those Me-110s myself yesterday. It had me fooled for a while. When I dived down, I saw what I believed to be four engines was really only our old friend the Me-110, packing two huge rocket guns under its wings beside the motors."

Hofer was the epitome of the confident, jaunty fighter pilot, and his story is one of bravery, humour, and adventurism. However, as so often happens in war, he lost his life and youth on July 2, 1944, when his P-51 was shot down by German anti-aircraft fire during a strafing run on an airfield at Mostar Sud, Yugoslavia. His body was removed from the wreckage of his Mustang and returned to the US for burial.

"All of us had hoped that he might someday return to Salem to receive the tribute from his friends as a real hero of the sky," the *Salem News* lamented. "His failure to return will only add glory to the fine record of this boy of the Ozarks established in the finest company known."

LEFT: Former pilots of the RAF Eagle Squadrons, now with the USAAF 4th Fighter Group, are shown with a Supermarine Spitfire fighter at RAF Debden in 1943. Public Domain

357th FIGHTER GROUP

The most successful P-51 Mustang fighter group of World War Two was also the first in the US Eighth Air Force to become active with the aircraft. The 357th Fighter Group, comprising the 362nd, 363rd, and 364th Fighter Squadrons, received the aircraft in December 1943, at RAF Raydon. The group trained with the Mustang for just a few weeks before entering combat with the P-51B on February 11, 1944, flying from its later base at RAF Leiston.

Active for three years and nine months during World War Two, the 357th Fighter Group's Mustangs, along with a single squadron of the 4th Fighter Group, were the first Allied fighter planes in the skies over Berlin on March 4, 1944. During the war, 357th pilots flew 313 combat missions and destroyed 595½ enemy planes in the air and 106½ on the ground. Some 43 pilots became aces, the highest number in the Eighth Air Force. The group was awarded two Presidential Unit Citations.

Activated on December 1, 1942, at Hamilton Field, California, the group was formed around a cadre of experienced officers from the 328th Fighter Group, some of whom had been in the Philippines during the early days of US involvement in the war. The pilots trained elsewhere in California and in Wyoming, flying the Bell P-39 Airacobra. Most of these aircraft were well used, having been inherited from the 354th Fighter Group. After a six-day passage across the Atlantic aboard the liner *Queen Elizabeth*, 357th personnel boarded a train for RAF Raydon in Suffolk on November 29, 1943. By the end of December, there were 15 Mustangs in service with the group. Flight training was limited, and most of the characteristics of the P-51 were learned on the job, flying combat missions.

At the end of January, the Eighth Air Force acquired the 357th, swapping with the Ninth Air Force to obtain the Mustang outfit in exchange for the 358th Fighter Group, flying P-47 Thunderbolts. The swap was prompted by the primary role of the Mustang as a long-range escort fighter protecting bombers while the Thunderbolt had already acquired a sterling reputation as a limited range escort and superb tactical ground support platform. In late January, the 357th was established at its new home at RAF Leiston as a component of the 66th Fighter Wing. The group gained the nickname of the Yoxford Boys, in reference to a village that was close to RAF Leiston.

Initial combat missions were flown in co-operation with the 354th and 4th Fighter Groups, and these were led by Major James Howard, a Medal of Honor recipient, and Lieutenant Colonel Don Blakeslee, who was also destined to gain fame as a P-51 ace. Escort missions were conducted against German V-1 buzz bomb launch sites in the Pas-de-Calais in mid-February, and from the 20th through the 25th, the group was heavily engaged in Big Week, an all-out commitment by Eighth Air Force strategic bombers against industrial targets and infrastructure in Germany. The 357th scored 22 air victories and lost eight Mustangs during the five days of intense combat. During its first full month of operations, its pilots claimed 59 kills for the loss of 14 Mustangs in 15 missions, a ratio advantage of nearly 3.6 to 1.

Bomber protection

Two days after the first fighter-escorted Eighth Air Force bombing of Berlin, the 357th was again protecting B-17 Flying Fortress bombers over the Nazi capital. For action on March 6, 1944, and again over Leipzig on June 29, the group earned the Presidential Unit Citation. Referring to the Berlin raid, the citation read: "The 35 P-51 aircraft went directly to Berlin and picked up the first formations of B-17s just before their arrival over the city. They found the bombers being viciously attacked by one of the largest concentrations of twin-engine and single-engine fighters in the history of aerial warfare. From 100 to 150 single-engine and twin-engine fighters, some firing rockets, were operating in the immediate target area in groups of 30 to 40 and singly. In driving enemy fighters away from the bombers, 20 Nazi fighters were destroyed. On withdrawal, one flight of five P-51s strafed a large enemy airfield in central Germany, damaging three twin-engine and single-engine aircraft on the ground

and killing 15-20 armed personnel before regaining altitude and returning to the bombers."

During August 1944, Mustangs of the 357th escorted bombers during Operation Frantic, shuttling missions over targets in Germany, landing in the Soviet Union, and then hitting oil production facilities in Poland before returning to their temporary base Southeast of Kiev, Ukraine, to re-arm and refuel. The bombers took off again to strike enemy airfields in Romania before heading to bases in Foggia, Italy. The 357th's Mustangs were with them, operating at San Severo before covering a mission to rescue downed Allied airmen in Yugoslavia on August 10 and attacking German communication centres in France before returning to England on the 12th. The top-scoring aces of the 357th were Major Leonard 'Kit' Carson and Major

John B England, both of the 362nd Fighter Squadron, with 18½ and 17½ victories, respectively. Major Richard 'Pete' Peterson of the 364th Fighter Squadron shot down 15½ enemy planes, while future general and aviation legend Charles E 'Chuck' Yeager contributed 11½ kills with the 363rd Fighter Squadron.

The third highest scoring ace of the 357th was Major Clarence 'Bud' Anderson with 16¼ victories. Anderson ended his military career as a brigadier general after 30 years of service, but he gained lasting fame as a 22-year-old hotshot P-51 pilot. He nicknamed a series of aircraft *Old Crow* after the cheapest bottle of bourbon whiskey available anywhere at the time. His first confirmed kill came on March 8, 1944, with a high-angle attack against an Me-109. His second air victory was against an Me-109 on April 11. During the same mission, he damaged another Messerschmitt and shared in the destruction of a Heinkel He-111 bomber.

During the famous Leipzig mission of June 29, 1944, Anderson shot down three enemy Fw-190 fighters. He reported: "We dropped our tanks and started forward when eight Fw-190s went under me. We followed. I dived from above and lined up on one. He broke down, so I picked the leader, gave him a short burst from about 350yds dead astern, got quite a few hits. He did a roll to the right straightened out skidding violently. The canopy flew off and he snapped over on his back bailing out. I then saw another one heading for the clouds. I attacked from the rear, getting quite a few hits all over. I flew alongside and saw fire break out in the cockpit. He slowly rolled over and went straight in from about 8,000ft, making a huge explosion." The third Fw-190 took no evasive action until it was too late. Anderson wrote: "Streamers were coming off his wing tips and tail surfaces and he spun right on in from 8,000ft exploding. No chute came out."

Anderson shot down two more Fw-190s over Berlin on December 5, 1944, and flew 116 combat missions during World War Two. He later served as a test pilot and a wing commander during the Vietnam War. At this time of writing, he remains active aged over 100.

During Operation Market Garden in September 1944, the 357th Fighter Group accounted for 50 enemy aircraft in two days of combat. On January 14, 1945, near Derben, in the vicinity of Berlin, Mustang pilots of the 357th flamed an amazing toll of 50½ German planes and earned their second Presidential Unit Citation. It was by far the highest single day tally of an Allied fighter group in the war. The 357th flew its last mission on April 25, 1945, having operated the P-51B, C, D, and K variants.

Deactivated in Germany on August 20, 1945, the legend of the 357th Fighter Group passed into history. Its honours, lineage, and legacy remain alive today in the care of the Ohio Air National Guard.

MAJOR LEONARD 'KIT' CARSON

RIGHT: Major Leonard 'Kit' Carson sits in the cockpit of his P-51 Mustang *Nooky Booky*. Public Domain

At the age of 20, Leonard Kyle Carson joined the US Army Air Forces in his native Nebraska, earning his wings on April 12, 1943. Assigned to the 362nd Fighter Squadron, he became the highest scoring ace of the 357th Fighter Group with 18.5 aerial victories.

Flying first the P-51B and then three P-51D Mustangs, nicknamed successively *Nooky Booky* and *Nooky Booky II-IV*, he completed two combat tours in the skies over Europe, all with the 362nd Squadron based at Leiston. Carson survived World War Two and remained in the US Air Force, retiring in 1968 with the rank of colonel and then pursuing a career in the aerospace industry. On a single mission November 27, 1944, Carson was flying escort for other fighters and bombers en route to strike targets near Magdeburg, Germany. He shot down five German fighters that day and vividly remembered that eventful encounter in an after-action report.

"I was leading Blue Flight of Dollar Squadron," Carson recalled. "We were in the vicinity of Magdeburg, Germany, when two large formations of bandits were reported. One of the formations, still unidentified, made a turn and came toward us at eight o'clock. We dropped our tanks and turned to meet them. We tacked on to the rear of the formation, which consisted of 50-plus Fw-190s. I closed to about 300 yards on the nearest one and fired a medium burst with no lead, getting numerous strikes. He started to burn and went into a turning dive to the left. I believe the pilot was killed. He never recovered but crashed into the ground and exploded."

Carson had entered the swirling dogfight with determination, and his hunt was on. "I returned to the main formation, again closing to the nearest one at the rear," he continued. "I opened fire at about 300yds, firing two short bursts, getting strikes all over the fuselage. He started to smoke and burn. He dropped out of formation and turned to the right until he was in a sort of a half split-S position, never recovering from this attitude. I saw him crash and burn. The pilot did not get out.

"Closing again on the main formation, I pulled on to the nearest man, at about 400yds. I fired a short burst, noting a few hits. He broke violently to the left and I broke with him. I picked up a lead on him and fired two more bursts, getting strikes

on the cockpit and engine. He started to smoke and burn badly. The pilot jettisoned the canopy and bailed out. I watched him fall for quite a distance but did not see his chute open. The Fw-190 crashed about 50yds from a house situated in a small town.

"I could still see the main formation about a mile ahead of me. While starting to catch them, I saw a straggler on the deck. I dropped down to engage him, but he saw me coming. He turned away from me and I gave chase for about three minutes before I caught him. I opened fire at about 400yds, getting strikes on the right side of his fuselage. He turned sharply to the right and I picked up a few degrees lead, firing two more bursts, getting more strikes on the fuselage. The pilot jettisoned his canopy and bailed out. As I was chasing this one, another formation of 40 Fw-190s passed about 500ft above and 400yds in front of me. They made no attempt to engage me or to help their fellow Jerry. They continued on a heading of 20 to 30 degrees.

"I pulled up after my last engagement and set course for home base when another Fw-190 came in at my wingman and me from seven o'clock high. We broke into him, and he started a zooming climb. I chased him, gaining slowly. Suddenly he dropped his nose and headed for the deck. I gave chase and caught him in four or five minutes. I opened fire at 400-450yds but missed. I closed further and fired another burst, getting several strikes on the fuselage. The plane started to smoke. I fired again as he made a slight turn to the right, observing more hits on the fuselage. Then the pilot jettisoned his canopy, and I broke off my attack to the right. I waited for him to bail out, but he didn't, so I turned to engage him again. I was still about 700yds away when the pilot pulled the nose up sharply and left the ship. His chute opened a couple seconds later. I claim five Fw-190s destroyed in the air. Ammunition: 1,620 rounds expended."

RIGHT: This P-51D Mustang is painted to resemble Kit Carson's fighter *Nooky Booky IV.* Creative Commons Alan Wilson via Wikipedia

RIGHT: One of them painted to resemble Kit Carson's P-51D *Nooky Booky IV*, a pair of Mustangs flies during a 2011 demonstration. Creative Commons Tony Hisgett via Wikipedia

MAJOR JOHN B ENGLAND

"Two pilots bailed out, two did not." So wrote Major John B England of the 362nd Fighter Squadron, 357th Fighter Group after an escort mission near Magdeburg, Germany, on November 27, 1944. While England shot down four German fighters on the day, squadron mate Major Leonard 'Kit' Carson flamed five in the same air battle.

England, born January 15, 1923, in Caruthersville, Missouri, had joined the US Army in April 1942 and qualified as an aviation cadet. He trained in Arizona with future US Senator Barry Goldwater as his flight instructor. Earning his wings in March 1943, England flew his first combat mission in the P-51 Mustang from RAF Leiston on February 11, 1944. He ended World War Two with 17½ confirmed aerial victories.

His succinct encounter report for that day in November 1944 read: "I was leading Dollar Green flight when I observed a large gaggle of enemy aircraft coming in formation from 10 o'clock slightly low. I approached them from above and to the right. Just as they went beneath me, I peeled down and pulled up behind them, around 800yds to 1,000yds away. There were around 40-50 Fw-190s, flying in a bunch and, as far as I could observe, in no particular type of formation. I pulled up behind the rearmost E/A (enemy aircraft) to within 600yds, opened fire from 600yds and saw strikes around his cockpit and smoke and fire coming out around his engine nacelle. This E/A flipped over, and the pilot bailed out. I was busy and did not have a chance to watch the chute open.

"I pulled up behind another Fw-190, closing to 300yds, and fired a long burst. He broke, but I got good hits on his wings and cockpit while he was breaking and during one or two turns immediately after his break. His canopy and pieces of his wings came off. The pilot bailed out, but I believe he was seriously injured.

"By this time, we were heading for the deck, when what was left of the gaggle which had stayed together was observed. I pulled up behind another Fw-190, firing a long burst. He flipped over and went straight into the ground. The pilot was definitely killed.

"Then I pulled up behind another Fw-190 and went through the same procedure, starting to fire from 800yds and closing to 150yds, observing strikes in his cockpit. The plane dived straight forward, went into the ground and exploded.

"This was one of the best shows I have ever seen since being in combat. Our whole squadron had tacked on to the rear of the enemy A/C (aircraft) and opened fire simultaneously. I believe these enemy planes were part of a huge force intending to rendezvous with another force and attack our bombers, which were bombing southwest of this vicinity. I claim four Fw-190s destroyed (air). 1,840 rounds."

Major England remained in the US Air Force after the war and formed a P-51 demonstration team called the Red Devils. He flew six combat missions in the F-86 Sabre during the Korean War and was credited with damaging an enemy MiG-15 jet. He was promoted to lieutenant colonel in October 1953 and was killed in the crash of his fighter on approach to an airfield in Marseille, France, amid adverse weather conditions on November 17, 1954.

TOP: John B England flew six missions in the F-86 Sabre during the Korean War and was promoted to lieutenant colonel.
Public Domain

ABOVE: North American P-51 Mustang fighters sit on the ground at RAF Leiston.
Public Domain

LEFT: Major John B England shot down four Focke Wulf Fw-190 fighters in a single mission.
Public Domain

MEMORABLE MUSTANG MISSIONS

RIGHT: Major Pierce McKennon commanded the 335th Fighter Squadron and was rescued by Lieutenant George Green. Public Domain

Major Pierce McKennon, a P-51 Mustang ace with a total of 19 victories in the air and on the ground, was leading the 335th Fighter Squadron, 4th Fighter Group in a strafing mission against Prenzlau airfield, roughly 40 miles from the German capital Berlin.

By March 18, 1945, the end of World War Two in Europe was in sight. But there were dangerous missions to be completed. McKennon flew into a maelstrom of flak and took a hit in the engine. Forced to bail out at 4,000ft, he came down in an open field. Among the 25 other members of the 335th flying that day, Lieutenant George Green watched his commanding officer descend.

For McKennon, Green had been a discipline problem, grounded four times for breaking the rules and even swiping his commander's Jeep for a ride. More than once, McKennon had threatened to throw Green out of the squadron. However, he also realised that Green was a fine, aggressive pilot. This day, McKennon had given the troublesome Green another chance and allowed him to fly as his wingman. And he was glad that he did.

RIGHT: Major Pierce McKennon sits in the cockpit of his Mustang fighter nicknamed *Ridge Runner III*. Public Domain

BELOW: Captain Bruce Carr stands before his P-51 nicknamed *Angels' Playmate*. He commanded the 353rd Fighter Squadron, 354th Fighter Group. Public Domain

Green knew it was strictly forbidden to land in enemy territory to attempt the rescue of a downed fellow airman. But true to form, he did it anyway. When he saw German soldiers running toward McKennon, he called other Mustang pilots in to strafe them while he came down in the field. As McKennon sprinted toward the P-51, Green tossed everything he could get his hands on out of the cramped cockpit, including his own parachute. McKennon threw his parachute away too.

The confines of the P-51 cockpit were tight for one man, but Green sat in McKennon's lap and gunned the Merlin engine, taking flight seconds later. Flying at 18,000ft, McKennon passed out from lack of oxygen, and Green roused him. The two then shared a single mask the rest of the way home. When Green was asked why he had done it, he quipped: "I figured I owed the guy a favour."

For a P-51 Mustang pilot in wartime, every mission was probably memorable. Flying in hostile airspace and living to tell the tale meant so much. But then, some missions were indeed extraordinary.

While No 414 Squadron Royal Canadian Air Force flew reconnaissance and support missions over Dieppe on August 19, 1942, Flying Officer Charles 'Smokey' Stover was flying at only about 50ft when he was jumped by a German Fw-190 fighter. Forced to take evasive action, Stover clipped a telephone pole that promptly tore off about three feet of his right wing and half the aileron. He managed to return safely to base, demonstrating his flying skill and the toughness of the Mustang.

Captain Glendon Davis of the 364th Fighter Squadron, 357th Fighter Group, brought his damaged Mustang home after a gut-wrenching encounter when the victor was almost downed by the victim, an enemy Me-109. Davis recalled of the March 16, 1944, incident above the city of Ulm, Germany, "I closed on him – firing steadily all the way and observing my bullets completely riddle his plane. Just as I pulled off to avoid collision he exploded. Pieces

of his plane hit the top and leading edge of my right wing, smashing it flat. I climbed back up to 29,000ft and came home alone, not being able to locate my second element. I can truthfully say that I owe my life to the excellence of American materials and workmanship."

Davis finished the war with 7½ air victories, all in the P-51.

Most harrowing mission

Captain Bruce Carr of the 353rd Fighter Squadron, 354th Fighter Group, ended the war with 15 kills, all in the P-51. He remained in the US Air Force, rising to the rank of colonel and flying 57 missions in Korea and 286 in Vietnam. However, he never forgot the most harrowing mission of his life. Shot down on a strafing run over Czechoslovakia in November 1944, he hid from German patrols for a time and stayed near an enemy airfield.

Noticing that a particular Fw-190 fighter had been fuelled and moved to a rather isolated place, Carr decided to take his chances. He dashed for the unattended plane, leaped into the cockpit, and began flipping switches, hoping to find the starter and crank the engine. This Focke Wulf fighter was an Fw-190A-8, which featured a single switch that controlled several vital

functions, and within half an hour of climbing aboard, Carr was airborne.

The Germans were roused as the engine coughed to life, and as they sprinted toward him, Carr was unable to line up properly on the runway. Instead, he opened the throttle and roared across a corner of the airfield between two hangars and into the air. Once aloft, he figured out how to retract the landing gear. The next concern was to avoid being killed by his own anti-aircraft fire or an Allied fighter pilot. He flew low, just above the treetops, and sweated every minute of the 200-mile flight back to his airfield in France.

When he determined that he was close to home, Carr tried to get the landing gear back down, but he failed. The best option then was to belly land the German fighter before the surprised Americans on the ground had time to fire their .50-calibre anti-aircraft guns at him. The tactic worked, but there were a few anxious moments as Carr climbed out of the Fw-190. Several rifles and pistols were pointed directly at him.

Once Captain Carr let loose with a few expletives, the guns were lowered! He related the story to awe-struck listeners and the wrecked Fw-190 was proof enough that his account was accurate. A few days later he was

back in the air. He went on to shoot down five enemy planes in a single mission on April 2, 1945. Along with three other P-51 pilots, he took on a swarm of 60 German fighters and became a Mustang ace in a day. For that act of heroism, he received the Distinguished Service Cross.

The story of Major Fletcher Adams of the 362nd Fighter Squadron, 357th Fighter Group recounts a wartime atrocity. At times, an Allied airmen who was captured alive met a terrible fate. On May 30, 1944, Adams flew his P-51B nicknamed *Southern Belle* on an escort mission to Bernburg, Germany.

During the heat of battle, *Southern Belle* was hit. Lieutenant Gilbert O'Brian reported on what he observed. "I last saw Capt. Fletcher E Adams at approximately 12.30pm on the May 30, 1944, in the vicinity of Celle, Germany. I was leading Capt. Adams' element at about 25,000ft, trying to overtake our bombers, when four Bf-109s came down on us from behind and out of the sun. They were at about seven o'clock. Before I knew what was happening, tracers were going over my wing and into my plane. I broke straight down, calling for the rest of the flight to follow suit. As I broke, I looked up and got a flashing picture of a Bf-109 firing from close range at Capt. Adams. I saw him streaming coolant or coolant smoke. Shortly after this Capt. Adams' aircraft rolled over on its back and split-S'd. His ship was in a controlled roll and apparently, he himself had not been hit."

Adams did bail out and survive the crash of his P-51 and was taken into custody by three German soldiers. Shortly afterwards, members of the local militia took control of the prisoner. The leader of the militia in the area, a sergeant named Funke, ordered two others, Gustav Heidmann and Erich Schnelle, to execute Adams. The three men »

took their captive into the nearby forest and fatally shot him.

Adams' fate was unknown until evidence was heard by a US military court at Dachau, Germany, in July 1946. Funke was apparently never brought to trial, but Heidmann was found guilty of murder and sentenced to death. Schnelle was sentenced to 20 years in prison. Later, however, Heidmann's sentence was reduced to 20 years, and he was released in 1954. Schnelle was paroled in 1950. Adams left behind a wife and infant son.

Student pilots?

"My first encounter with the Luftwaffe came recently when our 78th FG tangled with 24 Me 109s," wrote Captain Duncan McDuffie of the 83rd Fighter Squadron. "I am still trying to figure out whether those German pilots were flying students or whether they were full-fledged combat airmen. I believe they were the latter because they tried to fight. If so, then the German air force has sunk a long way from the early days of 1940 when it was rated the best in the world."

McDuffie also reported that the entire fight was over in eight or nine minutes. And in that short time, he shot down four German Me-109s, quite a tally for a first time tangling with Luftwaffe fighters in the air.

On March 2, 1945, an escort mission had developed into a dogfight. "Enemy aircraft, which turned out to be 24 plus 109s, were called out

ABOVE: Major Fletcher Adams flew the P-51B *Southern Belle* with the 362nd Fighter Squadron, 357th Fighter Group. Public Domain

LEFT: Flying from Iwo Jima, Captain Jerry Yellin has been credited with completing the last combat mission of World War Two in his Mustang. Creative Commons Bobeldridge via Wikipedia

at six o'clock low," McDuffie wrote. "The enemy aircraft were in a large loose formation in a left-hand pattern. We made a 180 degree turn and then a left turn, positioning us on their tails at about 15,000ft.

"I pursued one which broke to the left. We made a half turn when I gave him a lead while he was in a gentle climb," McDuffie continued. "After a good squirt, I saw generous hits on the canopy and engine. He flipped on his back and went down. I figured he'd been had so continued in the turn and found myself on the tail of another 109. This was a repeat of the first situation except the enemy aircraft was on fire when he went in.

"I was then at cloud level, so went beneath them and saw a 109 on the deck that apparently never saw me. I bounced him, gave him a long burst and the Jerry burst into a huge mass of flame and ploughed in.

"I sighted the fourth enemy aircraft at about 7,000ft. He saw me and evaded into one of the semi thick clouds. I followed, gained on him, and fired a short burst. Hits showed and he dodged back for a cloud. I followed and got in another short burst when he headed for another cloud. This dodging from cloud to cloud went on for

LEFT: Ground crewmen arm the weapons of an Me-109 fighter of JG-51, the Luftwaffe fighter group of ace Major Gunther Schack. Creative Commons Bundesarchiv Bild via Wikipedia

RIGHT: In August 2017, Captain Jerry Yellin talks with Don Brown, author of the book 'The Last Fighter Pilot'. Creative Commons Bobeldridge via Wikipedia

RIGHT: P-51 Mustangs sit at North Field on the island of Iwo Jima in 1945. Mustang squadrons flew VLR missions to Japan from Iwo Jima. Public Domain

Startling discovery

Mustang pilots took part in Operation Frantic shuttle missions, escorting bombers to targets in Germany, flying on to the Soviet Union, refuelling and re-arming to strike other targets on the return flights. During one of these missions on August 6, 1944, Major Gunther Schack, a Luftwaffe ace of Jagdgeschwader 51 (JG 51) with 174 confirmed kills was startled.

Expecting Soviet bombers to be his aerial opponents, Schack had taken off from an airfield at Lyke in East Prussia along with eight other Me-109s. As he closed on a bomber formation, he was shocked to see American fighters, P-51 Mustangs, rapidly closing the distance towards him.

One of the Mustangs got on Schack's tail, and the veteran ace took immediate evasive action, turning and jinking. But the American pilot was experienced as well. Lieutenant Hollis 'Bud' Nowlin of the 357th Fighter Group was flying his Mustang nicknamed *Hells Bells*. Credited with five enemy planes damaged or destroyed by the end of the war, he was determined to score and poured fire into Schack's Me-109. Smoke began to stream from the German fighter's engine, but Nowlin was nearly out of ammunition and running low on fuel with a long flight home. He peeled away, leaving Schack to make a belly landing in a field. Soviet soldiers came running, but German troops got to him first. Schack had cheated death – just.

For nearly 40 years, Schack wondered why the American Mustang pilot had allowed him to escape and had refrained from finishing his stricken plane off in the air. The two former foes finally met decades later in Germany,

BELOW: Captain Bruce Carr flew a Focke Wulf Fw-19A-8 like this one to freedom after hopping aboard at a Nazi airfield. Public Domain

about four or five passes with hits showing each time. On my next to last pass, I saw that his left elevator was completely gone and part of his right wing. On my last pass I saw hits on the engine and canopy. The enemy aircraft jerked, and glycol began streaming, and the airdrome over which we had been fighting commenced firing at me.

"The enemy aircraft slid off on one wing in a steep dive," concluded McDuffie, "and I, feeling that the enemy aircraft was done for, and to avoid the flak, climbed through the clouds."

ABOVE: Pilots of the 83rd Fighter Squadron pose with a P-47 Thunderbolt fighter in July 1944. The 83rd also flew the P-51, and Captain Duncan McDuffie shot down four Me-109s in the Mustang.
Public Domain

RIGHT: Mustangs like this P-51B of the 354th Fighter Squadron took part in Operation Frantic.
Public Domain

RIGHT: Boeing B-29 Superfortress bombers of the 468th Bomb Group fly over Japan. Jerry Yellin and his fellow Mustang pilots flew hazardous escort missions with the big bombers.
Public Domain

and Schack's question was answered. Nowlin was somewhat surprised to learn that he had in fact shot down the great ace and holder of the Knight's Cross with oakleaves that day. The two men became friends and met again, this time in the US at a 1991 reunion of the 357th Fighter Group.

The surrender of Japan, ending World War Two, was announced on August 14, 1945. But that morning, as far as the P-51 Mustang fighter pilots of the 78th Fighter Squadron, 15th Fighter Group knew, the war was still on. Captain Jerry Yellin, who had already flown 18 hazard VLR (very long range) missions from the recently occupied island of Iwo Jima to Japan, took off on a mission to strafe an enemy airfield near Tokyo.

The announcement of the Japanese surrender was made at noon local time, and Yellin's flight of Mustangs was already in the air. For some unknown reason, the pilots failed to receive the pre-arranged

message that meant the war was over. They continued and executed their strafing runs. Yellin and his wingman, 1st Lieutenant Phillip Schlamberg, roared into cloud cover, attempting to avoid anti-aircraft fire.

Yellin came out, but Schlamberg did not. The lieutenant's body was never recovered, and he is believed to be the last known American combat death of World War Two. Yellin has been credited with flying the last air combat mission of the war. He returned to Iwo Jima after hours in the cockpit and only then learned that it was over.

In his later years, Yellin dealt with post-traumatic stress disorder (PTSD), recovered, and became friends with Taro Yamakawa, a former Japanese pilot during the war, whose daughter had married Yellin's son.

Jerry Yellin wrote four books in his later years and became widely known for his efforts to reconcile with former enemies and for his work with other veterans who suffered from PTSD. He died in 2017 at the age of 93.

BILL OVERSTREET'S BATTLE

The life of a fighter pilot in the war-torn skies over Europe during World War Two was punctuated with moments of life-and-death engagement, of luck, and of skill and daring. Captain William B 'Bill' Overstreet Jr, a P-51B Mustang pilot with the 363rd Fighter Squadron, 357th Fighter Group for much of his career, had his share of such moments.

The most memorable occurred in the spring of 1944, when Overstreet was flying fighter escort for heavy bombers. At the controls of his Mustang, nicknamed *Berlin Express*, he engaged a German Messerschmitt Me-109 fighter. Within minutes, most of the Germans had broken off contact and headed back to their bases as the dogfight petered out near Paris. With Overstreet on his tail and regularly firing .50-calibre machine-gun rounds into his stricken plane, its engine coughing and streaming smoke, the Me-109 pilot decided to fly directly over the City of Light.

Reasoning that Overstreet would not chase him across Paris with the threat of German anti-aircraft fire in such a concentrated area, the German coaxed his engine for airspeed. Although the enemy ground fire grew in intensity, the impetuous American pilot stayed on the enemy's tail. In a last-ditch attempt to shake the Mustang, the German flew directly towards the Eiffel Tower, the symbol of France, and then directly underneath the towering monument. Overstreet would not be denied and continued to fire at the enemy plane until it went down, then following the course of the River Seine to safety. Observers on the ground were startled by the unusual encounter, which has become legendary in Mustang lore.

ABOVE: The modern P-51B Mustang *Berlin Express* takes off during the air show at Duxford, 2017. Creative Commons Alan Wilson via Wikipedia

LEFT: Bill Overstreet chased and shot down an Me-109 fighter over Paris. Creative Commons Bundesarchiv Bild via Wikipedia

"I had followed this 109 from the bombers when most of the German fighters left," Overstreet remembered. "We had a running dogfight, and I got some hits about 1,500ft. He then led me over Paris, where many guns were aimed at me. He figured I'd get around and he'd have time to get away. He was wrong. I was right behind him, right under the Eiffel Tower with him. And when he pulled up, I did get him. But listen that's a huge space. As soon as he was disabled, I ducked down just over the river, a smaller target for the Germans, and I followed the river until I was away from Paris."

Bill Overstreet had another close call in the spring of 1944 and barely survived. "While over enemy territory, a burst of flak cut my oxygen line," he recalled. "Since I was at about 25,000ft, I soon passed out. The next thing I knew, I was in a spin, engine dead since the fuel tank it was set on was dry. Somehow, I recovered from the spin, changed the fuel setting, got the engine started, and dodged the trees that were in front of me. Then, I looked at my watch. Ninety minutes were not in my memory. I had no idea where I was but remembered where I had been headed so I reversed it. I was able to find the coast of France and headed for Leiston."

Flying with infection

On yet another occasion, Overstreet took to the air while suffering from a sinus infection. While escorting bombers, he engaged an Me-109 at 30,000ft. When the German started to dive, the P-51 pilot followed at incredible speed. In seconds, the abrupt change in pressure caused his eyes to become swollen shut. Flying by instinct, Overstreet was able to maintain control of his Mustang, but he had no way to determine a correct direction or even to see his surroundings. He felt like a sitting duck. He called for help, and a squadron mate

LEFT: Captain Bill Overstreet shot down a German Me-109 after flying below the Eiffel Tower. Public Domain

»

BILL OVERSTREET'S BATTLE

was lost in action while being flown by another pilot, he decided to rename his replacement P-51 *Berlin Express*. On D-Day, June 6, 1944, the 363rd Fighter Squadron flew eight sorties in support of the Normandy landings, the first of these arduous missions lasting six hours. Through the next week, the American pilots strafed targets of opportunity, hitting German supply convoys, trains, river transport, and troop concentrations. On August 10, Overstreet engaged a German Fw-190 and dispatched the enemy fighter with fewer than 40 rounds of .50-calibre ammunition expended.

talked him through an orientation that put his plane on the proper course. The other P-51 pilot stayed with Overstreet, and he successfully landed in England under the voice coaching of the ground control. Several days were required before the swelling subsided and he could see once more.

While not dealing with difficult circumstances, Bill Overstreet demonstrated that he was a proficient fighter pilot. He engaged another German fighter on July 29, 1944, west of the city of Merseburg, Germany, reporting a bit of daredevil flying to make sure of the kill. "I was flying Cement Red #3, and my wingman and I were making a pass on a large field,"

he reported. "As we did, an Me-109 dived on us slightly to our right. I turned into him as soon as I was across the field, and he was fairly close. He turned right also, leaving me right behind him. Using the gyro gunsight, I fired about 30-degree deflection and got hits. I think the range was about 350yds. I closed in still firing and hit his coolant. He dropped down right on the ground and as my wing was in the grass I had to pull up. Pieces of the 109 made holes in my canopy." The Mustang pilot claimed the Me-109 as an aerial kill, destroyed an Fw-190 on the ground, and claimed another Fw-190 and Dornier Do-217 damaged on the ground.

Overstreet was born in Clifton Forge, Virginia, on April 10, 1921. He enlisted in the US Army Air Corps and waited several months for a slot to open as an aviation cadet. After graduating from pilot training, he was assigned to the 363rd Fighter Squadron, 357th Fighter Group in California. Flying the Bell P-39 Airacobra, he nearly lost his life when the plane went into an uncontrollable spin on June 28, 1943. His escape with only minor injuries was miraculous.

Overstreet flew the P-51 for the first time on January 30, 1944, from RAF Leiston. He nicknamed his first Mustang *Southern Belle*, but after it

The 357th Fighter Group later participated in Operation Frantic, the shuttle bombing missions of US Eighth Air Force bombers that struck targets in Germany and then flew on to land and refuel at bases in the Soviet Union. During one mission, the pilots traded .50-calibre bullets for vodka, emptying their weapons. The flight home became a bit dicey as the Mustangs were confronted by German fighters and managed to bluff their way through the encounter. One of the Me-109 pilots was so intimidated that he bailed out of his fighter without a shot being fired.

Overstreet's adventures also included flying escort during top secret Operation Aphrodite, when an explosive-laden bomber was deliberately crashed by remote control into Nazi submarine pens to demolish these U-boat facilities. He flew missions for the Office of Strategic Services (OSS), the forerunner of the US Central Intelligence Agency, recovering downed airmen, and returned to the United States in October 1944, leaving active duty a few months later while remaining in the reserves. After a combat experience that rivalled that of any other pilot in World War Two, Overstreet lived to age 92.

MUSTANGS IN THE MEDITERRANEAN

The P-51 Mustang entered service in the Mediterranean theatre of operations during World War Two with several fighter groups of the US Twelfth and primarily the Fifteenth Air Forces. The groups flew various types of fighter aircraft, including the British Supermarine Spitfire, the Curtiss P-40 Tomahawk, and the Republic P-47 Thunderbolt. By the time most of them received their P-51 Mustang fighters in the spring and summer of 1944, the pilots were veterans of aerial warfare, engaged against enemy aircraft, flying bomber escort, and strafing enemy installations and other targets on the ground.

Among the most famous of the fighter groups that flew the P-51 in the Mediterranean was the 332nd, the fabled Tuskegee Airmen, an all-black outfit that flew into history as the Red Tails – named for the distinctive paint scheme on its P-51s. The 332nd Fighter Group included the 99th, 100th, 301st, and 302nd Fighter Squadrons. Its pilots destroyed or damaged 400 Axis aircraft during the war and flew nearly 1,600 combat missions, earning the praise of bomber formation personnel who were escorted to targets across Nazi-occupied Europe.

The 325th Fighter Group, comprised the 317th, 318th, and 319th Fighter Squadrons transitioned from the P-47 to the P-51 in May 1944, and flew escort missions to the Soviet Union during the shuttle bombing programme. Missions were also flown against heavily defended targets such as the Messerschmitt assembly plant at Regensburg, Germany, the Daimler-Benz tank

factory on the outskirts of Berlin, the Nazi capital, and against oil facilities in Vienna, Austria, as well as across Czechoslovakia, Hungary, Romania, and the Balkans. The 318th Fighter Squadron alone was credited with the destruction of 173 enemy planes in aerial combat. The 325th Fighter Group's squadrons received multiple Presidential Unit Citations.

The leading Mustang ace of World War Two in the Mediterranean was Captain John J Voll of the 308th Fighter Squadron, 31st Fighter Group, which received its P-51s in March 1944, transitioning from the Spitfire after 19 months flying the British model. Some of the pilots of its 307th, 308th, and 309th Fighter Squadrons were reluctant to make the change. Voll took to the new fighter with gusto and shot down 21 enemy planes during an active period between June 23, 1944, and his reassignment to the China-American Composite Wing late in the year after 57 combat missions. Voll finished third among all Mustang aces of World War Two.

Voll's fellow pilots of the 31st Fighter Group embraced the P-51 soon enough. Flying fighter sweeps and escort missions over France, northern Italy, Austria, and Romania, the new Mustang jockeys flamed 98 German aircraft in their first two months with the Mustang. In June 1944, the 31st flew into Germany for the first time, and at the end of the month the tally of enemy aircraft stood at 52. In July, escort missions were flown over Munich, Friedrichshafen, Blechhammer, and Brux, as well as Budapest and Bucharest, the capital cities of Hungary and Romania respectively, and the oil refineries and storage facilities at Ploesti, Romania, which were hit by bombers four times. That month, the 31st Fighter Group score soared to 82 enemy planes destroyed. »

Highest scorers

On March 31, 1945, the 309th Fighter Squadron swirled in a dogfight with 30 German Messerschmitt Me-109 fighters, shooting down 18 of them in 20 minutes without any losses. By the end of World War Two in Europe, the 31st Fighter Group was the highest-scoring unit of its size in the Mediterranean with 570½ confirmed kills, a substantial number of them with the P-51.

Captain Robert Goebel of the 308th Fighter Squadron finished the war with 11 aerial victories in 61 combat missions flying the P-51. He remembered an encounter over Ploesti on July 3, 1944, that may well contradict an assertion made by Major Erich 'Bubi' Hartmann, leading fighter ace of all time with 352 victories. Hartmann recalled tangling with Mustangs that day and bailing out of his Me-109 after running out of fuel. He also remembered that the American pilot tailing him made a final pass and waved.

Goebel, however, recalled that he fired on an Me-109 and that hits from his .50-calibre machine guns made the German ace hit the silk. He was unaware that the enemy pilot was Hartmann. "I spotted two Me-109s above and about 5 o'clock," he wrote in his post-war memoir 'Five Down And Glory'. "The two 109s started down to attack the bombers below – it was a rash act indeed. Now the 109 almost filled my sight. Quickly raising the pipper almost to the tip of his tail, I fired again and was rewarded this time with strikes quick-flashing around the fuselage and wing roots, then his prop wash threw me off momentarily. Before I could get the sight back on him for another burst, the pilot left his airplane. Putting the gun switch in the 'Camera Only' position I made a pass at him, being careful to break off so my slipstream would not collapse

his canopy. As I passed to the side of him, I raised my gloved hand in a half wave half salute and then reformed my flight. The latest victory brought my total to four."

Whether or not Goebel shot Hartmann down that day, or the great ace abandoned his Me-109 due to dry tanks is still discussed to this day.

The 52nd Fighter Group operated as an element of the Twelfth Air Force until transferring to Fifteenth Air Force command in April 1944. During that same period, its pilots of the 2nd, 4th, and 5th Fighter Squadrons transitioned from the Spitfire to the P-51. Along with other groups the 52nd participated in shuttle bombing and escort missions to the Soviet Union in the summer of 1944 and on March 24, 1945, flew a 1,600-mile mission, escorting bombers in a raid on Berlin. The tail sections of the 52nd's Mustangs were painted bright yellow, and the group was commonly known as the Yellow Tails. During its combat tour, the 52nd flew missions from North Africa, Sicily, and Italy.

Among the prominent Mustang aces of the 52nd Fighter Group was Major James S 'Sully' Varnell of the 2nd Fighter Squadron. Varnell shot down 17 enemy aircraft and became the group's top-scoring ace. Born in Charleston, Tennessee, he was 21 years old when he began a productive onslaught against the enemy while flying from his base at Madna on the Italian coast of the Adriatic Sea. He became known for an aggressive instinct in the air, which contradicted his cool Southern demeanour while on the ground. Fellow pilots recalled that he possessed exceptional eyesight and in jest suggested that he carried binoculars in his cockpit.

On May 30, 1944, Varnell shot down a pair of German aircraft. The next

ABOVE: A Mustang ace of the 318th Fighter Squadron, 1st Lieutenant William Aron poses with his P-51 nicknamed *Texas Jessie*. Public Domain

LEFT: Pilots of the 332nd Fighter Group, the famous Tuskegee Airmen, discuss a mission. Public Domain

day while flying escort for bombers headed to Ploesti, he turned to hold off 30 enemy fighters and shot down two more. He became an ace in 11 days after downing his fifth enemy plane on June 9. A week later, the 2nd Fighter Squadron met at least 50 German planes in air-to-air combat, and Varnell claimed two more victims before his guns jammed. He spent the remainder of the mission bluffing attacks on German fighters that approached a crippled bomber.

Following up his rapid succession of kills, Lieutenant Varnell shot down three Me-109s in a swirling dogfight on July 9, 1944, that brought him close to flak batteries and even falling bombs. He shot down the first Me-109 quickly and then chased another through bursts of anti-aircraft fire, guns chattering as it erupted in smoke and flame. He latched onto a third Me-109 and saw strikes hit the target. However, the German continued towards a bomber formation, forcing Varnell to make a tight turn and hammer the enemy aircraft with machine-gun fire until it crashed.

Varnell scored his final kill, a Junkers Ju-52 transport, over Romania on August 4, 1944. He had shot down 17 enemy aircraft in the brief span of three months. Shortly after, he was ordered back to the United States to serve as a flight instructor. He was tragically killed in an air crash while flying a Curtiss P-40 at Pinellas Field, Florida, on April 9, 1945. He was the 10th ranked Mustang ace of World War Two.

LEFT: In this 1946 photo, members of the Tuskegee Airmen stand with a P-51 Mustang at Luke Air Force Base, Arizona. Public Domain

CAPTAIN JOHN J VOLL

In the capable hands of pilots like Captain John J Voll, the P-51 Mustang made its mark in the Mediterranean theatre. A pilot with the 308th Fighter Squadron, 31st Fighter Group, Fifteenth Air Force, based in San Servero and Mondolfo, Italy, Voll was the third highest scoring Mustang ace of World War Two with 21 aerial victories, and the highest scoring pilot of the US Army Air Forces in the Mediterranean theatre.

Voll was born on May 3, 1922, in Cincinnati, Ohio, and grew up in the town of Goshen. He enlisted in the Army Air Corps Reserve in August 1942, and received his pilot's wings on January 7, 1944. The young pilot completed his first combat mission escorting bombers in Italy while flying the Republic P-47 Thunderbolt fighter. In April, the 31st Fighter Group transitioned to the P-51, and while escorting Consolidated B-24 Liberator bombers during a raid on the oil refinery and storage complex at Ploesti, Romania, on June 23, 1944, he scored his first kill, downing a Focke Wulf Fw-190.

During another memorable mission on August 17, a squadron mate of Voll got into trouble, his P-51 hit repeatedly by enemy fire. As the other Mustang pilot hit the silk near the banks of the River Danube, Voll flew cover to prevent enemy fighters from strafing the surviving pilot in his parachute. As Voll turned for home, he got into a swirling dogfight, shooting down two enemy Messerschmitt Me-109 fighters, and claiming another Me-109 as probably destroyed.

Flying his P-51D nicknamed *American Beauty*, Voll continued to rack up an impressive number of aerial kills. In one amazing

LEFT: Captain John J Voll was the leading P-51 Mustang fighter ace of the Mediterranean theatre during World War Two. Public Domain

encounter, he accounted for three German fighters without ever using his .50-calibre machine guns. Finding himself under attack by the enemy aircraft, he violently manoeuvred his nimble Mustang, causing two of the German pilots to collide in a ball of fire. He then took advantage of the P-51's outstanding dive capability, coaxing another enemy fighter to follow. At the last moment, Voll pulled hard on the stick and clawed for altitude. The German was neither so lucky nor so skilled as he plunged directly into the ground and the plane exploded.

The fight of Voll's aerial combat sojourn occurred on November 16, 1944, as he led 308th Fighter Squadron Mustangs in an escort mission with Fifteenth Air Force bombers headed to the heavily defended city of Munich, in Bavaria. In their 1958 book 'Five Down and Glory: A History of the American Air Ace', authors Gene Gurney and Mark P Friedlander Jr, described the eventful five minutes in the skies near the Italian town of Udine along the northern coast of the Adriatic Sea.

"As Captain John J Voll, top-scoring ace of the 15th Air Force, climbed wearily from his plane after his 57th and last combat mission, he remarked: 'It was a helluva battle.' This was on 16 November 1944 and during his preceding five months in combat, he had flamed 17 German ships. On this last mission, he downed four more in the toughest battle of his fighting career, bringing his final total to 21 aircraft destroyed.

Good working over

"With his radio shot away, Captain Voll was returning early from a bomber escort mission in Germany. Alone over Northern »

LEFT: Captain John Voll sits in the cockpit of his Mustang fighter at an Italian airfield. Public Domain

LEFT: Captain John Voll and his crew chief pause for a photograph in 1944. Public Domain

CAPTAIN JOHN J VOLL

RIGHT: P-51 Mustangs of the 308th Fighter Squadron fly in formation.
Public Domain

Italy, he spotted a Junkers 88 and winged over after it. It led him on a merry chase across the Adriatic to a German air base and a hornet's nest of enemy aircraft. Out of the sun, seven Focke Wulfs pounced Voll's plane, while five Messerschmitts came in from another direction for what appeared to be an easy kill. Quickly closing on the Junkers, he blasted it out of the sky and wheeled around to take on the remaining 12 Germans. In the ensuing dogfight, he shot down two of the attacking Fw-190s and one of the Me-109s and gave the rest of the pack a good working over, getting two more probables, and damaging two more. Then he got a break and scrammed, eluding the other five."

The air battle had begun and ended swiftly, leaving Voll alone to return to his airfield and recount the incredible story. Word of the fight reached higher levels of command, and he later received the Distinguished Service Cross, the second highest award for valour in combat given to members of the US armed forces. His citation read in part: "After destroying a Ju 88 in the Udine area, Captain Voll was jumped by a dozen enemy fighters. Despite being heavily outnumbered, he remained in the fight, shooting down four more enemy to become an ace in a day."

Soon after the historic dogfight, Voll was withdrawn from air combat and reassigned to the China-American Composite Wing as a staff officer. He returned to the United States and then served briefly in the Pacific theatre. He was discharged from the military on November 13, 1945, just two months after the end of World War Two. Heading home to Goshen, he took a job as a high school science teacher in the autumn of 1946.

RIGHT: Pilots of the US 31st Fighter Group flew the British-made Supermarine Spitfire V in 1942.
Public Domain

RIGHT: Captain Voll and his comrades of the 308th Fighter Squadron escorted B-24 Liberator bombers such as these during raids on oil refineries at Ploesti, Romania.
Public Domain

Within months, however, Voll was back in the service, recalled to active duty with the US Air Force on October 26, 1948. He was stationed first with the 3525th Pilot Training Wing at Williams Air Force Base, Arizona, and then at Elmendorf Air Force Base, Alaska, with the 66th Fighter Interceptor Squadron. In October 1951, he transferred to California and Norton Air Force Base as an inspector and powerplant specialist. Various assignments with Air Defense Command were followed by a stint at Kimpo Air Base in South Korea. By late 1961, he had returned to the US, serving with the 27th Tactical Fighter Wing, commanding the 522nd Tactical Fighter Squadron, and working with the staff of the 832nd Air Division at Cannon Air Force Base, New Mexico.

During the Vietnam War, Voll served as air attaché to Singapore and then as chief of the plans division for the 6250th Support Squadron at Tan Son Nhut Air Base in South Vietnam. He was instrumental in planning Operation Rolling Thunder, a heavy strategic bombing campaign against targets in communist North Vietnam. His final active-duty assignment as commander of the 77th Aeronautical Systems Wing at McClellan Air Force Base, California, concluded in July 1974, and he retired with the rank of colonel after 32 years of military service.

Colonel Voll also received the Silver Star, Distinguished Flying Cross, Bronze Star, and Air Medal with multiple oak leaf clusters. He lived his later years in Lexington, Massachusetts, and died on September 12, 1987, at the age of 65. Erected in the town of Goshen, an Ohio state historical marker pays tribute to its native son, the fighter pilot whose record of aerial victories while flying the P-51 Mustang in the Mediterranean theatre of World War Two was unsurpassed.

EIGHTH AIR FORCE DAYLIGHT RAIDS

On August 17, 1942, the US Eighth Air Force executed the first of many missions against Nazi-occupied Europe. In the lead plane was General Ira C Eaker, head of the VIII Bomber Command. The raid against railroad marshalling yards near Rouen, west of Paris, consisted of a dozen Boeing B-17 Flying Fortress bombers escorted by eight squadrons of Royal Air Force Supermarine Spitfire fighters.

One US bomber was damaged by flak, but all the planes returned from the raid that dropped 18½ tons of bombs on the target. Although it was a relatively insignificant event in size and scale, it marked a turning point in the air war in Europe during World War Two. The RAF had been engaged in its own nocturnal bombing campaign against German cities and military targets for months under the direction of Air Chief Marshal Sir Arthur 'Bomber' Harris, who led Bomber Command. Harris had quoted the Biblical book of Hosea, noting that the enemy had "sown the wind and would not reap the whirlwind." And he was doing his best to make it so.

The Americans had a long way to go in the summer of 1942 if they were to make a significant contribution to the air war. Nevertheless, they were up to the task, and they brought with them the concept of daylight precision bombing coupled with their reliance on the state-of-the-art Norden bombsight and the belief that their heavily armed, four-engine bombers, specifically the Boeing B-17 Flying Fortress and the Consolidated B-24 Liberator, would always get through. The B-17, for example, was armed with 13 .50-calibre Browning machine guns and carried a crew of 10. A single Flying Fortress carried three tons of bombs at 300mph for a mission range of 2,000 miles. The type first flew in 1935, and by the end of the war, more than 12,000 had been built.

The Rouen raid bolstered the immediate desire of the American

ABOVE: Boeing B-17 Flying Fortress bombers of the US Eighth Air Force fly above Europe.
Public Domain

LEFT: A formation of B-17 Flying Fortresses bears down on the German city of Neumünster in April 1945.
Public Domain

air establishment to validate its doctrine, and General Henry 'Hap' Arnold, head of the US Army Air Forces (USAAF), commented: "The attack on Rouen again verifies the soundness of our policy of the precision bombing of strategic objectives rather than the mass bombing of large, city size areas." Arnold's pronouncement was somewhat premature, and the effectiveness of the doctrine is the stuff of controversy to this day.

The Eighth Air Force had been activated on January 28, 1942, in Savannah, Georgia, and the following month the initial cadre of officers arrived in Britain under the command of General Carl 'Tooey' Spaatz. By the late summer, its strength had grown from 2,000 to »

LEFT: North American P-51 fighter planes of the 375th Fighter Group fly in formation. The introduction of the P-51 altered the course of the air war in Europe.
Public Domain

ABOVE: Strafing US fighters shot up this German Focke Wulf Fw-190 on the ground. Public Domain

RIGHT: The Republic P-47 Thunderbolt was an excellent fighter bomber and shorter-range escort for Eighth Air Force heavy bombers. Public Domain

more than 30,000 personnel and from 200 assorted aircraft to more than 400 in three wings, one bomber and two fighter. By mid-1944, the Eighth Air Force comprised 200,000 personnel while it had reached a capacity to put more than 2,000 bombers and 1,000 fighters into the air in a single mission. As the war progressed, the US Fifteenth Air Force was established in North Africa in November 1943 and also mounted missions throughout the campaign in the Mediterranean.

Through the balance of 1942, Eighth Air Force raids were limited in scope, hitting German U-boat pens along the Atlantic coast, rail lines, marshalling yards, and factories in France and the Low Countries. B-24s joined in, and escorts consisted of Spitfires and American Lockheed P-38 Lightning and Republic P-47 Thunderbolt fighters. Eighth Air Force strength waxed and waned as fighter and bomber units were received and some diverted to the growing Mediterranean theatre. By the end of the year, more than 700 American bombers had dropped more than 1,700 tons of bombs on France, Belgium, and the Netherlands, but the US effort was still dwarfed by the RAF campaign.

Bombing differences

During the Casablanca Conference of January 1943, one of the major points of discussion was the effective utilisation of Allied bombing capacity, particularly whether the USAAF

should continue its daylight precision bombing or join the RAF with night area raids. Eaker interceded to head off Churchill's request for a change, convincing the prime minister that bombing the enemy around the clock would produce dramatically positive results. The notion that Allied air power alone might bring Nazi Germany to its knees was still considered plausible.

At the same time, Churchill and President Franklin D Roosevelt issued a directive known as 'Pointblank' that would guide the initiative of the Combined Bomber Offensive against the Nazis. Targets were prioritised in order: German submarine construction, German aircraft production, transportation, oil refineries and storage facilities and enemy industrial and war-related infrastructure. The objectives of Pointblank were to cripple the German capacity to make war while also establishing air superiority over Western Europe in support of the anticipated D-Day invasion that would occur in Normandy on June 6, 1944.

The size and intensity of Allied bombing increased after Casablanca, but the potency of the Luftwaffe did as well. At peak strength in 1943, the German air force was a skilled adversary with veteran pilots flying fighter interceptors that took an increasingly heavy toll on Allied planes. The Messerschmitt Me-109 and Focke Wulf Fw-190 pilots took advantage of an Achilles heel in the Allied effort. The primary escort fighters, the P-38, Spitfire, and P-47, were formidable but did not possess the range to escort American bombers on daylight raids deep into Germany. The veteran Luftwaffe pilots would regularly ravage the bomber formations as they penetrated beyond the range

killed or captured and a like number wounded. A single bomb group, the 'Bloody 100th', lost 17 of 19 planes committed.

Such catastrophic losses staggered the command of the Eighth Air Force, but the Americans returned to Schweinfurt on October 14. That date has lived on in history as Black Thursday. Some 60 of the 291 attacking Eighth Air Force bombers were shot down by German fighters and flak. Seventeen others were junked due to heavy damage, and

of escorting fighters en route to and returning from their targets.

One US bomber crewman said of the German pilots: "No matter the target they were defending, they were balls to the wall. They were brave. They didn't hesitate."

On August 17, 1943, USAAF planners organised a pair of major raids into Germany against the Messerschmitt assembly plant at Regensburg and the ball bearing facility at Schweinfurt. A total of 376 B-17s were allocated along with 18 squadrons of P-47s and Spitfires. In the event, bad weather threw the timetable off, and the American formations were hammered by determined Luftwaffe fighters and anti-aircraft fire. When it was over, the butcher's bill was horrific: 565 airmen were killed, wounded, or captured, and 60 big bombers had been shot down. Another 20 per cent of the attacking force was so heavily damaged that it was written off.

Dozens lost

Routinely, American bomber formations lost dozens of aircraft and valuable crews in a single raid. During a September 6, 1943, mission to bomb Bosch company production facilities in Stuttgart, 45 B-17s were lost. A raid on the shipyards at Bremen on October 8 resulted in the loss of 30 bombers with 300 aircrew

BELOW: This B-17 Flying Fortress is painted in the livery of the 91st Bombardment Group, Eighth Air Force. Public Domain

more than 100 planes had sustained damage. Of the 2,900 air personnel that participated, 650 were lost, an appalling 22 per cent casualty rate. Despite the short range of escort fighters and the deadly earnest Luftwaffe defence, the USAAF had continued to ply its doctrine of daylight precision bombing. However, such an attrition rate was unsustainable. Daylight raids deep into Germany were subsequently suspended until the situation could be redressed.

That redress came as the morale of Eighth Air Force personnel was at its nadir. The long-range North American P-51 Mustang fighter changed the balance of power in the skies over Europe, and along with it came a refocus of Pointblank priorities that set the Luftwaffe on its heels. It had become apparent that air superiority could not be won in the run-up to the Normandy invasion without inflicting substantial losses on the German fighters. The Mustang arrived in Britain in late 1943 and was soon routinely escorting Eighth Air Force bomber formations deep into Germany.

Another significant change was the perspective of the fighter pilot's role in both protecting the bombers and winning air superiority through the defeat of the Luftwaffe. In early 1944, General Spaatz was in command of the three US air forces in Europe, the Eighth, Ninth, and Fifteenth. General Eaker had been reassigned to the Mediterranean, and General Jimmy Doolittle, a legendary airman, was brought to Britain to command the Eighth. Doolittle reimagined the escort role. He believed the American fighters, particularly the P-51s, would win air superiority by destroying German planes in the air and on the ground.

To do so, however, the Mustang pilots could not be totally tethered to the bomber formations. Doolittle ordered them, along with other fighter pilots, to assume the offensive, harnessing the natural aggressiveness and offensive capability of their P-38s, P-47s, and P-51s to search for and shoot down enemy planes wherever and whenever possible. On the long missions to Germany, this was a priority for the Mustang pilots, and on their return to base in England they were to strafe targets of opportunity with any unused ammunition, shredding German planes on the ground and shooting up airfields. The bombers would benefit from an improved escort while dropping their damaging payloads, and they would in fact serve as bait, luring the Luftwaffe into the air, where its combat efficiency was steadily eroded.

In February 1944, the Eighth Air Force and RAF launched Big Week,

LEFT: The Consolidated B-24 Liberator heavy bomber participated in many Eighth Air Force raids on Nazi-occupied Europe.
Public Domain

LEFT: After completing the 25-mission requirement of Eighth Air Force, the crew of the B-17 *Memphis Belle* poses for a photograph on June 7, 1943.
Public Domain

an all-out effort to annihilate the Luftwaffe in the air and on the ground, while blasting production and assembly facilities that fed the German air effort. On the 20th, 1,000 American bombers and 900 fighters participated in the largest US air raid of the war to date. The bombers attacked aircraft manufacturing facilities at Leipzig, and when the German pilots rose to defend, they were astonished to see American fighters in the air. The results were favourable. Some 21 bombers and four fighters were shot down, but estimates placed the German fighter losses at 153, a shattering blow.

The Germans were resilient, adjusting their tactics, and the bomber formations lost more than 200 planes during the remainder of Big Week. Still, during the offensive more than 600 Luftwaffe fighters were downed with the loss of nearly 20 per cent of the best German pilots. Air superiority in the skies over Europe was achievable and soon accomplished.

On March 6, 1944, the Eighth Air Force executed its first raid against the Nazi capital Berlin, a round trip of 1,100 miles and five hours over Germany. Losses were high during the month and through the end of April, but clearly the tactics were working. Other targets, including oil production and transportation

centres, were hit regularly, and German fighters were noticeably absent above the Normandy invasion beaches on June 6. As Allied forces advanced towards the frontier of the Third Reich, the air campaign continued. By the spring of 1945, massive raids were relentlessly pounding areas that remained under German control.

Although the cost was high – the Eighth Air Force lost over 5,000 aircraft and more than 47,000 casualties during the war – its contribution to ultimate victory was substantial. And the introduction of the P-51 made a critical difference in the outcome. By 1945, every Eighth Air Force fighter group, with one exception, was flying the Mustang.

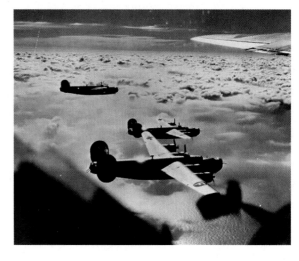

BELOW: A formation of B-24 Liberators of the 445th Bombardment Group departs from RAF Tibenham for a target in Nazi-occupied Europe.
Public Domain

MUSTANGS OVER BERLIN

ABOVE: A P-51 Mustang of the 375th Fighter Squadron flies with external fuel drop tanks attached.
Public Domain

RIGHT: A formation of Boeing B-17 Flying Fortress bombers leaves vapour trails en route to a target.
Public Domain

RIGHT: The Consolidated B-24 Liberator heavy bomber flew many missions to Berlin during the air war.
Public Domain

Reichsmarschall Hermann Goring, chief of the Luftwaffe, made many empty promises during World War Two. One of those was proven erroneous when the first Allied bombs fell on the Nazi capital Berlin as early as 1940. The Reichsmarschall had boasted: "You can call me Meyer!" if such an event occurred.

By the spring of 1944, another shocking revelation took place. Goring realised that the days of the Third Reich were numbered. "When I saw Mustangs over Berlin, I knew the jig was up," he told Allied interrogators after the war ended. The days of reckoning for Goring occurred in early March when the initial Eighth Air Force bombing raids on Berlin were launched.

On March 4, more than 500 B-17s of the 1st and 3rd Bombardment Divisions were ordered to attack industrial targets on the outskirts of Berlin, but bad weather hampered the plan, with only one wing of 30 bombers form the 3rd Division hitting its assigned target. The remainder either returned to their bases in England or, in the case of more than 200, hit targets of opportunity in the Ruhr, the industrial heart of Germany. The 2nd Division Flying Fortresses were alerted to the adverse weather conditions and aborted their missions before crossing into continental airspace. Of those that did attack, enemy fighters and flak shot down 10 B-17s.

The day was a disappointment. Compounding the frustration, 770 fighter planes of the US Army Air Forces (USAAF) had pulled escort duty for the raids, and the hope had been that they would not only protect the heavy bombers but also shoot down as many Luftwaffe fighters as possible. In the event, 33 P-51s of the 363rd Fighter Group took to the air, but 11 Mustangs were lost – not to the enemy but to accidents related to foul weather that broke up their formations over the Dutch coast.

A total force of 121 P-51s were sent aloft from the 363rd, 4th, 354th, and 357th Fighter Groups on the day, and 16 aircraft failed to return, three of them belonging to the Eighth Air Force, two from the 4th and one from the 357th Fighter Groups. The three pilots survived to be taken prisoner. The remaining Mustangs that were lost, two from the 354th Fighter Group and the 11 of the 363rd, were from the tactical Ninth Air Force's IX Fighter Command. All 13 pilots from these two groups were killed. Another Mustang was damaged beyond repair, crashing as the pilot was killed trying to touch down upon return. Another P-51 was damaged, and in exchange for these losses the Americans claimed five German aircraft shot down, along with others as probables or damaged.

Two days later, on March 6, 1944, the raid that is considered by most historians to be the first concerted USAAF daylight attack on Berlin occurred. The Eighth Air Force put 504 B-17s and 226 Consolidated B-24 Liberators in the air. Again, though their primary objectives were industrial targets in the city, many of the bombers were compelled to attack secondary targets on the outskirts or targets of opportunity elsewhere as thick cloud cover restricted visibility. Luftwaffe opposition has been described as concentrated and fierce. Owing to the previous attempts to hit Berlin and the pre-emptive bad weather, the Germans had been aware of USAAF intent and so were given time to co-ordinate their defence.

Severe losses

Losses were severe as heavy flak shook the bomber formations, some planes absorbing direct hits. Meanwhile, Luftwaffe fighter pilots pressed home their attack. A total of 53 B-17s and 16 B-24s were shot down, while 293 Flying Fortresses and 54 B-24s sustained damage. Five of the B-17s and a single B-24 were beyond repair and written off. During the action, the 100th Bomb Group (Heavy) sustained a loss of 15 B-17s,

the highest loss of aircraft in a single day by an Eighth Air Force group to date. Immediate count of casualties revealed 117 known dead, 686 officially missing, with many of these probably killed, and 31 wounded.

A total of 801 USAAF fighters accompanied the bombers, including 86 P-38 Lightnings, 615 P-47 Thunderbolts, and 100 P-51 Mustangs. Along with their pilots, five P-51s, five P-47s, and a single P-38 were lost to enemy action. Among the Mustang pilots who fought the Luftwaffe in the vicinity of Berlin that day, Major Henry L Mills, commander of the 334th Fighter Squadron, 4th Fighter Group, claimed his sixth aerial victory, shooting down an Fw-190 near Brandenburg. However, minutes later Mills took enemy fire and was forced to hit the silk as his engine failed. He was taken prisoner but escaped from Stalag Luft III in March 1945, and returned to England.

Both 1st Lieutenant Glenn T Eagleston of the 353rd Fighter Squadron, 354th Fighter Group, and 1st Lieutenant Pierce McKennon of the 335th Fighter Squadron, 4th Fighter Group, became aces on the day. Eagleston shot down an

Me-109 near Burg, while McKennon claimed a Messerschmitt over Berlin at 12.45pm.

Although the bombers had taken serious losses, the Germans had their proverbial noses bloodied as well. The Luftwaffe pilots were startled to see the P-51s over their capital city, and just between 11.30am and 3pm, American fighters of all types shot down 81 of their number, including fighters and attack planes, either along the bomber routes or in the air above Berlin itself. For Goring and the rest of the Luftwaffe command, the implication was clear. The presence of the Mustang escort fighters all the way to Berlin and back meant greater attrition for the Germans. And these were losses that would not easily be replaced. American industry, on the other hand, was producing aircraft at a phenomenal rate.

The experience of Captain Glendon V Davis, 364th Fighter Squadron, 357th Fighter Group, illustrates the difference that the Mustangs made on March 6. He reported: "We had set course for home and were climbing up above the 'Big Friends' when I noticed a B-17 straggler with an FW-190 sitting on his tail at

around 19,000ft. We dived down on the enemy aircraft but couldn't close on him as the tail gunner of the bomber was firing at him. We broke to the side of the enemy aircraft and at that time he saw us and broke into us. We turned into him and then he started for the deck in a tight spiral. We followed him down indicating from 450-500mph. We were forcing him to keep a tight spiral by cutting on the inside of him when he tried to widen it out. At 10,000ft he dropped his belly tank. At 5,000ft his plane appeared to be stalling as he tried to pull out. His canopy flew off, but the plane went right on into the ground without the pilot ever getting out. We circled the flaming wreckage taking a picture of it, then came on home without incident. I claim an FW-190 and pilot destroyed."

Two days later, Davis shared in the destruction of another Fw-190, and on March 16, he shot down an Me-109. A month later, he bailed out of his P-51, nicknamed *Pregnant Polecat*, over France due to mechanical failure. With the help of sympathetic French civilians, he evaded capture and ended the war with 7½ victories.

On March 6, 1944, the Luftwaffe lost 160 aircraft to American fighters. The day's air battle was a harbinger of things to come.

Eleven months later, on February 3, 1945, the Eighth Air Force unleashed its largest raid of the war against Berlin, 1,500 heavy bombers and more than 1,000 fighters. Only 36 attacking planes were lost, and USAAF raids would continue through April until the war's end.

Such results were evidence of the dwindling potency of German anti-aircraft defences, and even more so of the defeat of the once-vaunted Luftwaffe. Clearly, the Mustang, in long-range escort and offensive pursuit of enemy planes, had tipped the balance in the outcome of the air war in Europe.

ABOVE: An aerial mishap damages a B-17 during a bombing run over Berlin. Public Domain

LEFT: A section of Berlin lies in ruins after heavy Allied bombing in this photo taken by a reconnaissance aircraft. Public Domain

LEFT: During a 2020 flyover of the White House, P-51s escort a B-17 Flying Fortress bomber. Public Domain

CAPTAIN RAY S WETMORE

RIGHT: With a dashing pose, Ray Wetmore is shown crouching on the wing of *Daddy's Girl.* Public Domain

Fighter pilot Captain Ray S Wetmore scored the first 4¼ aerial victories of his World War Two combat career flying the Republic P-47 Thunderbolt in early 1944. By April, his 370th Fighter Squadron, 359th Fighter Group was training with the new P-51B Mustang.

A few weeks later, Wetmore was in the air flying escort during a bombing mission deep into Germany with his new mount, nicknamed *Daddy's Girl.* During a fierce air battle on May 19, 1944, he became an ace as the American fighters took on dozens of German Messerschmitts.

"I was leading Yellow Flight, escorting bombers to Berlin when approximately 100 Me-109s started an attack on them," he wrote in his follow-up encounter report. "I dived on the rear of the Hun formation, picked a target, and closed to 100yds before starting to fire. I noticed

RIGHT: Mustang ace Captain Ray Wetmore is shown at the wheel of a Jeep at RAF East Wretham. Public Domain

BELOW: P-51D Mustang fighters of the 359th Fighter Group USAAF line the field at RAF East Wretham in 1944. Public Domain

strikes on tail and fuselage. The Me-109 burst into flames and went into a spin out of control.

"I made a turn and saw another Me-109 attacking a P-51, so I dived on him. I followed him down to 12,000ft, firing when in range. He kept diving in and out of the clouds so much that it was hard to get a long burst in. Finally, he dived into a large cumulus cloud, and I went over the top, catching the Jerry as he came out. I gave him a long burst at 200yds, noticing strikes all over the Me-109. The pilot rolled it over and bailed out. By this time, I had lost my #2 and #3 men so with my #4 man, I came home. I claim two Me-109s destroyed in the air."

These were the first of an impressive tally that Wetmore racked up in the P-51 during the coming weeks. By the end of May, the hotshot pilot had reached 8¼ kills, and when he finished his second tour of duty

in the war-torn skies of Europe, he had amassed a total of 21¼ aerial victories. Wetmore flew the P-47, P-51B, and P-51D, each of them bearing the moniker *Daddy's Girl.* Born September 30, 1923, in Kerman, California, he was only 21 years old and held the rank of major by the time the war in Europe was over. Wetmore joined the Army Air Corps in November 1941 and earned his pilot's wings in July 1942.

After deploying to Britain, Wetmore was consistently engaged in escort duty and experienced some of the war's most intense dogfights. On November 27, 1944, he encountered a huge swarm of enemy fighters north of Munster, Germany. "Bandits were reported," he wrote in his encounter report. "The Sqdn got split up due to some heavy intense flak. At this time, I saw two gaggles of bandits of approximately 100 planes each.

One bunch was Me-109s and the other Fw-190s. I continued to follow them, remaining high and to the rear of their formation. A few minutes later, my second element had to return home due to engine trouble. By this time, the Jerries found out I was there and started sending out several four ship flights after us. I continued to call in the Jerries until we had to bounce them to save our own necks as they were starting to bounce us.

"I closed in on an Me-109 to around 600yds before firing and as soon as I started firing, the Me-109 burst into flames and went down spinning, pouring out black smoke. I then broke into the Jerries bouncing us. I got a good burst at one from about 300yds with a 20-degree deflection. The enemy aircraft lit up with strikes and went into a tumble pouring out black smoke. The last time I saw the Me-109, it was in flames spinning. I claim this enemy aircraft destroyed. I saw another Jerry making a pass on me, so I turned into him. We went around and around from 30,000ft to the deck. He seemed very aggressive and was darn good with his Me-109. Although I could out turn him, he was on my tail a lot of times. I finally ran out of ammo but by then I had hit him several times. I made another pass at him, and he bailed out. I then took a picture of him in the chute. Then for the next ten minutes I was attacked repeatedly by Fw-190s but managed to out manoeuvre them. They finally broke off and I came home. I claim three Me-109s destroyed in air."

Rocket power overcome

On February 14, 1945, Captain Wetmore flamed three more Fw-190s. Then, On March 15, he encountered a rocket-powered Me-163 Komet fighter while flying escort. "I was leading Red Section escorting bombers SW of Berlin when I saw two Me-163s circling at about 20,000ft 20 miles away in the vicinity of Wittenberg," he reported. "I flew over towards them, and while at 25,000ft started after one a little below me. When I got within 3,000yd, he turned on his jet, and went up into a 70-degree climb. At about 26,000ft, his jet quit, so he split-S'd. I dived with him and levelled off at 2,000ft on him at six o'clock. During the dive, my IAS (indicated air speed) was between 550mph and 600mph. I opened fire at 200yds. Pieces flew off all over. He made a sharp turn to the right, and I gave him another short burst, and half his left wing flew off, and the plane caught fire. The pilot bailed out, and I saw the enemy aircraft crash into the ground. I claim one Me-163 destroyed in air."

Wetmore remained in the service after the war, commanding the

1st Fighter Group at March Field, California, and serving as operations officer with the 37th Fighter Squadron, 14th Fighter Group at Dow Field, Maine. He commanded the 59th Fighter Interceptor Squadron at Otis Air Force Base, Massachusetts, and lost his life in the crash of his F-86 Sabre jet fighter on February 14, 1951. He was a 27-year-old lieutenant

colonel and father of four children at the time.

The accident occurred as Wetmore made a landing approach on a cross-country flight from Los Angeles, California. As he came in, the plane was seen to lurch upward and then nose into the ground. An investigation revealed that he had radioed difficulty with slowing the aircraft and an inability to bail out. He notified ground control heroically: "I'm going to go up and bring it down in Wakeby Lake, so I don't hit any houses."

During his combat career, Wetmore received the Distinguished Service Cross with bronze oak leaf cluster, Silver Star with bronze oak leaf cluster, Distinguished Flying Cross with silver and bronze oak leaf clusters, and the Air Medal with two silver and two bronze oak leaf clusters. He was the highest scoring pilot of the 359th Fighter Group and ranked eighth among all American fighter aces in the European theatre of World War Two.

ABOVE: Mustang pilots of the 370th Fighter Squadron gather round a mission board at their RAF East Wretham base. Public Domain

LEFT: Pilots of the 370th Fighter Squadron celebrate VE Day and the end of World War Two in Europe. Public Domain

LEFT: Captain Ray Wetmore shot down a German Messerschmitt Me-163 Komet like this on March 15, 1945. Public Domain

MAJOR GENERAL CHUCK YEAGER

RIGHT: Mustang ace and test pilot extraordinaire Chuck Yeager wears the rank of brigadier general in this portrait. Public Domain

FAR RIGHT: Captain Chuck Yeager posed for this photo in 1944 and went on to become a Mustang ace. Public Domain

BELOW: Chuck Yeager achieved most of his aerial victories flying the P-51D Mustang *Glamorous Glen III*. Public Domain

The sky was clear on October 14, 1947, and the experimental Bell X-1 jet aircraft was slung beneath the belly of a Boeing B-29 Superfortress bomber for a half-hour climb to 20,000ft. From there, the X-1 would be released and its pilot, Captain Charles E 'Chuck' Yeager, would take control, rapidly ascending to 42,000ft and shattering the sound barrier for the first time in history. Yeager flew at Mach 1.06 on this ninth flight of the X-1 that he had christened *Glamorous Glennis* after his wife.

Yeager streaked across the sky above Rogers Dry Lake in southern California and into history, a towering figure in the growth of modern aviation, not just in the United States but around the world. Perhaps it is more fitting to say that Yeager flew further into history that day. He did go on to achieve great fame as a test pilot in the early years of the Jet Age. However, he was already a hero, an ace pilot of the 357th Fighter Group, US Army Air Forces (USAAF) with 12½ aerial kills during World War Two.

Yeager flew the vaunted North American P-51 Mustang fighter during much of his combat career, logged 64 combat missions in the hostile skies over Europe while completing 270 hours in the cockpit, and survived being shot down to evade capture and return to duty in a harrowing exercise of wit and cunning.

Chuck Yeager was born on February 13, 1923, in the little town of Myra, West Virginia. As a boy, he became a crack shot with a .22-calibre rifle, often bringing rabbits home from forays into the woods to augment the family's food supply. His father worked as a driller for a natural gas company and enjoyed working with engines and mechanical contraptions of all kinds. The boy inherited his father's natural aptitude for such activities.

Although he had no native interest in flying, Yeager possessed a natural curiosity about the world outside his hometown of just 400 people, secluded in the rugged Allegheny Mountains. At the age of 18, he enlisted in the USAAF on September 12, 1941. Immediately, he put his skills as a mechanic to good use, tearing down engines and putting them back together easily. However, he expressed a distaste for some other aspects of life as an enlisted man on the ground.

Therefore, Yeager applied for a 'flying sergeant' programme that waived the normal requirement that USAAF pilots have at least two years at college to their credit. Once accepted, there was a daunting obstacle to overcome. His first flight made him violently airsick. He persevered and conquered the issue, then showed rapid proficiency as a pilot. He gained his wings on March 10, 1943, and was assigned to the 357th Fighter Wing in Tonopah, Nevada, where he gained experience flying the Bell P-39 Airacobra. He survived a fiery training crash but was hospitalised for some time with a broken back.

Precious commodity

Yeager recovered and, with his country at war, trained fighter pilots were a precious commodity. By November 1943, the 357th Fighter Group was in Britain with its P-51B Mustangs, flying both escort missions with heavy bombers raiding Nazi-occupied Europe and strafing and fighter bomber runs against ground targets. His first mission occurred on February 11,

GOOD LUCK!
Chuck Yeager

LEFT: Chuck Yeager stands in front of the Bell X-1 jet aircraft nicknamed *Glamorous Glennis*, in which he broke the sound barrier. Public Domain

LEFT: Chuck Yeager smiles from the cramped cockpit of *Glamorous Glennis* in September 1947. Public Domain

Handed off to a group of Maquis, members of the French resistance, Yeager remained with these guerrillas for some time. It was March, and winter weather prohibited an attempt to reach Spain through passes in the Pyrenees Mountains. Weeks lapsed, and when the weather improved, Yeager was assisted into the rugged mountains along with another downed American airman whom he knew simply as Pat, a former member of a Consolidated B-24 bomber crew. The Americans slogged through the difficult terrain, and German troops were active in the area. One enemy patrol opened fire on the party, seriously wounding Pat. Yeager had refused to leave his side until he was sure that his travelling companion was going to die. Years later, he discovered that Pat had been found by Spanish authorities and had survived the ordeal.

Finally, Yeager arrived in Spain, turning himself in to local authorities who checked him into a hotel in the resort town of Alhama de Aragón. The American attaché arranged for his return to England, but he spent six weeks recuperating in luxury surroundings. The diplomat made a deal with the Spanish, officially neutral but well known as pro-German, exchanging a quantity of gasoline for six American airmen, including Yeager.

Supposedly disqualified

After his return, Yeager was supposedly disqualified from further service as a fighter pilot. Having evaded capture, he could possibly compromise identities and other sensitive information regarding his French rescuers should he be shot down and captured alive. Undeterred, Yeager proved himself relentless, even securing a few minutes with General Dwight D Eisenhower, Supreme Commander of Allied Expeditionary Forces in Europe, to plead his case for reinstatement as a fighter pilot. He was convincing enough to »

BELOW: Colonel Chuck Yeager holds a scale model of the experimental North American X-15 aircraft in 1950. Public Domain

1944. Flak bursts bounced the planes around, but no enemy fighters were encountered.

That circumstance would soon change. During the first mission of Eighth Air Force bombers to Berlin on March 4, Yeager shot down his first enemy aircraft, an Me-109 fighter that crashed to the ground. However, the next day his luck changed dramatically.

Seemingly from out of nowhere, an enemy Focke Wulf Fw-190 fighter latched onto Yeager's tail, and without warning the Mustang was pounded by 20mm cannon fire. Its engine smoked and tongues of yellow flame licked back toward the cockpit. The stricken P-51 rolled and spun earthward, but the fortunate pilot managed to bail out at 16,000ft. He came to earth with a thud.

The French countryside was otherwise empty, at least temporarily, and he assessed his situation – cuts, bruises, and a nasty gash to his forehead, but miraculously he was otherwise unhurt. He watched

German planes circle above and was relieved when they finally flew away. He held his .45-calibre Colt pistol tightly in case a German patrol stumbled across his hiding place. The first night was chilling. He munched a chocolate bar and then settled into fitful sleep beneath the shreds of his parachute.

The next morning, the downed pilot jumped an unsuspecting French civilian who was carrying an axe. Pointing his pistol at the man, he tried to overcome the language barrier, and finally the Frenchman was able to communicate that another individual could perhaps help. Soon enough, an old man who spoke English told Yeager that it was safe to follow. They avoided German patrols and reached a stone farmhouse. The American heard German voices from his spot in a small closet and broke into a heavy sweat. When the Germans finally left the house, he was treated by a French doctor, given food, and then moved along.

win his argument, but shortly before his departure for his squadron, a German V-1 buzz bomb exploded near his hotel. He was shaken by the blast but unhurt.

By late summer 1944, Yeager was back with his 363rd Fighter Squadron. His new P-51D Mustang was nicknamed *Glamorous Glen III*, and his most productive dogfight of World War Two occurred on October 12, when he became an ace in a day with five Me-109s downed. His first two victims had seen his Mustang bearing down on them, and when one took evasive action, he crashed into the other. Both pilots bailed out, and Yeager had two kills without firing a shot.

Next, Yeager came upon a third German and 'observed strikes all over the ship, particularly heavy in the cockpit'. He skidded off to the left and was smoking and streaming coolant and went into a slow diving turn to the left. The fourth and fifth victims were shot down swiftly. Yeager reported: "I gave about a three

second burst and the whole fuselage split open and blew up after we passed. Another Me-109 to the right had cut his throttle and was trying to get behind. I broke to the right and quickly rolled to the left on his tail. I got a lead from around 300yds and gave him a short burst. There were hits on wings and tail section. He snapped to the right three times and bailed out when he quit snapping at around 18,000ft."

On a November 15, 1944, mission escorting a flight of fighters that was to strafe targets south of the German city of Magdeburg, Yeager shot down four Fw-190s in a single swirling dogfight. After a report of bandits at 11 o'clock, he led his Mustangs into a fight with an estimated 150 enemy aircraft. At 32,000ft, Yeager lined up on a German and reported: "I jumped the last enemy aircraft, which was a FW-190. He went into a rolling dive to the right and then pulled up into a tight turn to the right. I shot a side deflection shot from his right

and got hits from around 200yds. He snapped and the tail flew off and I saw no chutes."

Describing his second kill, Yeager said: "I got many strikes on the fuselage and the enemy aircraft started smoking and went into a dive. I followed it down to about 15,000ft and the enemy aircraft flew apart. There were no chutes." Yeager dispatched the third Fw-190 with a 30-degree deflection shot from 100yds. The fourth German was shot down with hammer blows to the cockpit area, and the American ace reported: "All the hits were concentrated in the cockpit and a sheet of flame came out of the cockpit and the enemy aircraft nosed down in a dive on fire."

In a late 1944 mission, Yeager caught a German Me-262 jet fighter trying to land at its airfield, pounced, and shot the plane full of .50-calibre bullets before being driven off by intense enemy anti-aircraft fire. He flew his last combat mission of World War Two on January 15, 1945, and returned to the United States the following month. He went on to hold numerous squadron and wing commands with the US Air Force during the 1950s and 60s. As a test pilot, he was one of the first Americans to fly the Russian-built MiG-15 jet fighter after a North Korean pilot defected, flying the plane to a United Nations airfield during the Korean War.

After 34 years of service, Yeager retired from the military in 1975. He died at the age of 97 on December 7, 2020.

Chuck Yeager achieved the rank of major general after retiring from one of the most storied, pioneering, and adventurous careers in military aviation history – and a big part of that career took place in the cockpit of the P-51 Mustang.

TUSKEGEE AIRMEN

Captain Charles 'Buster' Hall shot down a German Focke Wulf Fw-190 fighter on July 2, 1943, while flying his Curtiss P-40 Tomahawk fighter.

It was his eighth combat mission, and on that day his 99th Fighter Squadron, 33rd Fighter Group was escorting Consolidated B-24 Liberators attacking the Axis air base at Castelvetrano in southwestern Sicily. When he returned to base, Hall was greeted with a chilled bottle of Coca-Cola to celebrate the occasion. It was the squadron's first air-to-air kill, and he was to receive the Distinguished Service Cross. Further, it was the first aerial victory for a black fighter pilot of the US Army Air Forces in World War Two. Hall went on to shoot down two more Fw-190s before returning to the US as a flight instructor, but that day marked a historic point in the storied sojourn of the Tuskegee Airmen. Hall's Fw-190 was the squadron's only kill of 1943.

Hall's fellow fighter pilots of the Tuskegee Airmen went on to blaze a trail for black people in the US Military and compiled an outstanding combat record. They flew the Bell P-39 Airacobra, the Curtiss P-40 Tomahawk, the Republic P-47 Thunderbolt, and most famously the North American P-51 Mustang.

On June 9, 1943, six pilots of the 99th Fighter Squadron swept low over Pantelleria Island in the Mediterranean Sea in a fighter sweep as operations were underway to secure the spit of land in preparation

for the Allied invasion of Sicily. The capture of Pantelleria, located between the North African coast and Sicily, was a prerequisite for Operation Husky, and the thousands of German and Italian soldiers there had to be eliminated.

As the Americans completed their sweep and headed for their base in North Africa, they were jumped by a dozen German Fw-190s. The Americans were inexperienced but held their own in the swirling dogfight, sending the enemy planes scurrying for home without loss to themselves. First Lieutenant Charles Dryden had commanded the pilots in their first encounter with the enemy in the air.

The pilots of the 99th Fighter Squadron were all black Americans and graduates of the US Army Air Corps Advanced Flying School at

Tuskegee, Alabama. The 99th was later added to the 100th, 301st, and 302nd Fighter Squadrons to comprise the 332nd Fighter Group. After gaining experience in other types, »

ABOVE: This modern P-51C is painted in the colour scheme of the Red Tails, the famed 332nd Fighter Group. Creative Commons RadioFan via Wikipedia

LEFT: Tuskegee Airman Edward M Thomas posed for this portrait in March 1945. Creative Commons Toni Frissell via Wikipedia

BELOW: A first class of Tuskegee airmen stands at attention with Vultee BT-13 trainers at the Alabama airfield in 1941. Public Domain

RIGHT: A war bond poster features the striking image of a determined Tuskegee Airman.
Public Domain

the 332nd was equipped with the P-51B Mustang in July 1944 and as the war progressed the airmen also flew the P-51C and P-51D. When the Mustangs arrived, the men of the 332nd painted their tail sections in vivid red, along with red propeller spinners, bands on the noses, and other accents that made their planes distinctive and garnered the nickname 'Red Tails', one that would resonate through history.

Courage abounds

During their World War Two service, the Red Tails of the 332nd Fighter Group flew 1,578 combat missions, destroying or damaging an estimated 400 enemy aircraft in the air and on the ground while also sinking an enemy destroyer and strafing Axis convoys, troop concentrations, and rail traffic with reckless abandon. Stories of their courage abound, and some observers have proffered that while flying escort missions

for Boeing B-17s and Consolidated B-24 Liberator heavy bombers, the Red Tails never lost a bomber to enemy action. Such a statement has since been scrutinised but the simple pronouncement of such a feat is an accomplishment.

After the initial air engagement of the 99th Fighter Squadron, the official Air Corps history recorded of the Pantelleria Island mission: "The American Negro fliers, led by First Lieutenant Charles W Dryden, parried the Nazi thrust, damaged two German fighters, and forced the remainder to retire. The Americans all came home safely."

It had been a long road for the Tuskegee Airmen, from earning the right to train as pilots to deployment in combat. A significant lobbying effort was undertaken by the black press and with the support of such notable individuals as First Lady Eleanor Roosevelt. In March 1941, an experimental unit

Keep us flying!

BUY WAR BONDS

was formed at Rantoul, Illinois. In June, the US Congress authorised the formation of the 99th Pursuit Squadron at Tuskegee Institute, a small historically black college, and the original nucleus of personnel transferred there.

The first graduating class at Tuskegee included 12 cadets and a single cadet officer, Captain Benjamin O Davis Jr, who later became the second black officer in the US military to achieve general officer rank. Class 42C graduated on March 7, 1942, but due to a lack of confidence in the ability of black pilots and inherent discrimination, the unit did not receive orders to deploy for several months. Such circumstances were not unusual for the times and the formation, training, and deployment of black units in all branches of the US armed forces was a polarising issue. Still, black people were willing to serve, and did so in great numbers. Between 1942 and 1945, no fewer than 2.5m black men registered for the draft and more than a million were inducted into the service. Black women volunteered for service as well, and at historically black Howard University, more than 4,000 students and faculty members answered the call to enlist.

Even after entering the service, black personnel were usually relegated to support roles. Rarely were they given the opportunity to serve in combat units. They were often assigned to work detachments and served as stevedores, truck drivers, cooks, or manual labourers. Black soldiers were commanded by white officers, and the few black officers in the service were not allowed to command white soldiers.

At long last, the 99th Fighter Squadron was deployed to North Africa in April 1943, and initially attached to the 33rd Fighter Group. Original orders to send the squadron

RIGHT: In the spring of 1942, a group of Tuskegee Airmen stand before a Curtiss P-40 fighter.
Public Domain

BELOW: Pilots of the 332nd Fighter Group pose before the P-51 nicknamed *Skipper's Darlin' III* at Ramitelli Airfield, Italy.
Public Domain

ABOVE: Captain Roscoe C Brown Jr (right) and ground crewman Marcellus Smith inspect the engine of a P-51 Mustang in Italy. Brown shot down a German Me-262 jet fighter. Public Domain

RIGHT: Pilots of the 332nd Fighter Group attend a pre-mission briefing at an airfield in Italy, 1945. Public Domain

to Liberia were cancelled, and in May it reached an advanced base in Tunisia. At that time, the historic missions were flown in support of the invasion of Sicily.

Grudging respect

As the Italian campaign progressed in the autumn of 1943, the 332nd Fighter Group relocated to bases in Italy at Montecorvino, Capodichino, and then Ramitelli with the Fifteenth Air Force. With Davis in command, the airmen gained grudging respect from their comrades and their enemies alike. The Germans referred to them as Der Schwarze Vogelmenschen, or the black birdmen. Some bomber groups were so impressed with their skill that they were said to have requested the 332nd for fighter escort.

During World War Two, 96 pilots of the 332nd received the Distinguished Service Cross. While 992 pilots were trained via the Tuskegee programme, 335 were deployed to combat duty, and 66 were killed in action. Thirty-two Tuskegee airmen were shot down by enemy fighters

RIGHT: President George W Bush presents the Congressional Gold Medal to Dr Roscoe C Brown Jr, during 2007 ceremonies honouring the Tuskegee Airmen. Public Domain

or flak and taken prisoner. The 332nd Fighter Group earned three Presidential Unit Citations.

The Red Tails distinguished themselves in a memorable mission on March 24, 1945, while escorting B-17 Flying Fortress bombers of the 5th Bomb Wing in a raid against the Daimler-Benz tank production facilities in Berlin, the heavily defended Nazi capital. The entire flight covered 1,600 miles and lasted more than eight hours. When the relief fighter squadron that was to take up escort failed to appear, the Red Tails stayed with the big bombers for the duration of the flight.

On that day, three pilots of the 332nd engaged and shot down German Messerschmitt Me-262s, the first operational jet fighter in history. Red Tail pilots Earl Lane, Charles Brantley, and Roscoe C Brown, Jr, were credited with kills against the jets while flying their P-51 Mustangs, and at least 25 Me-262s were thought to have been in the air, flying from their base at Brandenburg Briest and intent on attacking the bombers over Berlin.

Captain Brown, a 23-year-old native of Washington, DC, remembered his aerial combat against the Me-262. He said: "We knew the German jets were faster than we were. Instead of going directly after them, we went away from them and then turned into their blind spots."

The bombers neared their target, and anti-aircraft fire rocked the air around them. Brown recalled: "As we got over the outskirts of Berlin, I first saw these streaks, which I knew were jets. They were coming up to attack the bombers. I ordered the other P-51 pilots, 'Drop your tanks and follow me'."

Spotting one of the enemy Me-262s hurtling toward a formation of bombers, Brown reacted instinctively. "He didn't see me,

and then I turned into his blind spot, put on my electronic gun sight, and there he was," the pilot reported after the action. "I pulled up at him in a 15-degree climb and fired three long bursts at him from 2,000ft at 8 o'clock to him. Almost immediately, the pilot bailed out from about 24,500ft. I saw flames burst from the jet engines of the enemy's aircraft. The attack on the bombers was ineffective because of the prompt action of my flight in breaking up the attack."

Brown later learned the pilot of the Me-262 he shot down that spring day in 1945 was Oberleutnant Franz Kulp, an ace of Jagdgeschwader 7 with 10 air victories who was severely wounded but survived the war. Brown graduated from Tuskegee's air training programme a member of class 44-C-SE in March 1944. He served as a flight leader and operations officer with the 100th Squadron, 332nd Fighter Group and was elevated to command of the squadron after the war ended. He received the Distinguished Service Cross for the jet encounter, and a week after his shootdown of the Me-262, he also flamed an enemy Focke Wulf Fw-190 fighter, ending the war with three kills.

After leaving the military, Brown received his doctorate and became a professor at New York University, and in 1950 he became director of the NYU Institute of Afro-American Affairs. From 1971 to 1986, he hosted a radio show called The Soul of Reason. He held numerous prestigious positions, serving as president of Bronx Community College for 16 years. He joined other Tuskegee Airmen in the rotunda of the US Capitol on March 29, 2007, when the veterans were presented the Congressional Gold Medal by President George W. Bush. Brown died on July 2, 2016, at the age of 94.

GENERAL BENJAMIN O DAVIS JR

RIGHT: In flight gear, Benjamin O Davis Jr stands before a Thunderbolt fighter. He flew both the P-47 and the P-51 Mustang in the Mediterranean theatre. Creative Commons Schreick's Photo Service via Wikipedia

Benjamin O Davis Jr was a pioneer of American military aviation, commanding the 99th Fighter Squadron and then the 332nd Fighter Group during World War Two. He personally flew 67 combat missions flying the Republic P-47 Thunderbolt and the North American P-51 Mustang fighters. He received the Silver Star for completing a hazardous strafing run against ground targets in Austria and the Distinguished Service Cross for heroism during a bomber escort mission in June 1944.

Davis was born in Washington, DC, on December 18, 1912, the son of Benjamin O Davis Sr, at the time one of only two black officers in the US Army. He was the first black cadet to attend the US Military Academy at West Point during the 20th century and only the fourth black cadet to

do so in the academy's history. He graduated and was commissioned a 2nd lieutenant in 1936. He became an infantry officer at Fort Benning, Georgia, and then relocated to the Tuskegee Institute in Alabama as a reserve officer instructor.

During his junior year at West Point, Davis applied for the Air Corps but was rejected because it did not accept black people. At Tuskegee, he was accepted into the first pilot training course for black aviation cadets and graduated in March 1942. The first black officer to fly solo in an Army Air Corps plane, he was promoted lieutenant colonel and given command of the 99th Fighter Squadron, leading it into combat in World War Two during operations in North Africa and the invasion of Sicily. He was given command of the 332nd Fighter Group in the autumn of 1943 after returning temporarily to the US. In December, he brought the 332nd into the Mediterranean to absorb the 99th Fighter Squadron in Italy.

The Tuskegee Airmen of the 332nd Fighter Group distinguished themselves during World War Two and, with the rank of colonel, Davis led more than 1,000 pilots and ground crewmen during the conflict in the Mediterranean.

After the war, Davis remained in the US Air Force, and when President Harry S Truman signed Executive Order No. 9981 ending racial segregation in the US military, Davis assisted in the composition and implementation of the directive in the Air Force. During service as a staff officer

at the Pentagon, he helped to establish the Thunderbirds air demonstration team, which is now world famous.

During the Korean War, Colonel Davis commanded the 51st Fighter-Interceptor Wing and flew combat missions in the North American F-86 Sabre jet fighter. He performed valuable service in the Far East and was promoted brigadier general in the autumn of 1954. Remaining in the Far East, he led the Thirteenth Air Force at Clark Air Force Base, Philippines, during the 1960s. Following service as deputy commander of US Strike Command at MacDill Air Force Base in Florida, he retired in 1970 with the rank of lieutenant general.

After retirement, Davis served as director of public safety for the city of Cleveland, Ohio, and director of Civil Aviation Security. During the Reagan administration, he was appointed Assistant Secretary of Transportation. In 1998, President Bill Clinton promoted Davis to the rank of full general on the retired list.

Davis died at age 89 on July 4, 2002. His legacy as a fighter pilot flying the P-51 Mustang, a commander of military personnel, and a leader in shattering the colour barrier in the US armed forces remains a stirring chapter in his nation's history.

RIGHT: General Benjamin O Davis Jr led the 332nd Fighter Group, the Tuskegee Airmen, during World War Two. Public Domain

BELOW: Future Four-Star General Benjamin O Davis Jr leads a flight of F-86 Sabres of the 51st Fighter Interceptor Wing during the Korean War. Public Domain

FLIGHT LT MAURICE H PINCHES

In early February 1944, Flying Officer Maurice Henry Pinches joined No 122 Squadron, No. 122 Expeditionary Air Wing, Royal Air Force, transferring from No. 41 Operational Training Unit, which had been formed in September 1941 at RAF Old Sarum in Salisbury, Wiltshire, for the purpose of training tactical reconnaissance pilots.

At the time of Pinches' transfer, No. 122 Squadron was just converting to the North American Mustang Mk III. Pinches went on to become the highest scoring RAF ace at the controls of a Mustang during World War Two, claiming nine aerial victories against German aircraft. With a lineage tracing back to the Great War, the squadron had been reformed in 1941 at RAF Turnhouse in Edinburgh and initially equipped with the Supermarine Spitfire I to perform convoy escort patrols along the Firth of Forth. Soon afterwards, the squadron transferred south to the Hornchurch Wing, its Spitfires flying sweeps over the English Channel and northern France while participating in the ill-fated Dieppe Raid in August 1942. In the autumn of that year, No. 122 Squadron received the Spitfire IX, while Squadron Leader Frantisek Frajtl, the first Czech pilot to lead an RAF squadron, became its commander.

After acclimatising to their new Mustang aircraft in January 1944, the pilots of No. 122 Squadron performed escort duty for bombers hitting targets in France and the Low Countries. Squadron Leader Ernest Joye led the

pilots in a refocusing to tactical air support during the run-up to D-Day. The Mustangs attacked targets in Nazi-occupied France and penetrated deeper into enemy territory after moving to the continent following the success of the Normandy invasion.

Within weeks of his arrival, Flying Officer Pinches was credited with five aerial victories. He received the Distinguished Flying Cross on June 23, 1944, and his citation read: "This officer has proved himself to be a determined and resolute fighter. Within a short period, he has destroyed at least five enemy aircraft, two of which he shot down in one sortie recently. His example has been most praiseworthy."

After three months of intense combat, No 122 Squadron was withdrawn from France and became part of the ADGB (Air Defence Great Britain), combating the fiendish Nazi pulse rocket terror weapons generally known as the V-1 Buzz Bomb, while continuing to provide long-range fighter escort for bombing raids into Germany. By the spring

of 1945, the squadron had taken delivery of the new Mustang Mk. IV and was frequently flying escort for de Havilland Mosquito and Bristol Beaufighter formations, raiding targets in Scandinavia under the auspices of RAF Coastal Command.

Flying Officer Pinches, however, had been the victim of significant misfortune. In a case of mistaken identity, his Mustang was accidently shot down by an American Lockheed P-38 Lightning fighter on August 10, 1944. Pinches bailed out and suffered only a few slight burns in the mishap. He was promoted flight lieutenant and returned to duty. He continued to fly until October 11, but suddenly fell ill with jaundice. The diagnosis was of unexplained origin and perhaps related to the earlier incident with the P-38. His condition rapidly deteriorated, and he died later that month.

On October 20, 1944, Pinches posthumously received a bar to his Distinguished Flying Cross, the citation noting: "Flight Lieutenant Pinches has now destroyed four more enemy aircraft and damaged several others. He continues to display a fine fighting spirit and great gallantry."

He was 25 years old.

ABOVE: Before transitioning to the Mustang, pilots of No. 122 Squadron flew the Supermarine Spitfire such as this one at RAF Hornchurch.
Public Domain

LEFT: Flight Lieutenant Jimmy Talalla, a mate of Flight Lieutenant Maurice Pinches, stands before his P-51 Mustang fighter.
Public Domain

LEFT: Ground crewmen of No. 122 Squadron RAF play a game of draughts waiting for their airmen to return from a mission over France.
Public Domain

GENERAL JOHN C MEYER

RIGHT: Intrepid ace John C Meyer was a top scoring Mustang pilot in the European theatre of World War Two. Public Domain

During a 35-year career with the US Air Force, John C Meyer rose to the highest echelon of command. He served as commander-in-chief of Strategic Air Command and director of Joint Strategic Target Planning and attained the rank of four-star general.

However, his headiest days were those spent in the cockpit of the P-51 Mustang fighter during World War Two. Meyer was the second highest scoring Mustang ace of the war, with 21 of his 24 aerial kills in the P-51, while ranking fourth overall among American aces. He also destroyed 13½ German aircraft on the ground.

Meyer's most famous foray against the Luftwaffe came late in the war. On January 1, 1945, the Germans launched a desperate air offensive to redress the growing superiority in numbers of the Allied air forces in Europe. Their plan was to attack Allied fighters on the ground, surprising them before they had a chance to get into the air to give battle. Operation Bodenplatte, or Baseplate, as it was called, became a costly failure for the Germans in that their losses were irreplaceable, while the Allies could easily replenish the planes destroyed that day.

RIGHT: General John C. Meyer welcomes then-Vice President Gerald Ford during a 1974 visit to Offutt Air Force Base. Public Domain

One of the reasons for the outcome of Bodenplatte was the heroism of John Meyer. While serving as deputy commander of the 352nd Fighter Group, Meyer and his fellow pilots were based at airfield Y-29, near the Belgian town of Asche. According to some contemporaries, Meyer had a knack for 'thinking like a German'. He believed the enemy might well try

BELOW: The Soviet-made MiG-15 fighter, this one shown in Hungarian livery at a museum, was a primary adversary of John C Meyer and American Sabre pilots in Korea. Creative Commons Varga Attila via Wikipedia

to pull a fast one on the Americans based at Y-29, thinking perhaps that they would be sleeping off late hours of New Year's Eve revelry. He was said to have postponed the 352nd Fighter Group's celebration for a day in anticipation of an enemy move.

Early on the first morning of 1945, Meyer led a dozen P-51s of the 487th Fighter Squadron into the air, but just as they were preparing to take off, about 50 Luftwaffe fighters appeared overhead. The Mustangs were weighed down somewhat with full auxiliary wing tanks, but that was no hindrance for Meyer. While he raised his landing gear and climbed off the runway, he blasted an enemy Focke Wulf Fw-190. Then, as the 45-minute melee unfolded, he flamed a second Focke Wulf. Altogether, due in large part to Meyer's prescience, the pilots shot down 23 German fighters on the day and later received the Presidential Unit Citation. For Meyer, it resulted in his third award of the Distinguished Service Cross.

College dropout

Born in Brooklyn, New York, on April 3, 1919, Meyer dropped out of the prestigious Dartmouth College to become an army aviation cadet in 1939, later returning to earn his degree from the Ivy League university. By July 1940, he was commissioned 2nd lieutenant and assigned as a fighter pilot to the 33rd Pursuit Squadron, flying the Curtiss P-40 Tomahawk, at Mitchel Field, New York. As the government of President Franklin D Roosevelt sought to aid the British before the US entry into World War Two in Europe, Meyer and the 33rd Fighter Squadron flew patrol missions from their base in Iceland, covering trans-Atlantic convoys.

In the autumn of 1942, Meyer was given command of the newly formed 34th Pursuit Squadron, a component of the 352nd Fighter Group. In January 1944, the unit received its P-47 Thunderbolt fighters at New Haven, Connecticut. By the spring, the 34th was redesignated the 487th Fighter Squadron, arriving at RAF Bodney. The commanding officer scored the squadron's first kill on November 26, 1943, one of three he recorded in the Thunderbolt before the 487th transitioned to the P-51 and became widely known for the blue noses and cowlings of its Mustangs.

Meyer earned the first of his Distinguished Service Crosses on May 8, 1944, while flying escort for heavy bombers. He and his wingman became separated from the rest of the squadron but nevertheless attacked a formation of 15 enemy fighters. He shot down two and then bagged a third just before turning back to RAF Bodney.

Four days later, while flying bomber escort over Frankfurt, Lieutenant Colonel Meyer shot down an enemy Me-109 fighter and a Heinkel He-177 'Greif' bomber. The situation then became uncomfortable, and he later wrote of the experience in his report of the action.

"As I pulled up, I observed an Me-109 on my tail at 250yds firing. He was painted robin egg blue on bottom and sides and either black or dark brown on top. In about a turn and a half I was on his tail then he dropped some flaps, and I was unable to get sufficient deflection. Unlike other Huns who in similar situations have broken for the deck and set themselves up, this Jerry continued his tight turn and seemed willing to continue the fight. I tried dropping 10 degrees and then 20 degrees of flaps and although this helped momentarily to decrease the radius of turn, my airspeed dropped off so much that I think nothing was gained by this. At this time, I was receiving groundfire from the field directly below, this combat taking place at about 3,000ft. Just then, another 109 joined in the fight, climbing above, and dropping down behind me and, as he lost ground, climbing up again and attacking as I completed the next orbit. I then broke for the deck, flying as low as possible, and headed south into the sun using valleys and hills for evasion. The Huns followed me for a while but always out of range. I pulled 67in for 30 minutes and somewhere in that time lost them."

Meyer went on to raise his total of aerial victories consistently. On September 11, 1944, he claimed three Me-109s and an Fw-190 in the crowded skies over Germany. After mixing it up for several minutes with a large formation of enemy planes, he said: "I saw a lone Me-109 emerging from a cloud in the vicinity of the large enemy gaggle. Only my right-wing guns were now firing so I opened at 200yds, closing to point blank range and 10 degrees deflection. I saw strikes all over the enemy aircraft and pieces flew off the tail and fuselage. He caught fire at his left-wing root. I broke off the attack and headed for the deck and home. Shortly after,

two Me-109s attacked me from slightly below and directly astern. Occasionally they would pull up their noses and fire but then drop behind. They chased me from the vicinity of Kassel to Bonn, breaking off their attack as I reached the Rhine River."

At times, the instinct for survival served the fighter pilots in Europe's war-torn skies as well as the drive to attack the enemy. Meyer maintained a balanced approach in combat. On November 11, 1944, he shot down four enemy fighters, and 10 days later, he shot down three more over Leipzig and gained his second Distinguished Service Cross.

During the Korean War, Colonel Meyer engaged in aerial combat while leading the 4th Fighter Wing. He participated in the first documented dogfight solely between opposing jets in history, the F-86 Sabres downing six communist Mig-15s without loss. He later shot down two MiG-15s and finished his career in air combat with 26½ **victories and well over 200 combat missions flown.**

As SAC commander during the Vietnam War from 1972 to 1974, Meyer oversaw the controversial Christmas bombing of North Vietnam, Operation Linebacker II. He suffered a heart attack and died at the age of 56 on December 2, 1975.

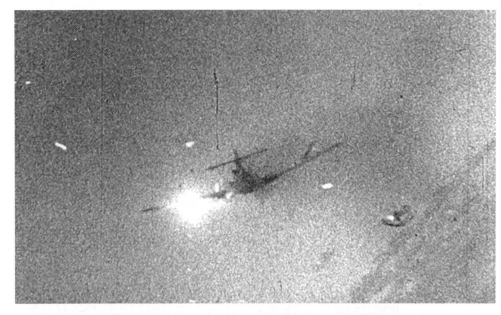

ABOVE: Pieces fly off a stricken German Messerschmitt Me-109 under the guns of an US fighter in 1944.
Public Domain

LEFT: General John C Meyer, second from left, stands with other high-ranking military officers and Speaker of the US House of Representatives Carl Albert in 1971.
Creative Commons Carl Albert Archives via Wikipedia

LEFT: General John C Meyer presents a medal for exceptional civilian service in 1970.
Public Domain

MAJOR GEORGE E PREDDY

RIGHT: Mustang ace Major George Preddy holds up six fingers in relation to his famous mission of August 6, 1944. Public Domain

The top-scoring P-51 fighter ace of World War Two scored his Mustang victories in the European theatre. However, he was lucky to survive being seriously injured in a mid-air training crash while flying a Curtiss P-40 Tomahawk fighter on the other side of the world.

George E Preddy underwent emergency surgery in July 1942, and spent weeks in hospital in Australia before transfer orders to the US Army Air Forces' 352nd Fighter Group meant transit aboard the luxury liner turned troopship Queen Elizabeth bound for Scotland, arriving at the Clyde on July 5, 1943. Although his flying experience was limited, Preddy had a leg up on his fellow pilots even though he had to forget much of his knowledge of the P-40 and learn the characteristics of the Republic P-47 Thunderbolt fighter.

RIGHT: George Preddy waves from the cockpit of his P-51D fighter *Cripes A' Mighty 3rd.* Public Domain

Preddy and other American fighter pilots felt the helplessness as US bomber formations were left unescorted for much of the distance during their raids into deep German-occupied territory. His P-47 did not have the range to fly with the big B-17s and B-24s through enemy skies swarming with Luftwaffe fighters and blackened with puffs of anti-aircraft fire, but he was determined to fight where he could. He was a gambler, and he believed that shouting 'Cripes A'

RIGHT: Major George Preddy posed in dress uniform for this portrait. Note the Eighth Air Force patch on his shoulder. Public Domain

Mighty!' when throwing dice would bring him good luck. It followed, then, that his aerial mount should be christened as such.

Flying with the 487th Fighter Squadron, Preddy claimed his first aerial kill on December 1, 1943, a Messerschmitt Me-109 fighter that was literally blown apart by his 'jug's' eight .50-calibre machine guns. Soon afterwards, the young officer shot down an Me-210 that was harassing a crippled B-24 named *Lizzie* and

then lured other enemy fighters away from the limping bomber in fruitless pursuit east of the Zuider Zee. He received the Silver Star for his heroism. Just after Christmas, he shot down an Fw-190 but took hits from an enemy flak gun, bailing out and surviving in the frigid water long enough to be rescued.

Preddy had packed a lot of adventure into fewer than five months of aerial warfare, but he was just getting started.

Born in Greensboro, North Carolina, on February 5, 1919, George Preddy had attended two years of college and worked in a cotton mill before learning to fly and becoming a barnstormer pilot, performing aerial stunts to the delight of crowds below. In 1940, he joined the North Carolina National Guard, and soon he tried to qualify as a US Navy pilot but was rejected three times. Opting for the Army, he gained his pilot's wings on December 12, 1941, just five days after the Japanese plunged the United States into World War Two with the attack on Pearl Harbor.

Turning point

The turning point in Preddy's fighter pilot career occurred in early 1944, when the 352nd Fighter Group swapped its P-47s for the new North American P-51 Mustang. He embraced the new fighter, a sleek and nimble aircraft possessing the range, speed, and firepower to duel with the enemy in the skies across Europe. The Mustang pilots escorted bombers on a long mission to hit the German cities of Hamm, Koblenz, Bonn, and Sost on April 22. Preddy and two other pilots strafed the Luftwaffe airfield at Stade and chewed up a twin-engine Junkers Ju-88 bomber as it was taking off. The three pilots each received credit for 1/3 of a kill.

Eight days later, Preddy shot down an enemy Fw-190, igniting a string of aerial victories that made the hotshot and his P-51 *Cripes A' Mighty II* the centre of attention. From the end of April through to D-Day on June 6, 1944, Major Preddy accounted for 4½ kills. At the time, he had completed a 200-hour tour in the combat area and received a pair of 50-hour extensions. He requested and received a third 50-hour extension, focusing on his tally of kills and suppressing any thoughts of going home on leave. During the next eight weeks, he shot

down nine more German aircraft, including four during a single mission on July 18.

After reading the weather report for August 6, 1944, Preddy was confident that there would be no air operations that day. So, on the night of the 5th, he participated heavily in the festivities of the 352nd Fighter Group's war bond drive party. Forgetting momentarily the stress of combat, he imbibed well into the night and the wee hours of the morning before sliding into bed shortly before daybreak. In less than half an hour, he was roused with the news that the weather had improved. A bombing raid was scheduled, and he was to lead the fighter escort. The target: Berlin.

Preddy was virtually incoherent during the mission briefing. He was placed in a chair by several other pilots, unable to deliver any instruction, and fell off the speaker's platform at one point. To help revive him, an oxygen mask was held over his nose, cold water was thrown into his face, and he was slapped a few times with a wet towel. After regaining some of his faculties, he

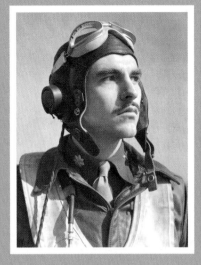

LEFT: Major George Preddy, highest scoring Mustang ace of World War Two, was killed by friendly fire. Public Domain

was strapped into the cockpit of *Cripes A' Mighty II*. He took to the air in a clear, almost cloudless sky.

Picking up their assigned flight of B-17s, Preddy's pilots scanned the distance for the approach of Luftwaffe fighters. They did not have long to wait. Soon enough, 30 Me-109s approached at high speed. Preddy singled out one German fighter and fired. The plane spun into the ground and exploded. »

LEFT: The nose of the modern *Cripes A' Mighty 3rd* is emblazoned with crosses signifying aerial kills. Creative Commons Valder137 via Wikipedia

BELOW: Painted to resemble *Cripes A' Mighty 3rd*, a modern P-51 Mustang takes wing. Creative Commons Valder137 via Wikipedia

ABOVE: The 487th Fighter Squadron P-51 Mustang nicknamed *MoonBeam McSwine* sits at an airfield in England.
Public Domain

RIGHT: Artistic ground crewmen paint the nose of a 352nd Fighter Group P-47 Thunderbolt at RAF Bodney. Prior to flying the P-51 Mustang, George Preddy flew the Thunderbolt.
Public Domain

RIGHT: The 487th Fighter Squadron was recognised by its jaunty emblem.
Public Domain

In seconds, he was on another target, stitching the port wing root of an Me-109 with .50-calibre bullets. The plane began to blaze, and the pilot took to his parachute.

The American fighters had approached the attackers from the rear, and while the Germans were intent on catching the bombers, several fatal minutes elapsed before the hunters realised they had become the hunted. Preddy quickly shot down two more enemy planes before the Germans finally began to take evasive action, several of them with Mustangs already firmly latched onto their tails. After shooting down his fifth enemy plane on the day, Preddy and other P-51 pilots watched the Germans descend to altitudes of just 5,000ft as they attempted to manoeuvre out of harm's way.

Too quick

Preddy got behind yet another Me-109, and the pilot violently jinked to the left to perhaps use Preddy's diving airspeed against him and get on the Mustang's tail. Preddy was too quick. He passed above the German and made a quick turn that

put him in close firing position from behind. The P-51's machine guns chattered, and this German pilot hit the silk as his stricken plane plunged towards the ground. By the time he touched down, Preddy's cockpit was foul with the former contents of his stomach. But he had pulled off one of the greatest feats of aerial combat in World War Two, downing six German fighters in a single mission.

The major staggered away from his plane and did not stop to report his success, aware that there had been plenty of witnesses to his exploits and that gun camera footage would substantiate the demise of the half dozen enemy planes.

In the days that followed, the news wires buzzed with reports of Major George Preddy's astounding accomplishment. He became a celebrity, and his smile was the focus of photographers' cameras, even though a few shots of a pale, nauseous pilot had been snapped just after he touched down at his airfield on August 6. Only six days after the historic mission, Preddy was presented with the Distinguished Service Cross by

Brigadier General Edward H Anderson, commander of the 65th Fighter Wing. Preddy's commanding officer, Lieutenant Colonel John C Meyer, had recommended the Medal of Honor and was incensed that his heroic pilot's award had been downgraded. Preddy, however, did not appear dismayed.

After his third extension expired, Preddy did go home to Greensboro. Amid seven weeks in the US, he was chafing to return to air combat. He felt a sense of duty that he expressed to his pastor simply saying: "Reverend, I must go back." He was shocked to find out on his return to England that *Cripes A' Mighty II* had been reassigned to another pilot after his departure, the personnel responsible thinking he was not going to return to the air. He was given command of the 328th Fighter Squadron of the 352nd Group, and when he received a brand now P-51D, Preddy would not fly a mission in the plane until its name, *Cripes A' Mighty 3rd*, was emblazoned on its fuselage.

There was good reason to hand the veteran fighter ace George Preddy the 328th. Its score of enemy aircraft was the lowest in the group. The new commander set about showing his charges how to fight in the air and win. On November 2, 1944, the squadron was aloft to escort bombers on a raid against the city of Merseburg in central Germany. Scanning the sky, the veteran pilot noticed several contrails streaming behind aircraft at 33,000ft. He instantly knew that German fighters were attempting to dive on a bomber formation.

Preddy caught an Me-109 and destroyed the plane in seconds, while the remaining Mustangs broke up the Luftwaffe fighter gaggle before it reached the vulnerable bombers. A day later, Preddy shot down another Fw-190.

Abruptly afterwards, however, the skies seemed rather empty of German fighters as the Luftwaffe had experienced significant losses in planes and pilots through attrition. The weeks dragged by, and then the calm was shattered when the Germans launched their Ardennes Offensive on the ground

planes in a steep dive. Preddy shot down a pair of Me-109s in rapid succession and then spurred his flight ahead in pursuit of the enemy that was fleeing toward the city of Liege, Belgium.

Preddy spotted an Fw-190 flying at high speed and treetop level trying to escape. He roared in to attack and opened fire on the German. Almost simultaneously, an American antiaircraft unit had spotted Preddy's plane. The battery opened fire on the Mustang, and before the gunners realised they were shooting at one of their own planes, tragedy struck. They ceased fire, but not before the Mustang had been damaged and a .50-calibre bullet had struck Preddy in the right thigh.

Cripes A' Mighty 3rd crashed to the ground a short distance from the anti-aircraft emplacement, and infantrymen rushed to the scene, administering first aid, and loading Preddy for transport to a field hospital as soon as possible. The wound, however, was fatal. With a severed femoral artery, the 25-year-old George Preddy bled to death en route.

At the time of the friendly fire incident, Preddy had scored 26.83 aerial victories, the vast majority of them flying the P-51 and had been credited with five more enemy planes shot up on the ground. He was one of a relatively few US pilots to fly missions against the Axis in both the European and Pacific theatres, and reports indicate that he had participated in damaging two Japanese Zero fighters while flying the Curtiss P-40 fighter.

Preddy was buried in the Lorraine American Cemetery near Saint-Avold, France.

A few weeks later, his 20-year-old brother, William, a P-51 pilot of the 503rd Fighter Squadron, 339th Fighter Group with two air victories, was shot down by enemy antiaircraft fire and killed while strafing an airfield near Pilsen, Czechoslovakia. He was buried beside George.

on December 16, 1944. The resulting Battle of the Bulge raged, and the Germans nearly succeeded in reaching their objective, the Belgian port city of Antwerp, and driving a wedge between the Allied armies north and south. And for a week, foul weather kept the 328th Squadron and other Allied aircraft from flying missions against the enemy.

Low ceiling

Finally, the frustrated pilots of the 328th were given the go-ahead for sorties on December 23. Flying from their airfield in Belgium, the Mustangs encountered a dangerously low operational ceiling as thick cloud cover blanketed the vicinity. They found no enemy planes to fight amid contradictory reports of enemy activity and false sightings of Me-109s and Fw-190s. Some of the pilots dodged tall trees as they made their way back to base. By this time, both pilots and anti-aircraft gun crews had grown edgy.

On Christmas Day 1944, Preddy took off with 10 more Mustangs in search of targets, either in the air or to strafe in the open on the ground. For three hours, the pilots searched in vain. And then reports of enemy aircraft near Koblenz crackled across their radios. At last, they spotted their quarry and attacked the enemy

MAJORS DON S GENTILE AND JOHN T GODFREY

RIGHT: Major Don Gentile sits on the wing of his P-51B Mustang *Shangri La*. Public Domain

RIGHT: Major John T Godfrey sits in the cockpit of his P-51B fighter in 1944. Public Domain

BELOW: General Dwight Eisenhower presents the Distinguished Service Cross to Don Gentile. Colonel Don Blakeslee stands at right. Public Domain

The two Mustang pilots were a combat team – one an acknowledged expert at the controls of a high-performance fighter plane and the other keeping pace, watching his comrade's '6' and becoming a legendary wartime ace in his own right.

Major Don S Gentile and Major John T Godfrey were inseparable, in the air and often during down time on the ground. Their exploits were known far and wide among the pilots of the Allied air forces based in England, and they earned praise even from British Prime Minister Winston Churchill, who called the pair 'Damon and Pythias', legendary characters of Greek mythology. General Dwight D

Eisenhower, supreme commander of Allied forces in Europe, called Gentile a 'One Man Air Force.' The pilots had other nicknames too – the Two Man Air Force, Captains Courageous, and the Messerschmitt Killers.

Both men had engaged in air battles well before the United States entered World War Two. They flew with the legendary Eagle Squadrons of the Royal Air Force and got to know the superb flying characteristics of the British Supermarine Spitfire. When the US Army Air Forces absorbed the Eagle Squadrons, they flew with the 4th Fighter Group, first in the heavy-duty Republic P-47 Thunderbolt, nicknamed the Jug due to its silhouette's resemblance to a milk bottle, and then in the sleek North American P-51 Mustang, the thoroughbred of Allied combat aircraft.

Gentile hailed from Piqua, Ohio, where he was born on December 6, 1920. At the age of 17, he bought a homemade plane for $300 and nearly killed himself while flying it. Then, undeterred, he persuaded his father to help him purchase a World War One-vintage biplane for $1,400. He flew solo in the wood and canvas relic on the day the previous owner set it down in an open field near Piqua and closed the deal. From that point, he flew with irrational exuberance and gained a reputation

as a troublemaker with the local law enforcement. He buzzed the town of Piqua with regularity, blew the laundry off clothes lines, and caused general mayhem.

In later years he remembered: "On Saturday afternoons, I would beat up the town in my plane, and the cops chased me. I could see their cars running after me, trying to get my number. I'd raise the hair on everybody's heads with my propeller. I'd blow in the curtains on Betty Levering's house and make the geraniums in Marge Dill's front yard give up their petals."

In the autumn of 1939, the war in Europe was underway. Gentile wanted to enlist in the US Army Air Corps but did not have the two years of college required. He convinced his father to sign enlistment papers for the Royal Canadian Air Force (RCAF). There was only one condition. He promised that he would earn a high school diploma when he had the time.

Off to Britain

Gentile was soon shipped to Britain, where he completed Royal Air Force pilot training and was assigned to No. 133 Squadron RAF, flying the famed Spitfire V. He earned his first aerial victories on August 9, 1942, shooting down a Focke Wulf Fw-190 fighter and a twin-engine Junkers Ju-88 bomber. During that period, he also met his friend and partner in air combat, John Godfrey.

Born in Montreal, Canada, on March 28, 1922, Godfrey and his family moved to the mill town of Woonsocket, Rhode Island, when he was a year old. With the outbreak of World War Two, Godfrey skipped his senior year of high school and tried to enlist in the Canadian army. When that attempt was derailed, he tried twice to join the RCAF before

LEFT: This statue of Don Gentile stands in his hometown of Piqua, Ohio.
Public Domain

accomplishing the task on the third try. His parents were frustrated, their hopes that he would attend college set aside, but his father once found the teenager at a train station in Boston before dragging him home, while his mother called the FBI to track down her impetuous son.

It was a hard sell, but Godfrey did finally convince his parents to allow him to enlist in the RCAF in the autumn of 1941. About that time, his brother Reggie was killed when the ship SS *Vancouver Island* was torpedoed in the Atlantic by a

German U-boat. Reggie had been among American civilians travelling to Britain to assist with the war effort. Godfrey finished his pilot training at Moncton, New Brunswick, and arrived in England to join No. 133 Squadron. He later nicknamed his fighter aircraft *Reggie's Reply* in memory of his brother.

Gentile was a veteran combat pilot when Godfrey joined him, both pilots flying the P-47, on an escort mission shepherding B-17 Flying Fortress bombers over Nazi-occupied Europe on September 27, 1943. Gentile had fought for his life in a harrowing escape from an Fw-190 in July 1942 and had gone on to become an ace in the Thunderbolt. During the return flight from their first mission, Gentile suddenly went into a steep dive. Godfrey followed and the P-47s roared down to 1,500ft. When they landed at RAF Debden, Godfrey asked the reason for the manoeuvre. Gentile replied that his gyrocompass had malfunctioned, nearly causing a crash. Godfrey had stayed with him like a good wingman should, and the friendship was cemented that day.

On December 1, 1943, Godfrey shot down a Messerschmitt Me-109, and he shared another kill three weeks later. Meanwhile, Gentile concluded his most harrowing mission with Lieutenant Bob Richards as his wingman on January 14, 1944. He

shot down a pair of German fighters, but two Fw-190s got on his tail and pumped 20mm cannon shells into his P-47. Twisting and turning for 15 minutes, he finally outlasted the German pilots who dogged him, the nearest enemy flier enraged as he ran out of ammunition. On February 25, Gentile shot down his sixth and last German plane while flying the Thunderbolt.

The situation was about to change dramatically for both Gentile and Godfrey. In January, Colonel Don Blakeslee took command of the 4th Fighter Group, and he immediately began to lobby for its transition to the P-51 Mustang. The pilots took to their new fighters, although »

LEFT: John T Godfrey (left) and Don S Gentile stand together at RAF Debden.
Public Domain

LEFT: The official badge of No. 133 Squadron RAF reflects its heritage as an Eagle Squadron.
Public Domain

there were early concerns regarding the liquid-cooled engine that was more vulnerable to enemy fire than air-cooled powerplants, as well as the four wing-mounted .50-calibre machine guns of the P-51B, apparently under-armed since the P-47 mounted twice that number.

On March 3, 1944, Gentile persevered through difficulties with his P-51 nicknamed *Shangri-La,* as he dealt with frost on the inside of his canopy before dodging an attacking Me-110 and three Fw-190s that flew head-on at him. He damaged a Dornier Do-217 bomber and then shot down an Fw-190 before some of his guns jammed. He then selected targets prudently and flamed an Fw-190 before heading home.

First mission

Godfrey flew his first mission in the P-51 on February 28, 1944, and with only 40 minutes of flying time in the new fighter. He gained his first air victory in the Mustang on March 6. Two days later, he joined Gentile once again for one of the most eventful missions of their combat careers. While escorting B-17s en route to bomb the Erkner ball bearing works on the outskirts of Berlin, they spotted a large group of Me-109s just before 2pm, making head-on passes at the big bombers.

They closed rapidly with the enemy fighters and latched onto a pair of Me-109s. Godfrey opened fire, and the German plane exploded in mid-air. Gentile stayed with his target in tight turns, finally resorting to the use of his flaps, slightly lowering them to close the distance to only 75yds. He fired, and a wisp of white smoke began to trail from the German plane before it snapped into a death spiral and hit the ground in a shroud of smoke and flame.

Gentile swiftly manoeuvred behind another Messerschmitt and opened up at a distance of 100yds. When the stream of .50-calibre bullets struck home, the German pilot hit the silk, abandoning his damaged plane. Two more Me-109s were within striking distance. Godfrey fired an accurate burst, and one of the Germans disintegrated. Gentile's next victim nosed over into a spin, and the pilot bailed out seconds before the plane smashed into the ground.

One German pilot bravely attacked Gentile and Godfrey, getting more than he could handle in return. The Mustang pilots moved into firing position, and Godfrey let loose, striking the Me-109 until his ammunition supply was exhausted. Gentile stepped in and poured .50-calibre fire into the enemy plane

ABOVE: A group of RAF pilots gathers to discuss a mission in the shadow of one of its Mustang fighter planes. Public Domain

LEFT: Gentile and Godrey flew the Spitfire V as pilots of No. 133 Squadron RAF. Creative Common Roodhullandemu via Wikipedia

until its auxiliary fuel tank, still slung under its belly, caught fire, convincing the German to bail out.

When the swirl of battle had subsided, the two pilots spotted a single B-17 of the 92nd Bomb Group, separated from its formation and flying alone towards home. Gentile and Godfrey pulled up alongside and escorted the bomber safely away from Berlin and all the way home to its airfield in East Anglia. After touching down safely, the bomber crewmen were tremendously grateful

and broadcast profuse thanks to their 'Little Friends' who had flown the Mustangs and brought them back safely.

In just a few minutes, the two Americans had thrown the German attack on the B-17s into disarray. Gentile had shot down three enemy planes, Godfrey had claimed a pair, and then for good measure they had shared a sixth Me-109. Godfrey had shot down his fourth and fifth aerial victories, becoming an ace. Gentile had been credited with 11.84

BELOW: Don Gentile and John Godfrey flew the Republic P-47 Thunderbolt during their combat careers as well as the P-51 and Spitfire. Public Domain

RIGHT: Pieces
fly off a stricken
Focke Wulf
Fw-190 during a
dogfight in 1944.
Public Domain

air-to-air kills to date, and a rivalry
began to develop with other aces,
particularly Duane Beeson of the
334th Fighter Squadron, 4th Fighter
Group with 16 kills and P-47 pilot
Bob Johnson of the 56th Fighter
Group with 22 at the end of March.

Momentous month

The month of March was momentous
for both Gentile and Godfrey. On
the 18th, Gentile engaged six Fw-190s
above Augsburg, Germany, and
chewed up one of them in a spiralling
chase that resulted in the German
pilot bailing out just 6,000ft above
the deck. Godfrey, meanwhile, scored
4.33 more victories and flew with
Gentile on the 29th to escort B-17s
attacking industrial targets in the
Brunswick area. When the bombers
came under attack, the intrepid pair
raced in. While Gentile shot down
three enemy planes, two Fw-190s
and an Me-109, Godfrey riddled a
pair of Fw-190s and sent them down
in flames before helping two other
pilots shoot down a Heinkel He-111
bomber. His score stood at 11 air
victories.

On April 1, Godfrey witnessed a
Gentile kill while they flew with
Blakeslee on an escort mission
with B-24 Liberator bombers over
Stuttgart. Four Me-109s were
attacking a bomber formation and
managed to shoot down one of the
'Big Friends' before Gentile started a
steep dive on an Me-109, descending
like an avenging angel from 23,000ft
to 6,000ft. The planes locked in a
tight spiral, but Gentile's gunsight
filled with the Messerschmitt and his
.50-calibre machine guns chattered.
Pulling back on the stick, he came
out of the dive while Godfrey saw
the German spin into an open field,

RIGHT: Sheep
graze around the
wreckage of a Nazi
plane damaged
by strafing and
abandoned.
Public Domain

BELOW: Allied
bombers attack
a rail marshalling
yard in France.
Gentile and
Godfrey flew many
escort missions.
Public Domain

raising a large cloud of fire and
smoke. Gentile now had 21 aerial kills
and was credited with destroying
three more on the ground.

Four days later, the entire
4th Fighter Group participated in
a sweep against the Stendal airfield
near Berlin. The Mustangs shot up
numerous German planes as they
were parked next to the runway.
At least 25 Junkers aircraft were
destroyed, as well as others. Records
vary somewhat, but Gentile was
credited with shredding four or five,
becoming the first fighter pilot of
the Eighth Air Force to score more
than 26 victories in the air and on
the ground, surpassing the American
record of Captain Eddie Rickenbacker
of the 9th 'Hat in the Ring' Squadron
who claimed 26 victories during
World War One.

On April 6, Godfrey's P-51B, never
christened as *Reggie's Reply* but
painted with the same chequerboard
scheme on the engine cowling as
Gentile's *Shangri La*, was damaged
beyond repair on a training flight
with another pilot at the controls.
He received a new P-51 and promptly
did name this mount *Reggie's Reply*.
On April 22, he shot down three
German aircraft. Two days later, he
flamed another.

Meanwhile, Gentile had shot down
two more enemy aircraft on April
8, both Fw-190s claimed over »

crashed his plane at a forward base on April 26, damaging it beyond repair. He did go up again on May 1, shooting down a single Me-109. Soon afterwards, he was ordered to join Gentile at Chorley. The pair went on a war bond tour in the US, lauded by the press and idolised by the public.

Major Gentile remained in the United States and test flew the Lockheed P-80 Shooting Star, an early American jet fighter, at Wright-Patterson Air Force Base in Dayton, Ohio. He left the military in the spring of 1946 but then thought better of the decision and returned to the service in late 1947. During his post-war years, he co-wrote his autobiography titled 'One Man Air Force' with war correspondent Ira Wolfert.

Unfitting end

Tragically, Gentile met a fate that did not seem fitting for a fighter

ABOVE: This P-51B Mustang crashed in Switzerland after being damaged in battle.
Public Domain

RIGHT: Don Gentile and John Godfrey flew the P-51B Mustang for much of their combat careers.
Public Domain

BELOW: Don Gentile was killed in the crash of a Lockheed T-33 Shooting Star trainer similar to this one.
Public Domain

Brunswick. Always a maverick and full of enthusiasm, his exuberance got the best of him on the return approach to RAF Debden. Showing off for a cluster of reporters, officers, and ground crewmen, he buzzed the field but came in too long, crashing *Shangri La* beyond the length of the runway. He suffered only bumps and bruises, but Blakeslee was furious. He had previously decreed that any pilot whose plane cracked up as the result of 'showboating' would be grounded. So it was with Gentile. It was his last combat mission, and he had score 15½ of his 21.84 air victories in the P-51.

Godfrey was unlucky again with *Reggie's Reply* as another pilot

ace of such dash and aplomb. On January 28, 1951, he was scheduled to make a routine proficiency flight from Andrews Air Force Base near Washington, DC. Mechanical issues emerged with his Lockheed T-33 Shooting Star trainer, and Sergeant Lawrence Kirsch of the ground crew asked for more time to evaluate the problems. Gentile agreed to postpone the flight until later in the day, but when he returned to the field, Kirsch still had misgivings about the jet's performance.

When Kirsch offered to go on the flight as an adviser in the event of trouble, Gentile accepted. Less than half an hour after take-off, the T-33 crashed in a field in the Maryland countryside, killing both men. Witnesses had seen the jet in a steep dive and were horrified as it clipped treetops and slammed into the ground.

After the war bond tour, Godfrey managed to talk his way back into action. On August 5, 1944, he shot down an Me-109, destroyed three Junkers Ju-52 transport planes on the ground, and blasted eight railroad locomotives with his wingman, Captain Otey Glass. A day later, he claimed an Me-410. However, within minutes he ran into trouble. Enemy anti-aircraft fire struck his Mustang during a strafing pass over a German airfield east of Berlin. Precious engine coolant streamed out of the perforated powerplant, and he pulled the canopy back, preparing to bail out. Seconds later, his 336th Fighter Squadron mate Fred Glover pulled up alongside and urged Godfrey to stay in the plane, suggesting that he use the primer pump to push raw fuel into the overheating engine cylinders. He reasoned that it just might cool the Rolls-Royce Merlin powerplant enough to coax the plane home. It worked.

For the next two hours, Godfrey continually plied the pump until his hand throbbed. He touched down at an advanced base at Beccles. He had beaten the odds and made it back, but soon his luck evaporated.

Low-level strafing runs were always dangerous business, and on August 24, Godfrey led a section of fighters against an airfield at Nordhausen in central Germany. The strafers made four passes, destroying four Ju-52s, but Godfrey's P-51 was hit. Instead of peeling away, he completed three more passes. When the engine petered out, he was forced to land on his belly in a field some distance beyond the German air base.

Godfrey eluded capture for a day before the Germans caught up with him and transferred him to Stalag Luft III in Zagan, Poland. He attempted to escape three times and was successful shortly before World War Two in Europe ended. In a bizarre twist, after his return to RAF Debden, he reviewed gun camera footage of the fateful mission and determined that friendly fire from his own wingman had been the source of the crippling damage to his Mustang. He flew no more combat missions and finished the war with 16.33 aerial

victories and an impressive tally of 13.67 German planes destroyed on the ground. He was promoted to major shortly after the end of the war and was discharged from the service in late 1945.

Godfrey returned to Rhode Island and found work in his wife's family business, manufacturing lace for the garment industry. In 1952, he ran successfully as a Republican for a seat in the state senate. Although the party urged him to seek the governor's mansion, he had no further political ambitions. By 1954, he had left the family business and relocated to Freeport, Maine, starting his own independent lace manufacturing facility.

Godfrey began to experience a distressing decline in health in the mid-1950s, and after suffering for months he was given a dreaded diagnosis of Amyotrophic Lateral Sclerosis, better known as Lou Gehrig's Disease after the famous

ABOVE: This model depicts Stalag Luft III, where John T Godfrey was held as a prisoner and escaped in 1945.
Creative Commons via Wikipedia

LEFT: Friedrich Wilhelm von Lindeiner-Wildau was commandant of Stalag Luft III.
Public Domain

New York Yankees baseball player. The prognosis was grim – less than two years to live.

There was no viable treatment for the disease, and Godfrey spent his last months reminiscing about the days of glory in the skies over Europe and dictating comments for his book titled 'The Look of Eagles'. He died at the young age of 36 on June 12, 1958, and the autobiography was published after his death.

Together, Don Gentile and John Godfrey had blazed a war-winning trail in aerial combat with the 336th Fighter Squadron, and in doing so they had helped secure a prominent place in military history for the formidable P-51 Mustang.

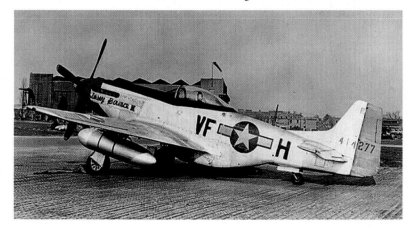

LEFT: This P-51D Mustang of the 336th Fighter Squadron sits at RAF Debden.
Public Domain

THE BLOND KNIGHT AND THE MUSTANG

Major Erich Hartmann, the highest-scoring fighter ace of all time, recorded an astonishing 352 aerial victories during World War Two flying the Messerschmitt Me-109 fighter with Jagdgeschwader (Fighter Wing) 52, 53, and 71. His Me-109 was familiar to friend and foe with the recognisable black tulip engine cowling, and the vast majority of his kills were recorded on the Eastern Front flying against the Soviet air forces.

During his lengthy combat career, Hartmann, nicknamed the 'Blond Knight of Germany', received the Knight's Cross with oakleaves, swords, and diamonds. He is known to have shot down 11 Soviet aircraft in a single sortie on at least two occasions. He was forced to crash land his aircraft due to hostile fire or mechanical problems 16 times but survived World War Two and lived to the age of 71. He died on September 20, 1993, at his home in southern Germany. After the war, he held the rank of colonel in the West German Air Force and trained on post-war jet aircraft at Luke Air Force Base in Arizona.

Although some post-war revisionist research has called his claims against the P-51 Mustang into question, and dates and accounts may vary according to source, he did tangle with the American fighter while serving with JG-52 in defence against

heavy bombing raids on the large oil refineries and storage facilities at Ploesti, Romania. His score against the P-51 is generally believed to have been seven air victories. According to records, he encountered the Mustang for the first time on May 21, 1944, near the Romanian capital of Bucharest. He claimed two were shot down.

Defending Ploesti on June 1, Hartmann shot down four P-51s, and a few days later he claimed two more. On that day, however, he incurred the wrath of the Mustangs. Eight P-51s chased the great ace for some distance, forcing him to bail out of his Me-109 when its fuel supply was exhausted. Hartmann's assertion that he had run out of fuel is somewhat contradicted in 'Mustang Ace: Memoirs of a P-51 Fighter Pilot', the

autobiography of Lieutenant Colonel Robert Goebel, an ace of the US 31st Fighter Group, who finished the war with 11 victories, and believes that his machine-gun fire compelled the German ace to bail out.

Nevertheless, in an interview conducted many years after the war, Hartmann recounted his impressions and encounters with the P-51. He remembered contemplating a fight with American pilots as the war turned against Nazi Germany. "I don't recall anyone talking of defeat," he said. "But I do know that we talked about some of the great pilots killed already, and the news of the American Mustangs reaching deep into Germany, and even further. Few of us had any experience against the Americans, although many old

timers had fought the British. Those who fought Americans had done so in North Africa, and their insights proved interesting."

Dread and anticipation

Reflecting on his encounters with the P-51, he said: "Then there were the American Mustangs that we both dreaded and anticipated meeting. We knew they were a much better aircraft than ours – newer and faster, and with a great range."

His first fight with American Mustangs was memorable. "This was in the defence of Ploesti and Bucharest and also over Hungary," he recalled. "When the bombers came in and they had heavy fighter escort. I was re-called to take over command of I/ JG-52, and this was 23 June 1944. B-17s were attacking the railroad junction, and we formed up. We did not see the Mustangs at first and prepared to attack the bombers. Suddenly, four of them flew across us and below, so I gave the order to attack the fighters.

"I closed in on one and fired, his fighter coming apart and some pieces hit my wings, and I immediately found myself behind another and I fired, and he flipped in. My second flight shot down the other two fighters. But then we saw others and again attacked. I shot down another and saw the leader still had his drop tanks, which limited his ability to turn. I was relieved that this pilot was able to successfully bail out. I was out of ammunition after the fight. But this success was not to be repeated

because the Americans learned, and they were not to be ambushed again. They protected the bombers very well, and we were never able to get close enough to do any damage."

During another mission, Hartmann rescued a fellow pilot. "I did have the opportunity to engage the Mustangs again when a flight was being pursued from the rear and I tried to warn them on the radio, but they could not hear," he said. "I dived down and closed on a P-51 that was shooting up a 109, and I blew him up. I half rolled and recovered to fire on another of the three remaining enemy planes and flamed him as well. As soon as that happened, I was warned that I had several on my tail, so I headed for the deck, a swarm of eight Americans behind me. That is a very uncomfortable feeling I can tell you!"

This was the mission in which Lieutenant Goebel engaged Hartmann. Flying with his wingman Carl Junger, Hartmann attacked American Mustangs one more time. "Once in Romania, we had an interesting experience with both Russians and Americans. It seemed the Americans and Russians were busy examining each other and were unaware that we were around," he said of the mission to intercept Soviet bombers over Prague.

"I gave the order to drop down through the Mustangs, then the Russian fighters, and through the bombers in just one hit-and-run attack, then we would get the hell out of there since there were only

the two of us. I shot down two P-51s quickly in my dive, and then I fired on a Boston bomber, scored good hits but it was not a kill. The second element also scored a kill against the Mustangs, and my wingman and I were all right. Suddenly, the most amazing thing happened. The Soviet fighters and Americans began fighting each other, and the confusion worked for us. They must have not realised that it was a swarm of Germans that started the whole thing! The Russian bombers dropped their bombs and turned away. I saw three Yaks (Soviet fighters) get shot down and a Mustang damaged, trailing white smoke. That was my last fight against the Americans."

Two of the Mustang pilots that are believed to have fallen victim to Hartmann were Lieutenant Joseph W Harper of the 318th Fighter Squadron, 325th Fighter Group and Lieutenant Howard F Welch, 319th Fighter Squadron, 325th Fighter Group. Both pilots remain listed as missing in action.

On two occasions, General of Fighters Adolf Galland asked Erich Hartmann to join the Luftwaffe squadrons then training to fly the new Messerschmitt Me-262 jet fighter. Hartmann, however, declined, choosing to remain with JG-52. Flying over Czechoslovakia on May 8, 1945, the last day of World War Two in Europe, he scored his final aerial victory, shooting down a Soviet Yak-9 fighter.

Hartmann soon surrendered along with his surviving pilots and ground crewmen to the US 90th Infantry Division. The Americans, per agreement with the Soviets, turned their prisoners over to the Red Army. The prisoner was later offered a post in the East German Air Force but refused to take the role or to embrace communism when pressed by his captors. He was charged and convicted of war crimes and finally released from Soviet captivity in 1955. In 1997, a Russian prosecutor reversed all charges of war crimes against the great ace who had arisen under the Soviet regime.

MUSTANG VERSUS ME-262

The first operational jet fighter in history, the Messerschmitt Me-262, appeared in combat too late and in numbers that were too few to alter the course of World War Two in Europe. However, its implications were obvious.

The Me-262 was powered by a pair of Junkers Jumo 4 axial flow turbojet engines that produced a maximum speed of 560mph at a range of 650 miles (1,050km). The Schwalbe, or Swallow, was more than 100mph faster than the P-51 Mustang at top speed. Its armament was deadly, with up to four 30mm nose-mounted MK 108 cannon, a single shell capable of ripping the wing off an opposing bomber or fighter.

From a research programme that began in 1939, the Me-262 made its first jet-powered flight on July 18, 1942, and entered combat in April 1944. About 1,430 were built during the war years, and German pilots

claimed more than 540 Allied aircraft shot down in roughly 13 months of combat. The old maxim that speed kills was certainly applicable to the Me-262, and it blazed the trail for future jet fighter development. Numerous examples were recovered and brought to Allied countries for study after the war, and its design influenced generations of aircraft to come.

On April 19, 1944, Erprobungskommando (Testing Command) 262 was formed at Lechfeld, south of Augsburg, Germany. In July, Major Walter Nowotny, a renowned fighter ace who scored 258 aerial kills in his career and a holder of the Knight's Cross with oakleaves, swords, and diamonds, took command and the fighter group was nicknamed Kommando Nowotny. Allied encounters with the Me-262 confirmed the Nazi jet's outstanding performance, but Mustang pilots took advantage of the vulnerability of the new enemy fighter as they were able.

The most effective technique to combat the Me-262 was to fly near known airfields where the jets operated and wait for them to either take off or return from a mission, attacking when the Swallow was flying at low airspeed and had not yet gained altitude or safely touched down. Of course, German anti-aircraft fire was accurate and heavy on most occasions, and Mustang pilots who executed air attacks against the Me-262 ran a high risk of being shot down themselves. Among the American P-51 pilots who scored victories over the Nazi jet were three members of the historic Tuskegee Airmen, the 332nd Fighter Group, and all-black fighter squadron.

Miraculous feat

On October 7, 1944, Major Urban Drew of the 375th Fighter Squadron, 361st Fighter Group, accomplished the miraculous feat of shooting down two Me-262s in action above Achmer Aerodrome, Germany. Drew enlisted in the US Army Air Forces (USAAF) on May 14, 1942, and trained as an instructor on the P-51 in the US before gaining a position as a Mustang flight instructor with the 56th Fighter Squadron, 54th Fighter Group. He then transferred to the 375th Fighter Squadron, the Yellowjackets, at RAF Bottisham. Later flying from RAF Little Walden, he claimed six kills piloting his Mustang nicknamed Detroit Miss.

On the historic day, Drew was leading a decoy squadron of fighters. He said: "We went down to join a fight that was going on under the box of bombers behind our box. I could not locate any enemy aircraft. I couldn't locate our bombers either, so I joined up with some red-tailed B-17s that were short on escorting fighters. I stayed with them until I spotted two aircraft on the airfield at Achmer. I watched them for a while and saw one of them start to taxi. The lead ship was in take-off position on the eastern runway and the taxiing ship got into position for a formation take-off. I waited until they were both airborne then I rolled over from 15,000ft and headed for the attack with my flight behind me. I caught up with the second Me-262 when he was about 1,000ft off the ground. I was indicating 450mph and the jet aircraft could not have been going over 200mph. I started firing from about 400 yds, 30-degree deflection. As I closed on him, I observed hits all over the wings and fuselage. Just as I passed him, I saw a sheet of flame come out near the right wing root. As I glanced back, I saw a gigantic explosion and a sheet of red-orange flame shot out over an area of about 1,000ft."

With the first German jet crashing to the ground, Drew took up the chase of the second Me-262. "The other jet aircraft was about 500yds ahead of me and had started a fast-climbing turn to the left. I was still indicating about 400mph, and I had to haul back on the stick to stay with him. I started shooting from about 60 degrees deflection, 300yds and my bullets were just hitting the tail section of the enemy aircraft. I kept horsing back on the stick and my bullets crept up the fuselage to the cockpit. Just then, I saw the canopy go flying off in two sections and the plane rolled over and went into a flat spin. He hit the ground on his back at about a 60-degree angle. I did not see the pilot bail out. The enemy aircraft exploded violently and as I looked back at the two wrecks, there were mounting columns of black smoke. I claim two Me-262s destroyed."

During the encounter, the gun camera of Drew's P-51 malfunctioned, and his wingman, Lieutenant Robert McCandless, was shot down and captured, unable to confirm the Me-262 kills. Therefore, Drew's recommendation for the Distinguished Service Cross was denied. He was awarded the Air Force Cross in 1983. Forty years after the double shootdown, a German pilot confirmed that from the ground, he had seen two jets shot down by a Mustang with a yellow nose. It was enough to validate Drew's claims.

Major Nowotny, a 23-year-old hero of the Luftwaffe and leader of

the jet fighter wing that bore his name, met his fate in the Me-262 on November 8, 1944. Nowotny had taken off, despite strict orders against flying personally, and shot down a B-17 Flying Fortress bomber and a P-51 that day, flying from his base at Achmer in Lower Saxony. He is thought to have encountered the failure of one engine and tried to restart it while the jet slipped into a gradual dive. At the same time, Mustangs of the 364th Fighter Squadron, 257th Fighter Group had been strafing targets west of the city of Hanover and spotted the German fighter in distress.

Captain Merle Allen and his wingman, 1st Lieutenant Edward 'Buddy' Haydon, quickly gave chase. Other American pilots joined in, and one of them, Captain Ernest Fiebelkorn of the 77th Fighter Squadron, 20th Fighter Group, lined up for a shot on Nowotny's Me-262. Just as he drew a breath to fire, Fiebelkorn was thwarted when Allen and Haydon crossed in front of him. Haydon appears to have been the only P-51 pilot who fired at Nowotny.

Within seconds, the German ace's Me-262 nosed up, arched steeply, and plunged into the ground in a ball of fire about five miles from the airfield. Haydon and Fiebelkorn were each given credit for half a kill.

General of Fighters Adolf Galland had been a witness to the aerial drama and remembered Nowotny's last moments. "I stepped outside to watch his approach to the field when an enemy fighter pulled away not far

from us. I heard a jet engine, and we saw this 262 coming down through the light clouds at low altitude, rolling slightly and then hitting the ground. The explosions rocked the air, and only a column of black smoke rose from behind the trees. We took off in a car and reached the wreckage, and it was Nowotny's plane. After sifting through the wreckage, the only salvageable things found were his left hand and pieces of his Diamonds decoration."

The debut of the Me-262 in combat during World War Two, though often plagued with mechanical issues and requiring extensive pilot training, was a harbinger of things to come in aerial warfare. The P-51 Mustang was the height of piston-engine technology at the time. The future would belong to the jet.

ABOVE: A German test pilot defected to the Allies with this Me-262 in March 1945. The plane was shipped to the US for study. Public Domain

LEFT: Adolf Hitler presents Major Walter Nowotny with oakleaves, swords, and diamonds to the Knight's Cross, October 1943. Public Domain

BELOW: A Luftwaffe Messerschmitt Me-262 jet fighter is serviced at a German airfield in April 1945. Creative Commons Bundesarchiv Bild via Wikipedia

ADOLF GALLAND AND THE MUSTANG

Perhaps the most famous Luftwaffe fighter pilot of World War Two, General Adolf Galland was credited with 104 aerial victories during the conflict. He was promoted to General of Fighters, but his candour often raised the ire of Führer Adolf Hitler and Reichsmarschall Hermann Göring, chief of the Luftwaffe. Nevertheless, he received the Knight's Cross with oakleaves, swords, and diamonds and emerged from the war as a chivalrous adversary who treated his foe with respect and even became friends with former enemies in later years.

During World War Two, Galland gained a tremendous respect for Allied fighter types, particularly the Supermarine Spitfire and the North American P-51 Mustang. In his post-war memoir titled *The First and the Last*, Galland acknowledged the prowess of the P-51. He said: "In December 1943, the P-51 Mustang was introduced into the Eighth AAF, the technical details of which we had known for some time. In the beginning of 1944, it was used more and more frequently. With the increasing strength of the Mustang fighter escort, we also lost more of our fighters."

Indeed, with his high rank, Galland had been ordered to refrain from combat missions as the war dragged one. However, on a bright spring day in 1944, he could not resist and strapped himself into the cockpit of a Focke Wulf Fw-190 fighter, hoping to engage formations of American heavy bombers headed for targets deep inside Nazi-occupied Europe and even the heartland of Germany itself. In company with fellow ace Colonel Johannes Trautloft, credited with 58 air-to-air kills stretching back to the Spanish Civil War, Galland spotted a straggling American bomber over the city of Magdeburg, Germany, and moved in to attack.

Suddenly, the tables were turned, and Galland later wrote: "Trautloft's voice cried over the radio, 'Achtung Adolf, Mustangs! I'm beating it – guns jammed!' And then – with the first bursts of four Mustangs – I sobered up. There was no mistake about the B-17. She was finished, but I was not."

Swiftly there were four Mustangs on the tail of the general of fighters, and he took evasive action. Twisting and turning, he tried to shake the Americans, but the drama was real. He wrote in his memoir years later: "I simply fled. Diving with an open throttle, I tried to escape the pursuing Mustangs, which were firing wildly. Direction East towards Berlin. The tracer bullets came closer and closer. As my Fw-190 threatened to disintegrate and as I had only a small choice of those possibilities which the rules of the game allow in such harassing situations, I did something which had already saved my life twice during the Battle of Britain. I fired everything I had into the blue in front of me. It had the desired effect on my pursuers, who suddenly saw the smoke which the shells had left behind coming towards them. They probably thought they had met the first fighter to fire backwards or that a second attacking German fighter was behind them. My trick succeeded for they did a right-hand climbing turn and disappeared."

Greater admiration

Given Galland's heart-throbbing account, it was a near-run thing.

GAUNTLET EN
AT NORMAL CRUISING S

He already appreciated the attributes of the P-51, but very likely his admiration of its capabilities grew even greater that day. The trailing Mustangs were probably pelted by spent cartridges from the Fw-190's guns, giving the American pilots the impression that German bullets were striking them. Apparently, they did see the smoke, and after their own tracer rounds had zipped past Galland's cockpit, they broke off the chase, allowing the German ace to return to his base, shaken but still alive.

Although there has been some questioning of this terrific encounter, Galland lived to the age of 83, dying in 1996. And he stuck to his story.

One tantalising account from the American side adds a bit of credence to the tale, and it comes from *Tumult in the Clouds*, the wartime memoir of Lieutenant Colonel James A Goodson, a veteran fighter pilot of the US Army Air Forces' (USAAF) 336th Fighter Squadron, 4th Fighter Group. Goodson had flown the British Spitfire and Hawker Hurricane with No 43 Squadron RAF and then No 416 Squadron RAF, before joining the USAAF in September 1942 after American entry into the war, seeing air combat in the Republic P-47 Thunderbolt fighter before the P-51.

Goodson finished the war a triple ace with 15 aerial victories, and he wrote of a fight with German aircraft that was somewhat like the story Galland lived to tell. He saw an enemy Fw-190, lost him, and, he said: "I spotted him again, in a shallow dive, but three Mustangs were behind him. They were firing, and maybe hitting but they weren't closing. I had the advantage from my vertical dive and was able to cut across and close slowly. I didn't get to within range until we were almost on the deck. I checked the fuel gauge and knew I should have turned for home ten minutes before.

"What was more, the 190 was streaking eastwards. I closed until I was about 300yds to 250yds – beyond

LEFT: Adolf Galland is pictured at left with Reich Armaments Minister Albert Speer. Creative Commons Bundesarchiv Bild via Wikipedia

my preferred range, especially when he was jerking and evading. I fired one burst and then another. Little puffs of smoke floated back from the 190. I gave another burst, but it was only for a second. I was out of ammunition. I broke away and headed for home with my three flight members. They too had shot their ammunition and were as low on gas as I."

Goodson's account sheds some additional light on the issue, adding more to the explanation for breaking off the chase than just the effectiveness of Galland's ruse. However, Goodson's observance that hits were achieved on the fleeing Fw-190 may well have been the smoke of Galland's firing at nothing.

On June 20, 1944, Goodson, well known for flying dangerously low during P-51 strafing missions, was shot down by German anti-aircraft fire during a pass over the enemy airfield at Neu Brandenburg. He was taken prisoner and handed over to the dreaded Gestapo. The story goes that he faced imminent summary execution but managed to charm his way out of trouble by teaching his interrogator how to blow smoke rings. He remained in the US Air Force and Reserves until 1959 and passed away peacefully in Massachusetts in 2014, aged 93.

Galland reportedly felt the sting of the Mustang on two other occasions.

LEFT: Mustang ace Major James Goodson smiles from the cockpit of his P-51 fighter. Public Domain

Late in the war, he championed the new Messerschmitt Me-262 jet fighter. In November 1944, he was present at a nearby airfield when the Me-262 piloted by Major Walter Nowotny, a Luftwaffe ace with 258 victories, was shot down by a P-51 pilot while trying to land. There has been speculation that the jet crashed due to mechanical failure, but a preponderance of the evidence points to .50-calibre machine-gun fire from an American fighter.

On April 26, 1945, Galland attacked a formation of US Martin B-26 Marauder bombers and shot down one. He damaged another, but soon his Me-262 was peppered by a Mustang's .50-calibre machine guns. The engines shut down, but he managed to get one of them restarted and returned to base. Wounded, he was in hospital at the end of the war.

Galland travelled to Argentina after the war to assist with training that nation's air force. He returned to Germany and engaged in private business, often attending reunion events of former enemies as an honoured guest. He befriended RAF legends Douglas Bader and Robert Stanford Tuck, visiting with the latter in Britain and taking Stanford Tuck on boar hunts in Germany.

LEFT: This P-51 fighter was assigned to ace James Goodson's squadron, the 336th of the 4th Fighter Group. Public Domain

MUSTANGS IN THE
CHINA-BURMA-INDIA THEATRE

RIGHT: A P-51 Mustang of the 311th Fighter Group flies over China in 1945.
Public Domain

RIGHT: Troops of Merrill's Marauders rest on a jungle trail. P-51 Mustangs supported their jungle operations.
Public Domain

RIGHT: General Clayton Bissell served as early commander of the US Tenth Air Force in the CBI.
Public Domain

Universal Engineering Company of Frankenmuth, Michigan, employed 500 workers during World War Two, and they were committed to their country's war effort. They did everything they could, working long hours and extra shifts, donating blood, and buying war bonds. But they wanted to do more.

Then someone got the big idea of purchasing a plane and handing it over to the US Army Air Forces (USAAF). Within days, the notion took hold, and enough money was raised to pay for a brand-new P-51 Mustang fighter. The story circulated widely when the reporters of the CBI Roundup, the official newspaper of American forces in the China-Burma-India theatre, got hold of it and published an account in its September 28, 1944, edition. That report came along with an update.

"That plane is making history in the CBI Theatre," read the article. "When it was turned over to the USAAF, it was named *Spirit of Universal*. When it got overseas it was renamed *Jackie*, in honour of Mrs Jacqueline England, wife of its pilot, Maj (then Capt) James J England, of Jackson, Tenn.

"To date, that plane – member of the Yellow Scorpion Squadron – has destroyed eight Japanese planes and damaged three over Burma. On several occasions, other pilots than England flew it, notably Lt William W Griffith. Between the two, they have two DFCs, two Air Medals, numerous clusters to each and the

Silver Star. England has credit for all the sky victories, while Griffith won the Silver Star for 'gallantry in action.'

"For the information of the good people of Universal Engineering Co, their plane has done considerable damage while flying air support over Burma, killing many enemy foot soldiers, and destroying fuel, ammunition and storage dumps, barracks areas, bridges, and sundry other installations.

"They are also appraised that they never would be able to recognise the ship today, because in its more than 100 combat missions and 600 hours against the enemy, it has been shot up quite frequently. Besides having had 58 different holes, 38 from one mission, it has had two new wing tips, two gas tanks, stress plate, engine change, prop, aileron assembly, tail section, stabiliser, electric conduit in the left wheel

and several canopies. Yet it still sees action regularly in combat.

"When Griffith won the Silver Star for his feat of bringing back the plane when it was theoretically unflyable, the Universal employees rewarded him and his crew chief, S/Sgt Francis L Goering with $100 war bonds."

Major England went on to record 10 air-to-air kills in the Mustang and remained in the US Air Force, retiring in 1968 with the rank of colonel.

The famous P-51 belonged to the 530th Fighter Squadron, 311th Fighter Group, which deployed to the CBI between July and September 1943 and was one of only three groups to utilise the A-36 Invader, the dive bomber variant of the P-51. Entering combat as the 311th Fighter-Bomber Group, it was comprised of the 385th, 528th, 529th, and 530th Fighter Squadrons, based in India and Burma with the Tenth Air Force and later in China with the Fourteenth

Air Force. Its pilots flew many ground attack missions, escorted transports flying supplies over the eastern end of The Hump across the Himalayas between India and China and supported the fabled Merrill's Marauders during action behind Japanese lines in the summer of 1944.

Scorpions sting

According to records, the pilots of the 530th were notified that during one escort mission, American bomber crews had trouble distinguishing the P-51s from Japanese fighters. So, the situation was remedied when the pilots and crews painted their prop spinners yellow. The infamous Japanese radio propagandist Tokyo Rose referred to the 530th as the Yellow Scorpions, and its pilots gained a fearsome reputation with a positive kill ratio. One pilot remembered shooting down an enemy Nakajima Ki-44 fighter plane. "The Tojo whipped over, trailing a long plume of flame," he reported.

On October 23, 1944, four P-51s escorted eight other aircraft in a mission against a Japanese supply dump at Kamaing, Burma, destroying the target and giving rise to numerous such forays along the length of Japanese-occupied Burma. Captain England, 530th operations officer, led the squadron on a long mission on Thanksgiving Day, 1944, escorting bombers to the Burmese capital of Rangoon and refuelling at a makeshift airstrip at Rau on the return trek.

The experience of the 530th Squadron is representative of the airmen and ground crews that flew and maintained the P-51 Mustang in the CBI from 1943 to 1945. Not only did they fight a tenacious enemy in the Japanese, but they also contended with a harsh climate, searing temperatures, dense jungle, and torrential seasonal rains.

The Tenth Air Force reached the CBI in 1942, developing the famed Hump airlift and executing transport, bombing, and fighter operations. Its 51st Fighter Group received the P-51D Mustang in 1945 after operating the Curtiss P-40 Warhawk and Lockheed P-38 Lightning and flew escort on the eastern end of the Hump as well as top cover for airfields around Kunming, China.

In March 1943, the China Air Task Force, a component of the Tenth Air Force, was dissolved, and its personnel incorporated into the Fourteenth Air Force operating in China under the command of Major General Claire Chennault, once commander of the famed American Volunteer Group, better known as the Flying Tigers.

Among the other units to fly the P-51 in the CBI, the 23rd Fighter Group, successor to the Flying Tigers, was a component of both the Tenth and Fourteenth Air Forces, operating in theatre from December 1941 through the end of the war. Its 74th, 75th, 76th and 449th Fighter Squadrons converted to the Mustang

LEFT: Major General Claire L Chennault commanded the US Fourteenth Air Force in the CBI. Public Domain

in November 1943 and were credited with destroying 621 Japanese planes in the air and 320 on the ground in 24,000 combat sorties. Thirty-two of its pilots became aces flying the various types of fighters. Among the leading Mustang aces in the CBI was Colonel Edward O McComas of the 118th Tactical Reconnaissance Squadron, 23rd Fighter Group, who shot down 14 Japanese planes, five in a single day.

The 1st and 2nd Air Commando Groups flew from bases in India in support of Chindit operations in Burma. Both groups included fighter squadrons equipped with the P-51 from late 1943 and 1944 respectively, the 1st swapping for P-47s for a time and then re-equipping with P-51s in the spring of 1945. These squadrons conducted fighter-bomber, ground support and bomber escort missions.

The Chinese-American Composite Wing of the Fourteenth Air Force included the 3rd and 5th Fighter Groups, which flew the P-51 from late 1944. The groups included both American and Chinese pilots, and the Americans were considered personnel of the Chinese Air Force, wearing its wings along with those of the USAAF. The 3rd Fighter Group received a Presidential Unit Citation for its role in stemming a major Japanese ground offensive in the CBI during the summer of 1944.

The 3rd Fighter Group included the 7th, 8th, 28th, and 32nd Fighter Squadrons, while the 5th Fighter Group was comprised of the 17th, 26th, 27th, and 29th Fighter Squadrons.

During its service in the CBI, the P-51 was the most proficient fighter on either side. Among its primary opponents in the air were the Japanese Nakajima Ki-84 Hayate, codenamed Frank by the Allies, the Mitsubishi A6M Zero, or Zeke, the Nakajima Ki-44 Tojo, the Mitsubishi J2M Raiden, or Jack, and the Kawasaki Ki-61 Hien, or Tony, which bore a passing resemblance to the P-51 in silhouette.

LEFT: These P-51 Mustangs of the Republic of China Air Force were photographed in the 1950s. Public Domain

LEFT: The Kawasaki Ki-61 Hien, or Tony, was sometimes confused with the P-51 due to a similar silhouette. Public Domain

SUBSCRIBE

THE SHEPHERD THE GREATEST STORY IN AVIATION?

The Heart Of Aviation Heritage

FlyPast

RHUBARBS, CIRCUSES AND RAMRODS
Fighter Command's European offensive

PINSTRIPE DELTAS
Test pilot Roly Falk

Another Spitfire flies from Biggin Hill

MERLIN
MAGIC

MACH BUSTER BELL X-2
Shattered dreams or the 'right stuff'?

JET PILOT PIONEER
Who was Brian Moloney?

FREE GIFT WORTH £33.95!

FlyPast is internationally regarded as the magazine for aviation history and heritage.

shop.keypublishing.com/fpsubs

HMS *TRIUMPH*: 'WHAT HAPPENED TO MY UNCLE'S SUBMARINE'

BRITAIN'S BEST-SELLING MILITARY MONTHLY

BRITAIN AT WAR

ISSUE 199

Blooming Marvellous
Inside the Poppy Factory

HEROES ON HORSEBACK

"They thundered past me while every gun in Germany fired at them"

THE DAY GOSPORT WENT BANG *Were communists to blame for ammunition depot explosions?*

FREE GIFT WORTH £35.95!

MISSING LINK: FINAL FORM OF FORGOTTEN TANK

Britain at War is dedicated to exploring every aspect of the involvement of Britain and her Commonwealth in conflicts from the turn of the 20th century through to the present day.

shop.keypublishing.com/bawsubs

ORDER DIRECT FROM OUR SHOP...
shop.keypublish

OR CALL +44 (0)1780 480404

(Lines open 9.00-5.30, Monday-Friday GMT)

KEY
Publishing

756/23

TODAY

SPECIAL! **FOCKE-WULF CENTENARY**

November 2023
Issue No 607,
Vol 51, No 11

AEROPLANE
HISTORY IN THE AIR SINCE 1911

BUTCHER BIRD

*An RAF ace test-flies the Fw 19...
and other Focke-Wulf legen...*

VIKING RESTORATION
Support a great British airliner project

IN THE FOOTSTEPS OF AN ACE
Al Deere's nephew: Spitfire warbird owner

FREE GIFT WORTH £28.94!

Aeroplane is still providing the best aviation coverage around. With focus on iconic military aircraft from the 1930s to the 1960s.

shop.keypublishing.com/amsubs

NEW 'OLD SALT': USS *NIMITZ*'S 1976 MAIDEN CRUISE

AVIATION NEWS
The past, present and future of flight · www.Key.Aero

FINNAIR
The first 100 years

PLUS CEO outlines network and fleet plans

WADDINGTON'S WAR GAMES
Inside Cobra Warrior 2023

A TALE OF TWO TERMINALS
Liverpool Airport at 90

ALL ABOARD THE FORD
Aviation on the biggest warship ever built

PLUS JAKARTA / KEMAYORAN 1983 / WHAT'S ON GUIDE / RADOM... REVIEW / AIRPORT & AIR BASE MOVEMENT / URBAN AIR MO...

FREE GIFT WORTH £30.95!

Aviation News is renowned for providing the best coverage of every branch of aviation.

shop.keypublishing.com/ansubs

ng.com

COLONEL EDWARD O McCOMAS

RIGHT: Colonel Edward O McComas was a 14-kill ace of the 23rd Fighter Group in China.
Public Domain

RIGHT: Colonel McComas stands at the wing of his P-51 Mustang in the CBI.
Public Domain

BELOW: Mustangs of the 118th Tactical Reconnaissance Squadron sit on the flight line at Laohwangping, China in June 1945.
Public Domain

The loss of Major Bob Weirman, commander of the 118th Tactical Reconnaissance Squadron, in a routine training mission on September 29, 1943, shook the pilots and ground crew to a man. Weirman had been an easy-going and well-liked leader. His Bell P-39 Airacobra fighter had apparently gone into an uncontrollable spin, and it appeared there had been no time to bail out due to low altitude.

Plans for the unit to deploy overseas, probably to the Pacific theatre, were abruptly postponed, and a pall was cast over the Aiken Army Airfield in South Carolina. But barely had the circumstances taken hold when another shocking event took place. Word circulated rapidly that Major Edward O McComas had been appointed to command the squadron. One history read: "The worst fears of many of the squadron officers and enlisted men were soon realised. Major McComas,

not exactly everyone's favourite candidate, was to become the new squadron commander!

"McComas was a hard driving individual, who on first acquaintance tended to intimidate and overpower those subordinates with which he came in contact," the history continued. "He proceeded to give the squadron the 'shock treatment' to restore its shattered morale. The relatively relaxed atmosphere was gone, and all hands began to feel the heat."

Like a good leader, though, McComas was probably never going to ask anyone under his command to do anything that he himself would not do. He was to prove his mettle as a leader and as a fighter pilot soon enough, flying the P-51B Mustang in the China-Burma-India theatre

of World War Two and emerging as one of the highest-scoring aces of the 23rd Fighter Group and the US Fourteenth Air Force with a total of 14 confirmed aerial victories and four Japanese planes destroyed on the ground.

Born on June 25, 1919, in Winfield, Kansas, McComas attended Southwestern College and the University of Kansas before enlisting in the US Army Air Corps in 1940 and receiving his pilot's wings the following year. He was assigned to the 66th Reconnaissance Group and the 118th Tactical Reconnaissance Squadron at Aiken, and after assuming command he led the squadron through extended training at Key Field near Meridian, Mississippi. Likely because of his

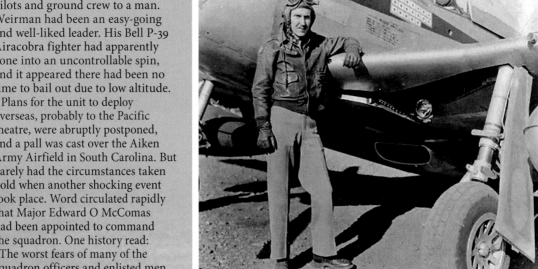

commanding presence and discipline, the 118th transitioned well to the P-51B Mustang and was deployed to India in January 1944, its initial task to provide fighter escort for big Boeing B-29 Superfortress heavy bombers that were to operate from airfields there against the Japanese.

Soon the 118th Squadron was on the move again, relocating to China and fighting the enemy in the air and on the ground. On September 29, 1944, McComas was forced to bail out of his heavily damaged Mustang, aggravating a serious back injury that he had sustained years earlier. Although he was rescued and returned to the squadron by Chinese Nationalist guerrillas, the back injury plagued him for the rest of his life. He also experienced other physical ailments but kept flying. Two weeks later, he was back in the air and claimed his first kill on October 16. On November 20, he shot down two Japanese planes. During this period, he was also promoted lieutenant colonel.

Hot streak

In December, McComas was on a hot streak. He downed his fifth enemy aircraft on the 19th and shot down his sixth that same day. Then, he added two more Japanese planes to his tally on the 21st. His crowning achievement in aerial combat occurred two days later.

Although he was often known to fly alone, McComas took to the air on December 23, 1944, in company with wingman Max Parnell. Their mission was to conduct reconnaissance of a Japanese airfield near the Chinese city of Canton. As the two Mustangs roared over the airfield, McComas caught an enemy aircraft and sent it crashing into the ground riddled with .50-calibre bullets. While the Japanese pilots on the ground scrambled to get to their planes, the Americans came around for another pass.

McComas sighted a pair of enemy fighters rising and shot both down just as they were clawing for altitude. Coming around again, he watched as two more Japanese fighters got

airborne. In their haste to avoid the chattering guns of his Mustang, the two enemy pilots collided in a fiery mid-air crash. McComas was credited with both enemy aircraft, and his total for the mission grew to five. He had become the only American pilot in the China-Burma-India theatre to achieve the title of 'ace in a day'. For good measure on December 24, McComas shot down another Japanese plane, his final air victory of World War Two.

On Christmas Day, General Claire Chennault, commander of the Fourteenth Air Force, is said to have presented McComas with a new P-51 fighter. The 118th had also earned the nickname 'Black Lightning'.

In just over seven months of flying in a combat zone, McComas had demonstrated tremendous skill in dogfighting. He received the Distinguished Flying Cross, Silver Star with oak leaf cluster, Legion of Merit with oak leaf cluster, Purple Heart with oak leaf cluster, and numerous other decorations for his outstanding performance. He was also said to have been involved in the sinking of a Japanese destroyer in Victoria Harbour, Hong Kong. In January 1945, he relinquished

command of the 118th Squadron due to the worsening of his back injury. He returned to the US and spent months in healthcare facilities.

After World War Two ended, McComas remained in the US Air Force, serving with the 12th Tactical Air Command in Germany. He was promoted colonel in 1949 after completing the Air Command and Staff School at Maxwell Field, Alabama. With the outbreak of the Korean War, he was ordered to Tokyo, Japan, as Chief of Combat Operations, Far East Air Forces (FEAF). He flew 35 combat missions in the Lockheed F-80 Shooting Star while in command of the 8th Fighter Bomber Group.

Continuing issues with his back injury prompted evacuation for treatment to the US after less than a year in Japan, and McComas was assigned to the Air Force War Plans Division at the Pentagon. During the next three years, he underwent numerous operations, but his physical and emotional condition deteriorated. At the age of 35, Colonel McComas committed suicide in his Virginia home on June 22, 1954. He was buried at Arlington National Cemetery.

LEFT: The distinctive emblem of the 118th Tactical Reconnaissance Squadron was also emblazoned on the unit's Mustang fighters.
Public Domain

LEFT: General Claire Chennault, commander of the 23rd Fighter Group, stands in front of a P-51 Mustang as he talks with pilots.
Public Domain

BELOW: Lockheed F-80 Shooting Star aircraft of the 8th Fighter Bomber Group sit at an airfield in Korea. Colonel Edward McComas commanded the 8th and flew 35 combat missions during the Korean War.
Public Domain

MUSTANGS IN THE PACIFIC

RIGHT: This P-51 Mustang of the 72nd Fighter Squadron was photographed at North Field on Iwo Jima in 1945.
Public Domain

RIGHT: P-51 Mustangs of the 506th Fighter Group sit on the dusty runway at Iwo Jima.
Public Domain

RIGHT: A P-51 Mustang takes off from Iwo Jima on a VLR mission in 1945. Public Domain

Despite the reputation of the P-51 as a formidable fighter with great range and agility, the reception for the Mustang in the Pacific was less than enthusiastic in some quarters. Lieutenant General George C Kenney, commander of the US Far East Air Forces, was a believer in the Lockheed P-38 Lightning, and for good reason.

Kenney's fighter squadrons were flying long-range missions, some of them more than 700 miles, routinely and over wide expanses of ocean. He believed that the twin-engined Lightning gave a pilot a better chance of coming home with a damaged plane than the single-engine Mustang would offer. Nevertheless, despite his concerns, the P-51 was coming. The first Mustangs to operate in the southwest Pacific were the F-6 photo reconnaissance variant with the 82nd Tactical Reconnaissance Squadron, while the 348th Fighter Group in the Philippines acquired the Mustang in late 1944 and early 1945, among the first in the area to do so. The 3rd Air Commando Group took on the P-51 in New Guinea in January 1945 prior to relocating to the Philippines.

While operating from the Philippine island of Mindoro, Captain William Shomo earned the Medal of Honor on January 11, 1945, as he and wingman Lieutenant Paul Lipscomb, relative newcomers to their F-6s, attacked a formation of 13 Japanese aircraft, a single bomber and 12 fighters. Shomo shot down seven enemy planes in six minutes, while Lipscomb claimed three more. It was one of the most

outstanding Allied fighter pilot accomplishments of World War Two.

Meanwhile, the 15th and 21st Fighter Groups of VII Fighter Command received the Mustang in late 1944 and trained for long-range escort missions accompanying Boeing B-29 Superfortress bombers, flying from bases in the Marianas archipelago, on raids against targets in the home islands of Japan. The groups began deployment to Iwo Jima, 675 miles from Tokyo, as that island was being secured in March 1945. The 506th Fighter Group followed in May. Iwo Jima would serve as an emergency landing strip for B-29s disabled during their bombing raids, while its airfields would also bring the Mustangs within escort range. The earliest Mustang pilots to arrive flew ground support missions for Marines still fighting on Iwo Jima and attacked targets in the nearby Bonin Islands.

The Mustang squadrons flying from Iwo Jima trained vigorously for

their upcoming B-29 escort missions. Hours in the air at the controls of a P-51, often compounded by harsh weather conditions, navigational challenges, and concerns with fuel consumption weighed upon the pilots, and such sorties were termed 'very long range' or VLR missions. And then, there were the Japanese defenders to contend with as well.

First mission

The first VLR mission took place on April 7, 1945, as 96 Mustangs escorted 107 B-29s of the 73rd Bomb Wing to Tokyo. Although fewer and fewer Japanese fighters would rise to oppose them later, on this day as many as 100 enemy planes came up to do battle. Three big bombers were lost, two to flak and one to Japanese fighters. However, the Mustangs claimed 21 Japanese planes shot down. Two Mustangs were lost in the 15-minute melee. Major James B Tapp of the 78th Fighter Squadron,

15th Fighter Group, who finished the war with eight victories flying his P-51 nicknamed *Margaret-IV*, got four confirmed kills that day.

The VLR missions were arduous tasks, and some P-51 pilots, thoroughly exhausted and suffering from severe muscle cramps, literally had to be lifted out of their cockpits upon returning to Iwo Jima. The weather was always a concern, and on June 1, 1945, a day veterans of the ordeal remember as Black Friday, tragedy struck. When 148 Mustangs were ordered to fly escort for B-29s conducting a raid on the city of Osaka, they encountered a severe storm front, although early reports from a B-29 weather plane had indicated that the front was passable. The P-51s became engulfed in thick cloud stretching from sea level to more than 20,000ft. Some pilots became disoriented, and there were mid-air collisions. Extreme turbulence and high winds buffeted others, and their pilots either crashed or ditched in the open sea.

Only 27 fighters made it through the roiling weather to find the B-29s, and the magnitude of the disaster was shocking. Twenty-seven P-51s were lost along with 24 of their pilots, and the 506th Fighter Group, which had become operational only two weeks earlier, lost 15 Mustangs and 12 pilots, several of whom had limited combat hours in the aircraft. The VLR missions were deemed so hazardous that just 15 were required to be completed before a pilot was given furlough back to the US. During a six-week period from July to mid-August 1945, no fewer than 85 US fighter pilots were killed on VLR

missions, the vast majority due to poor weather and navigational difficulties.

By the summer, Japanese fighter opposition was almost non-existent. Mustangs sought out targets of opportunity in enemy territory and shot up supply depots, airfields, docks, and vessels in the surrounding waters. Low-level strafing missions were always heart-pounding due to ever present anti-aircraft fire.

Five Mustang pilots flying from Iwo Jima became aces. The top scoring Mustang ace of VII Fighter Command was Major Robert W Moore of the 45th Fighter Squadron, 15th Fighter Group, who had one kill prior to reaching Iwo Jima and subsequently shot down 11 Japanese planes during VLR missions. During that first VLR mission of April 1945, Moore watched as four Japanese Mitsubishi A6M Zero fighters shot down the crippled B-29. He was too far away to intervene, but as the Zeros peeled away, he followed them, steadily closing the distance.

He said: "I closed in on number four, gave him a short burst from 600ft, and he exploded behind the cockpit. Then I gave my plane full throttle and closed on the number three man. I caught him at the bottom of their lazy eight and gave him about a three second burst that hit his engine and cowling. Then I looked up for the number two man and saw the leader of the formation turning into me. I told the flight to give it full throttle and dive away."

Another pilot confirmed that Moore's second victim on that mission had gone down in flames. The air battle had lasted just 45 seconds.

Following Moore and Major Tapp in the kill tally were Major Harry Crim of the 531st Fighter Squadron, 21st Fighter Group with six kills, Major John Mitchell with five while flying from Iwo Jima, and Captain Abner Aust Jr of the 457th Fighter Squadron, 506th Fighter Group, who became the final American ace of World War Two when he shot down two enemy Zero fighters on August 10, 1945.

The service of Major John Mitchell is worthy of note. Flying with the 15th Fighter Group and then commanding the 21st Fighter Group, his five confirmed aerial victories flying from Iwo Jima were added to his total of six aerial victories flying the P-38 in the Solomons earlier. He also led the P-38s of the 339th Fighter Squadron that shot down a Mitsubishi G4M Betty bomber carrying Admiral Isoroku Yamamoto over the island of Bougainville in April 1943, killing the commander-in-chief of the Japanese Combined Fleet. Mitchell went on to shoot down four communist MiG-15 jets during the Korean War for a combined total of 15 aerial victories.

The last Mustang VLR missions from Iwo Jima were flown on August 14, 1945, and more than 130 American fighters had been lost in the effort.

MAJOR WILLIAM A SHOMO

RIGHT: Major William A Shomo wears the Medal of Honor presented for his heroic action in the Philippines.
Public Domain

RIGHT: The Ki-61 Tony was an adversary in the air as Shomo and Lipscomb attacked.
Public Domain

RIGHT: A single Nakajima Ki-44 Tojo fighter engaged the American pilots on January 11, 1945.
Public Domain

The odds were long, or so it appeared, but Major William A Shomo and his wingman, Lieutenant Paul Lipscomb, hardly gave that a thought. The enemy was there, and they were intent on attacking.

On January 11, 1945, Shomo and Lipscomb were in the middle of a mission, flying the F-6D photo reconnaissance variant of the P-51D Mustang fighter. They had set out to gather intelligence on the Japanese airfields at Aparri and Laoag on the Philippine island of Luzon. If the opportunity presented itself, they intended to strafe targets of opportunity with their six wing-mounted .50-calibre Browning machine guns.

At the controls of his F-6D, nicknamed *The Flying Undertaker*, Shomo spotted a flight of enemy aircraft, 11 Kawasaki Ki-61 Hien (Flying Swallow) fighters known to the Allies as the Tony, a single Nakajima Ki-44 Shoki (Devil Queller) fighter known as Tojo in Allied parlance, and a twin-engine Mitsubishi G4M Betty bomber. The Japanese planes were around 2,500 ft above them, and the two American pilots executed Immelmann turns to come up behind the enemy.

"I had been in the war for almost 16 months at that time, but I had never had the opportunity to actually get a crack at an airplane in the air, that is a Jap airplane, while I was flying," Shomo told a newspaper reporter during a 1981 interview. "I'd seen

them while they were bombing our bases, but never while I was airborne. So, this was the opportunity of a lifetime. And at that point, I made up my mind I wasn't going to miss. I'd waited too long for the opportunity."

The sky seemed full of Japanese planes, and without hesitation Shomo and Lipscomb pitched into them. In a flash, the Americans were firing. Shomo closed to fewer than 40yds on his first pass and shot down four Tonys in rapid succession. He manoeuvred underneath the Betty and unleashed a torrent of machine-gun fire. The bomber lurched, and the pilot appeared to be attempting to make a belly landing somewhere below.

Two of the Tonys peeled away with the stricken bomber, but Shomo was already busy as the Tojo turned into him, its own guns twinkling. The

Japanese pilot fired steadily until his plane began to stall and he slipped into cloud cover. Meanwhile, the Betty crashed and exploded in a terrific fireball. As the Tonys pulled away from the scene, remaining at low altitude, Shomo put his Mustang into a dive and sent them both spiralling into the ground. In short order, he had downed an amazing seven enemy aircraft. The entire fight from start to finish had lasted only six minutes. Lipscomb had flamed three more enemy planes as well. Shomo was slightly wounded, and his F-6D was damaged by the Tojo's fire, much of its canopy shot away, but the daring pilot had continued the air battle to conclusion.

Three Japanese fighters had survived the onslaught of the two American pilots, and Shomo's impressive feat was second only to

that of carrier-based Grumman F6F Hellcat pilot Commander David McCampbell, highest scoring US Navy ace of World War Two, who downed nine Japanese planes in a single sortie in October 1944.

Success against odds

Shomo's exploits that day earned him promotion from captain to major and the coveted Medal of Honor, presented to him at Luzon by Major General Ennis Whitehead, commander of the US Fifth Air Force, on April 3, 1945. The citation read in part: "Although the odds were 13 to 2, Maj. Shomo immediately ordered an attack. Accompanied by his wingman, he closed on the enemy formation in a climbing turn and scored hits on the leading plane of the third element, which exploded in midair. Maj. Shomo then attacked the second element from the left side of the formation and shot another fighter down in flames. When the enemy formed for counterattack, Maj Shomo moved to the other side of the formation and hit a third fighter which exploded and fell. Diving below the bomber he put a burst into its underside, and it crashed and burned. Pulling up from this pass, he encountered a fifth plane firing head on and destroyed it. He next dived upon the first element and shot down the lead plane. Then diving to 300ft in pursuit of another fighter, he caught it with his initial burst, and it crashed in flames. Maj Shomo's extraordinary gallantry and intrepidity in attacking such a far superior force and destroying seven enemy aircraft is unparalleled in the southwest Pacific area."

Shomo later told a reporter that Medal of Honor recipients 'are extremely fortunate – and never forget for one minute that that medal belongs to a lot of people and not just to us'. During his career, he also received the Distinguished Flying Cross and the Air Medal with four bronze oak leaf clusters among numerous other awards. He flew more than 200 combat missions. Lieutenant Lipscomb received the Distinguished Service Cross for the action on January 11, 1945.

According to some sources, Shomo had already shot down one enemy plane two days before the historic mission of January 11. He had shredded a Japanese Aichi D3A Val dive bomber as it attempted to land at the enemy airfield at Tuguegarao on northern Luzon. He had seen only 14 enemy aircraft during his tour of duty in the Pacific and shot down eight of them.

Born in Jeannette, Pennsylvania, on May 30, 1918, Shomo worked as an undertaker prior to enlisting in the aviation cadet programme of the US Army Air Corps in August 1941. After earning his wings, he joined the 82nd Tactical Air Squadron flying the Bell P-39 Airacobra and Curtiss P-40 Tomahawk in ground attack and photo reconnaissance sorties. Based first in New Guinea and then at Morotai, the squadron moved to the Philippines at Mindoro and then Luzon, receiving its F-6Ds in December 1944. Shomo led his pilots in their first combat mission in early January.

After World War Two ended, Shomo remained in the US Air Force. He was promoted to lieutenant colonel in 1951 and held numerous operations and training posts. In the spring of 1952, he became commander and administrative officer of the 175th Fighter Interceptor Squadron at Ellsworth Air Force Base, South Dakota. He served as operations officer of the 31st Air Division in Minnesota and commanded the 14th Fighter Interceptor Squadron in Iowa and the 59th Fighter Interceptor Squadron at Goose Bay, Labrador. After holding several other posts, he retired from the Air Force in 1968. He died aged 72 on June 25, 1990.

That incredible day in 1945 remains a highlight of Shomo's service and of the Mustang's prowess in the air. A newsreel filming his return to base noted a victory roll, and then another and another until the narrator commented: "By the time he was making the fifth, the sixth, and seventh roll, no one would believe it. Seven victories seemed impossible. He was just showing off. Showing off? Perhaps, but with good reason."

LEFT: Major William Shomo was also credited with shooting down a Japanese Aichi D3A Val dive bomber.
Public Domain

LEFT: Shomo and Lipscomb flew the F-6D photo reconnaissance variant of the P-51 Mustang fighter.
Public Domain

BELOW: Prior to piloting the F-6D, Shomo flew the Bell P-39 Airacobra and the Curtiss P-40 Tomahawk, pictured here.
Creative Commons Alan Wilson via Wikipedia

MAJOR JAMES H HOWARD

RIGHT: Mustang ace and Medal of Honor recipient James H Howard wears the rank of colonel in this 1945 portrait.
Public Domain

FAR RIGHT: Mustang ace James Howard and a crewman prepare P-51B *Ding Hao!* for flight.
Public Domain

BELOW: Ace James Howard sits in the cockpit of P-51D Mustang *Ding Hao!* Note the victory tally on the fuselage.
Public Domain

To say the least, January 11, 1944, was an active day in the air for Major James Howard, commander of the 356th Fighter Squadron, 354th Fighter Group. That morning, Howard led 50 Mustang fighters into the air to escort the B-17 Flying Fortresses of the 401st Bomb Group on a mission to hit the Me-110 fighter production facilities at Halberstadt and Oschersleben in central Germany. It was the 14th mission for many of the bomber crews, and one of their most hazardous.

Heavy flak and enemy fighters had greeted the big bomber boxes, and the Mustang escort engaged the Luftwaffe squadrons that came up to oppose them. The air combat was bitter, and Howard quickly found himself in the thick of it. As the bombers completed their runs and turned back for England, he spotted a German Messerschmitt Me-110 twin-engine fighter and swooped low to shoot the enemy plane down. As he climbed back toward the bomber formations, he realised that he had become separated from the rest of his squadron.

No matter. Howard continued to shepherd the B-17s that were in the vicinity – alone and for half an hour. The bomber pilots who watched this single P-51 remain with them were astounded. In the meantime, Howard took on a swarm of around 30 German fighters, keeping them at bay. At least six of these enemy planes were attacking a single formation of 20 bombers, and the odds were long.

Without hesitation, Howard attacked a Focke Wulf Fw-190 fighter, riddling it with his P-51B's .50-calibre machine guns. The German pilot bailed out, and his canopy narrowly missed Howard's plane, nicknamed *Ding Hao!*, an English corruption of the Chinese phrase 'Ting Hao De', meaning 'Number One' or 'Very Good'. Pressing home his attacks, Howard shot down or damaged as many as six enemy planes that day. He was eventually credited with destroying the Fw-190 and two Me-110s. Remarkably, when he ran out of ammunition and his fuel became dangerously low, he continued to make passes at German fighters to disrupt their attacks on the retiring bombers. After he landed at RAF Boxted, the intrepid pilot counted only a single enemy bullet hole in *Ding Hao.*

News of Howard's exploit spread rapidly, and Major Allison C Brooks, a group leader with the bombers of the 401st, called the pilot a 'one man air force'. Brigadier General Robert F Travis, commander of the bomber force, crowed: "For sheer determination and guts, it was the greatest exhibition I've ever seen. It was a case of one lone American against what seemed to be the entire Luftwaffe. He was all over the wing, across and around it. They can't give that boy a big enough award."

Within a week, the story made the newspapers, and the January 19, 1944, edition of the *New York Times* identified Howard as the 'lone United States fighter pilot who for more than 30 minutes fought off about 30 German fighters'. The Army Air Forces organised a press conference in London, and Howard described the action. Andy Rooney, a correspondent for the *Stars and Stripes* newspaper and later a famed CBS News correspondent, christened the episode 'the greatest fighter pilot story of World War Two'.

Heroism downplayed

Howard downplayed his own heroism and remarked: "I never did see 30 or 40 of those planes all at once the way the bomber people tell it. I'd see one, give it a squirt, and go up again. I was quite busy in a constant merry-go-round, presenting a good enough bluff for them to break off and dive away."

Nevertheless, some sources assert that during the newly-famous mission, Howard had become the first ace of the 354th Fighter Group and the first to achieve such status while flying the Mustang with the Rolls-Royce Merlin powerplant. He was promoted to lieutenant colonel in February 1944, and on June 5 became the only fighter pilot in the European theatre during World War Two to receive the Medal of Honor.

General Carl Spaatz, commander of US Strategic Air Forces in Europe, presented the medal, and the citation read in part: "Col Howard lost contact with his group, and at once returned to the level of the bomber formation. He then saw that the bombers were being heavily attacked by enemy airplanes and that no other friendly fighters were at hand. While Col Howard could have waited to attempt to assemble his group before engaging the enemy, he chose instead to attack single-handed. With utter disregard for his own safety, he immediately pressed determined attacks for some 30 minutes, during which time he destroyed three enemy airplanes and probably destroyed and damaged others."

Adding to the lustre of his wartime exploits, Howard was already a fighter ace when he came to the European theatre in early 1943. Flying the Curtiss P-36 Hawk and P-40 Tomahawk as a pilot with the legendary American Volunteer Group, the Flying Tigers, he shot down six Japanese planes between August 1941 and July 1942. Rooney was probably right – Howard scored 12 confirmed victories while flying against both Japanese and German pilots prior to and after formal US entry into World War Two.

The son of an ophthalmologist then teaching surgical skills in China, James Howard was born in Canton

on April 8, 1913. His family returned to the United States in 1923, and he attended school in Montgomery, Pennsylvania, and St. Louis, Missouri, receiving a degree from Pomona College in California in 1937. Rather than following his father into the medical field, he chose the military and became an aviator with the US Naval Reserve, earning his wings at Naval Air Station Pensacola in 1939. Assigned to the aircraft carrier USS *Enterprise*, Ensign Howard served with Fighter Squadron VF-6 before leaving the navy in June 1941.

With strong emotional ties to China, which was then battling the invading Japanese, Howard responded to a call for volunteer pilots. He became commander of the Flying Tigers' 2nd Pursuit Squadron and served for 11 months in Asia. The American Volunteer

Group disbanded in mid-1942, and he returned to the US, accepting a commission in the Army Air Forces as a captain. He was promoted major in September 1943. After the extraordinary mission of January 11, 1944, he scored two more aerial victories while flying *Ding Hao!*, an Me-110 on January 30 and an Fw-190 on April 8, both in the vicinity of Braunschweig, Germany. He returned to the US in November 1944, attending gunnery school at Pinellas Army Airfield, Florida, and was promoted full colonel on November 25, 1945.

After World War Two, Howard was elevated to brigadier general in the US Air Force Reserve and commanded its 96th Bombardment Group. He retired in 1965. In 1991, at the age of 78, he completed his autobiography titled 'Roar of the Tiger'. Howard died on March 18, 1995, at the age of 81, and a permanent exhibit detailing his illustrious military career is in the terminal at Florida's St. Petersburg-Clearwater International Airport, previously the site of Pinellas Army Airfield.

TOP: This exhibit at the St. Petersburg-Clearwater International Airport honours Major James Howard. Attribution James G. Howes

ABOVE: Major James Howard receives the Medal of Honor from General Carl Spaatz in June 1944. Public Domain

LEFT: Major Howard stands at centre with 354th Fighter Group pilots who have just received the Air Medal. Public Domain

COLONEL GLENN T EAGLESTON

RIGHT: Colonel Glenn T Eagleston was the highest scoring fighter ace of the US Ninth Air Force during World War Two. Public Domain

The mission to Kiel had been long and costly on January 5, 1944, and as the bombers turned for home after blasting targets in the German port city, the P-51B Mustang fighters of the US Army Air Forces 354th Fighter Group covered their retirement. Glenn Eagleston caught a German Focke Wulf Fw-190 at 450 deflection and fired a short burst at the enemy fighter. It turned and plummeted earthward in seconds, exploding on impact.

Eagleston had scored the first aerial victory of his fighter pilot career, and he would go on to become the highest scoring ace of the US Ninth Air Force in Europe with 18½ kills. He tallied two more probables that were unconfirmed, damaged at least seven others in air-to-air combat, and shot five others to pieces as they sat on the ground.

Born in Farmington, Utah, on March 12, 1921, Glenn Eagleston joined the US Army Air Corps in 1940 and applied for pilot training.

He completed the programme in September 1942 and was promoted 2nd lieutenant. Assigned to the 79th Fighter Squadron, 20th Fighter Group, he flew the Bell P-39 Airacobra until January 1943, when he was transferred to the 353rd Fighter Squadron, 354th Fighter Group, nicknamed The Pioneers, and became acquainted with the magnificent North American P-51B Mustang fighter that autumn. He nicknamed his new fighter *Feeble Eagle*.

Initially during Eagleston's tour of duty, the 354th Fighter Group was detailed to bomber escort duty, with its first missions protecting the 'Big Friends' starting in December in the skies over Nazi-occupied France. It was during this escort duty period that Eagleston scored that first air-to-air kill, as the squadron flew amid intermittent bouts of foul weather that hampered effective operations. Nevertheless, the young pilot steadily scored, flaming four more enemy fighters, including three Messerschmitt Me-110s and an Me-109, in fewer than 40 days of flying from January 30 to March 6, 1944.

During the preparation for the D-Day landings in Normandy, the 354th Fighter Group resumed much of its original role as tactical air support, hitting German troop concentrations, fortifications, supply and logistics centres, and transportation. Within days of the

June 6, 1944, landings, the fighter group moved to the European continent, taking up station at an airfield near the French town of Cricqueville-en-Bessin. Eagleston completed a combat rotation with promotion to the rank of captain and 8½ kills to his credit. He took leave, returning to the United States for rest, and then came back to the European theatre for another tour of combat duty.

On October 29, 1944, Eagleston recorded the most productive day of his fighter pilot career, which reached a grand total of nearly 100 hazardous missions. Commanding the 353rd Fighter Squadron, he shot down three Me-109s during a dogfight that swirled across the skies for half an hour. He received the Distinguished Service Cross, his nation's second highest award for valour in combat. His citation noted officially: "The President of the United States takes pleasure in presenting the Distinguished Service Cross to Glenn T Eagleston, Captain (Air Corps), US Army Air Forces for extraordinary heroism in connection with military operations against an armed enemy. On this date, Captain Eagleston shot down three enemy aircraft in a single mission. Captain Eagleston's unquestionable valour in aerial combat is in keeping with the highest traditions of the military service and reflects great credit upon himself, the Ninth Air Force, and the US Army Air Forces."

RIGHT: Lieutenant Colonel Eagleston sits in the cockpit of his P-51 Mustang fighter in the spring of 1944. XXXXX

RIGHT: In addition to the P-51B Mustang, Colonel Glenn Eagleston also flew this Republic P-47 Thunderbolt fighter. Public Domain

Diminished opportunities

Eagleston's last combat kills of World War Two occurred on March 15 and 25, 1945. By that time, the opportunity to shoot down German planes had greatly diminished as the Allies controlled the skies and attrition had taken a tremendous toll on the Luftwaffe, both in pilots and aircraft. He returned to the US in October 1945, serving as assistant director of operations and training at Dover Field, Delaware, through mid-1946 and then as commander of Dow Field, Maine.

Among the earliest veteran combat pilots to complete jet fighter training at Williams Field, Arizona, Colonel Eagleston held several command posts before the outbreak of the Korean War in the summer of 1950. He was given command of the 334th Fighter Interceptor Squadron that autumn and the 4th Fighter Interceptor Group in Korea, flying combat missions with

the F-86 Sabre jet. He shot down two MiG-15 fighters in separate actions in December 1950 and April 1951, raising his final total in aerial victories to 20½.

During one harrowing mission on June 17, 1951, Eagleston nearly lost his life. His Sabre jet was badly shot up by Sergei Kramarenko, a veteran Soviet fighter pilot who had scored victories over Luftwaffe planes during World War Two. He survived the ordeal with the help of some Sabre flying comrades and made a belly landing of his badly damaged fighter at Kimpo Air Base. One of his rescuers was Lieutenant Colonel Bruce Hinton, the first Sabre pilot to engage and shoot down a Soviet-built MiG-15 on December 17, 1950.

Although Soviet pilots were flying in Korea on a clandestine basis, the Americans knew they were up against experienced combat aviators. Kramarenko was known to be

proficient in the air, and he earned the nickname of 'Casey Jones'. On that fateful day, the American Sabre pilots were on the hunt for Casey, and soon enough they were engaged in a heated air battle.

Lieutenant Colonel Hinton remembered the action and his effort to come to the aid of Eagleston, not realising that it was the colonel himself who was in grave danger. He said: "About 500ft behind the lone F-86 was a MiG, and he was pounding the F-86 with cannon fire. Both planes flew directly in front of me. As the two aircraft were passing in front of me, I noted that the MiG was firing his cannons and the rounds were hitting the Sabre with good results, with flame and fire marking the strikes on the Sabre fuselage. Pieces of the F-86 were flying, and some were very large pieces. One unassailable rule we had in the 4th was that no MiG was worth losing an F-86. The F-86 was now on fire, and I broke off my certain kill to try and beat off the MiG that was hammering the Sabre. I had no idea who was in the Sabre, let alone that it could be Eagle."

Kramarenko saw Hinton coming, and a series of violent manoeuvres ensued. Hanson noted: "This time the MiG had to fly through the spray from my six 50s. After he took that second burst, the MiG suddenly broke away. After landing, I rolled to a stop by the busted F-86. The airplane was a wreck. It was then that I learned that the pilot was my very close friend Glenn Eagleston."

After that brush with death, Eagleston returned to the US and held numerous command positions until retirement from active duty and a 27-year career. On May 16, 1958, he was given the honour of participating in the selection of the World War Two Trans-Pacific Unknown Soldier. He died aged 70 on May 17, 1991, one of the most successful fighter pilots in US military history and a champion of the P-51 Mustang. He was buried with full military honours at Arlington National Cemetery.

LEFT: With his P-51 *Feeble Eagle* in the background, Lieutenant Eagleston conducts a mission briefing with pilots in France.
Public Domain

LEFT: Lieutenant Colonel Eagleston (right) and comrades stand in front of *Feeble Eagle* in France.
Public Domain

BELOW: Now residing in a museum, this North American F-86 Sabre bears the markings of the USAAF 4th Fighter Interceptor Group. Creative Commons Kowloonese via Wikipedia

LIEUTENANT COLONEL DUANE W BEESON

RIGHT: This modern P-51C Mustang is nicknamed *Boise Bee* in a nod to Duane Beeson.
Creative Commons tataquax via Wikipedia

Duane Beeson was eager. Born on July 16, 1921, in Boise, Idaho, he travelled to Vancouver, British Columbia. The United States was not directly involved in World War Two yet, but Beeson intended to be. He joined the Royal Canadian Air Force a month before his 20th birthday, primarily since he had two years of college completed, a prerequisite to enlisting in the US Army Air Corps for pilot training.

Beeson then became a fine example of transition and adaptability. He earned his wings in February 1942 with just over 200 hours of flying time at training facilities at Prince Albert and Yorkton, Saskatchewan. Posted to No 71 Squadron and RAF Debden, he was assigned a Hawker Hurricane fighter. By then, the US was at war and Beeson was among the RCAF pilots who resigned their commissions to join the 4th Fighter Group, then being assimilated into the US Army Air Forces from the famed Eagle Squadrons, and he was given a Supermarine Spitfire fighter. Then, in early 1943, he was trained for his third mount, the Republic P-47 Thunderbolt fighter.

RIGHT: Pilots of the 334th Fighter Squadron flew Supermarine Spitfires like this one painted with American markings.
Public Domain

In the Thunderbolt, Beeson excelled, flaming a dozen German planes in air-to-air combat. Thus, he was already an ace when the fourth aircraft type he was to fly, the North American P-51 Mustang, was received in February 1944 by the 334th Fighter Squadron. Beeson got acquainted

RIGHT: Lieutenant Colonel Duane Beeson was an outstanding fighter pilot in four types of aircraft, including the P-51B Mustang.
Public Domain

with the P-51B quickly and shot down five more enemy aircraft with credit for another one-third of a kill. He was one of 10 American fighter pilots during World War Two to become aces in two types of fighter aircraft.

Beeson and his ground crew chief christened his Mustang the *Boise Bee*, and during his first combat flight at the controls of the P-51B, he shot up a Luftwaffe Junkers Ju-88 bomber on the ground.

On March 18, 1944, Beeson was leading 'Pectin Squadron' east of Mannheim, Germany, escorting bombers on a mission to Munich. He picked up a radio report of enemy fighters and soon confirmed that nine Messerschmitt Me-109s were directly below his position.

"We started down on them, but they began to dart in and out of cloud," he later reported. "I picked one and closed to 200yds before opening fire and fired a short burst but saw no results. Fired another short burst which must have hit his belly tank because the whole aircraft immediately blew up in my face.

A large sheet of flame suddenly appeared in front of my aircraft, and I tried to avoid it but was unable and flew through it, feeling pieces of 109 strike my aircraft before I could break clear. At the same time, I could feel the heat in my cockpit and upon breaking away, began to check engine instruments. Last saw what was left of the 109 going down, covered in flame.

"Later made two more passes at Me-109s but they went into the cloud and though I chased them down, was unable to find them below the cloud layer. One of these last two 109s was flying just above the cloud layer when three bursts of flak came very near him and a fourth appeared to hit him; then he fell off into cloud and we lost him." Beeson had fired only 76 rounds of .50-calibre ammunition.

Highest for a time

On March 23, Beeson flew his 93rd combat mission but one of just a handful in the Mustang. He put the powerful plane to the test once more, downing two Me-109s east of the city

LEFT: Pilots of the 334th Fighter Squadron posed for this group photo in January 1945. Public Domain

of Munster, Germany, and for a time becoming the highest scoring ace in the US Army Air Forces.

"I was flying Pectin White 1," he wrote. "I saw several bombers going down, one of them in flames, another minus a wing. P-38s could be seen circling above and around the bomber formation. There were many enemy aircraft around and then an Me-109 made a head-on pass through our squadron, circling around and behind as though to come in again, so I turned after him."

Beeson followed the Messerschmitt pilot into a dive and then an abrupt climb. He said: "At about 25,000ft, I was in range and got good strikes on him. He began to smoke and dived for cloud at 6,000ft. I got on his tail as he came out of cloud and clobbered him again, but he stuck to his airplane and crash-landed in a field. I strafed the aircraft on the ground, but as I came around again, I saw the engine beginning to flame and the pilot getting out of the cockpit. He ran very fast across the field and fell behind a fence post as I came over again."

For good measure, Beeson strafed a nearby freight train, riddling the locomotive with bullets. He then resumed his air activity.

"I climbed to cloud level at 3,000ft and saw an Me-109 flying with its wheels down so turned after him, but he went into cloud. Saw tracers going past my port wing, so made a quick break to starboard and saw another 109 behind. He pulled up into cloud and as I came around in the turn he dived down, allowing me to get on his tail. I fired short bursts and saw many flashes, and he jettisoned his hood, so I fired again, got more strikes and oil from the enemy aircraft covered my windscreen. The

pilot bailed out at about 1,000ft but the chute did not open. His aircraft crashed nearby and burst into flame."

In one other descriptive report, Beeson had waxed eloquent: "Then two more Me-109s came down from above and I fired a burst at one of them, 45 degrees head-on, seeing a few strikes on his port wing. Lieutenant Fraser fired at the other one. As our section started to come out at about 19,000ft, a lone Me-109 stooged by in front with his finger well up. I closed to about 150yds and shot him down, observing him strike the ground."

Although he had quickly become proficient with the P-51B, Beeson's days in combat were numbered. On April 5, 1944, he was shot down by German flak guns and taken prisoner. He was interrogated by Luftwaffe Obergefreiter Hanns Scharff, fluent in English and a master in the practice of extracting information from downed Allied airmen using tactics that he shared with American intelligence personnel after the war. Interestingly, Scharff was an accomplished artist. He emigrated to the US and created numerous magnificent mosaics, among them the adornment of Cinderella's Castle and the entrance ramps to EPCOT Centre at Disney World in Orlando, Florida.

Beeson was liberated by troops of the Soviet Red Army in April 1945. He had received promotion to major and the award of the Distinguished Service Cross while in captivity. He was later promoted lieutenant colonel. However, he fell ill suddenly in early 1946. Diagnosed with a brain tumour, he died at Walter Reed Army Hospital in Washington, DC, at the tender age of 25 on February 13, 1947, before surgery could be scheduled.

LEFT: The 334th Fighter Squadron was nicknamed the Fighting Eagles during World War Two. Public Domain

LEFT: During his fighting career, Lieutenant Colonel Duane Beeson flew this P-47D Lightning fighter as well as the P-51D Mustang. Creative Commons Newresid via Wikipedia

ACES IN A DAY

RIGHT: Lieutenant Colonel Wayne Blickenstaff became an ace in a day and covered Major Robert Elder, who accomplished the same feat. Public Domain

FAR RIGHT: Captain William R Beyer shot down five German fighters during a mission to Kassel on September 27, 1944. Public Domain

S hooting down five enemy aircraft and reaching ace status is quite an achievement for a fighter pilot. But to achieve such a feat in a single day is extraordinary.

Nineteen P-51 Mustang fighter pilots accomplished the task during World War Two, attesting that they were not only exceptional combat pilots but also possessed of a tenacious will to take the fight to the enemy relentlessly. And the Mustang gave them the weapon of war with which to succeed.

In addition to the exploits of famed Mustang pilots such as ace of aces Major George Preddy, Major Leonard 'Kit' Carson, Captain Chuck Yeager, Lieutenant Bruce Carr, and the others who became aces in a day in the European theatre, Captain William A Shomo and Lieutenant Colonel Edward McComas were the only two who reached that pinnacle in the Pacific.

When the Mustangs of the 353rd Fighter Group touched down at RAF Metfield on March 24, 1945, five of their number had been lost. However, the veteran pilots of the 350th and 352nd Fighter Squadrons had shot down 29 German fighters. Ten of these belonged to Major Robert Elder and Lieutenant Colonel Wayne Blickenstaff, who claimed five each. In 30 minutes of swirling air combat, both had become aces in a day. They were the only pair of Mustang pilots in the European theatre to do so while flying with the same fighter group in the same aerial action.

The Mustangs were flying toward the German city of Kassel on what Elder termed a mission of 'area support'. He spotted 15 Me-109s at 6,000ft flying cover for 15 Fw-190s that were at low altitude, or 'on the deck' as common fighter pilot parlance put it. "I positioned myself and my wing man, Lt Guthrie, directly behind two Me-109s that were still flying straight and level at about 4,000ft," he reported. "After closing to around 200yds, I opened fire and blew the left wing off this enemy aircraft which immediately went into an uncontrolled series of gyrations to the left and later crashed. Lt Guthrie set the Me-109 he was shooting at on fire, and I saw it go down burning."

Elder dispatched an Fw-190 flying at about 800ft, watching as it crashed in a cloud of flames. He then found himself in 'a big turning fight with about ten or 12 Fw-190s, all of us being at zero-1,000ft altitude'. He said: "These Jerries were plenty willing to fight, but occasionally one of them would reverse his turn and start out level as if to escape." Closing

to about 50yds, Elder opened fire on one of the violently manoeuvring Germans and observed: "I don't think the pilot was dead but extremely frightened and didn't realise our low altitude. He crashed, going straight in."

Spotting a fourth enemy Fw-190, Elder went into a dive and came up quickly on its tail. He said: "I closed to within 100yds dead astern and with very few rounds fired, I set this enemy aircraft on fire. He crashed immediately into the ground with a big, long splash of black smoke and fire. I pulled up right over this wreck.

"By this time," Elder concluded, "I had about three Fw-190s shooting at me and several others circling. As I was at only a few hundred feet altitude, I started screaming for help and Lt Colonel Blickenstaff, who was fighting Me-109s up above came down and said he was covering me. By this time, I was down to about 50 rounds of ammunition per gun since my tracers had just come out. With

BELOW: This P-51D Mustang was assigned to William Beyer's 361st Fighter Group. Public Domain

this top cover to encourage me, I managed to out-turn another Fw-190 and just as I was at about 30 degrees angle off, this Jerry reversed his turn (they are stupid that way!) and I latched onto his tail at about 100yds range. I got strikes all over the plane and he caught fire in the air and crashed burning. As I was shooting the above Fw-190 down, another Fw-190 got onto me and Lt Colonel Blickenstaff came down and shot him off. I saw this plane crash as I pulled up over my enemy aircraft."

Vivid impression

When Elder's plea for help came, Blickenstaff had already shot down two Me-109s. He commented: "Hurriedly looking around, I was left with the vivid impression of 109s and 190s going down in flames, and the fires of many exploded aircraft on the ground." The colonel's second kill occurred as he turned the tables on a German pilot. "I broke hard right

and after a 360-degree turn ended up on the enemy aircraft's tail in a 50-degree dive. The Me started to smoke after a few strikes and then half rolled into some trees. As I went by, I snapped a picture of the crash with my K-25 camera."

Blickenstaff looked around and found another dust-up to join. "A few minutes later I recognised Major Elder's airplane by the camouflage," he reported. "As I looked down, I saw numerous strikes on a 190 that he was shooting at. This enemy aircraft crashed into flames as I started down to help. I could easily cover Major Elder and noticed he was doing very well. He was shooting at another 190 in a left orbit when I saw another 190 close in from his rear. I told him to continue shooting and I would take care of the one behind." He did.

From there, Blickenstaff realised that only one of his .50-calibre machine guns was still working. He sighted an Fw-190 and called

to other pilots to shoot it down. When no response was received, Blickenstaff went after the German with just that single machine gun. "I slid in behind and raked across the cockpit," he reported. "This enemy aircraft also began to smoke, and I presume the pilot had been hit as the enemy aircraft slid off and crashed into the ground. Even though my camera exposed only 15ft of film and my gunnery wasn't as good as it could have been, there is no doubt whatsoever about the destruction of the aircraft. I saw each plane augur into the ground with its pilot and explode."

Elder's five kills were his total for the war in the air, and he was credited with destroying two more enemy planes on the ground. He went on to command the 353rd Fighter Group in the autumn of 1945. He retired from the US Air Force with the rank of colonel in 1960, after 20 years of service.

After that memorable day, Lieutenant Colonel Blickenstaff remained with the military through the end of the war and then pursued a career as an artist and illustrator. He finished his tour of duty with 10 aerial victories, one of them over a Messerschmitt Me-262 jet fighter and years later wrote a memoir of his career as a fighter pilot.

Elder was awarded the Silver Star and Blickenstaff the Distinguished Service Cross for their actions that day in the skies above Kassel. It had been an unforgettable experience of life, death, and pursuit.

The other Mustang pilots who achieved ace in a day status during World War Two were Colonel William A Daniel, Lieutenant Gordon H McDaniel, Captain Donald S Bryan, Lieutenant Carl J Luksic, Captain William T Whisner, Major William J Hovde, Captain William R Beyer, Captain Ernest E Bankey Jr, Lieutenant Colonel Sidney S Woods, Lieutenant William H Allen, and Captain William H Lewis.

F-82 TWIN MUSTANG

Although the P-51 Mustang made a tremendous impact on the outcome of World War Two, particularly the air war in Europe, its period of ascendency and dominion on the cusp of the Jet Age was relatively brief.

Still, the marvel that was the Mustang conjured imaginative and practical variations on the proven airframe of the P-51. Several variants were developed as modifications were introduced. The A-36 dive bomber and F-6 photo reconnaissance aircraft were deployed early in the war years. The 1944 project that fitted the fighter with ski landing gear and the aircraft carrier-based Mustang considered during Project Seahorse, which was terminated in the spring of 1945, along with other variants were proposed and either discarded or shelved. Although the innovative F-82 Twin Mustang was prototyped, tested, and put into production, it did not see action during World War Two.

The idea for the Twin Mustang came about during discussions surrounding a long-range fighter escort for Boeing B-29 Superfortress heavy bombers engaged in massive air raids on cities and industrial targets in the home islands of Japan in the spring and summer of 1945. But by the time the F-82 was operational, the war was over. The concept had also become less relevant with the capture of the islands of Iwo Jima and Okinawa.

However, in the autumn of 1943, such events were yet to unfold, and plans were formulated for an escort fighter with a range of more than 2,000 miles. An experimental lightweight Mustang, the XP-51F, modified by North American Aviation design head Edgar Schmued, served as the basis for

the F-82 (designated the P-82 until the change from 'pursuit' to 'fighter nomenclature in June 1948). A pair of fuselages, lengthened nearly 5ft each behind the cockpits to accommodate additional fuel tanks and equipment, were joined to a centre wing section, which housed six .50-calibre machine guns. Other potential armament configurations, including a removable pod with more machine guns and a 40mm cannon, were considered but never entered production. Retractable pylons were installed by a test group at Eglin Air Force Base, Florida, and were capable of mounting ten high velocity air rockets (HVAR) of 5in diameter. The conventional wings were strengthened to accommodate hard points that might carry 1,000lb of bombs or external fuel tanks. The tail sections were also joined by a horizontal centre section.

Early prototypes and the production models, the P-82B and P-82E, included two operational cockpits, allowing

for control in either space to provide relief on lengthy flights. Both cockpits contained throttle and propeller controls manipulated by levers, while the pilot's cockpit on the left housed standard instrumentation and the co-pilot instrumentation in the right cockpit was limited to the necessities of emergency and relief stints. The later P-82F and P-82G models substituted a radar operator in the right cockpit rather than a co-pilot.

Fully armed and fuelled, the P-82 did muster a range of more than 1,600 miles, and its top speed of 475mph was achieved with a pair of proven Rolls-Royce V-1650 Merlin engines licence-built in the United States by Packard. Later production models were powered by twin Allison V-1710-100 engines, while the Merlin was phased out. The switch was dictated by higher licensing fees from Rolls-Royce and the desire to make the Twin Mustang an all-American production affair. In practice, the

Allison engines were capable of a slightly slower top speed, and their performance was predictably inferior to the Merlin at high altitude. Nevertheless, the Merlin-powered P-82s were retained as trainers while the later production models were powered by the Allison engines.

Successful tests

The prototype Twin Mustang was flight tested successfully on June 26, 1945, and formally accepted by the US Army Air Forces (USAAF) on August 30. However, senior USAAF officers were so enthusiastic about the prospects for the P-82 that they approved an order for the P-82B in March 1945, three months before the first successful test flight. Some P-82s were completed before the end of World War Two, but these were not deployed due to a shortage of available engines that was not cured until 1946. A night fighter version of the Twin Mustang was also built, and the total production run topped out at 250 aircraft.

The prodigious range of the Twin Mustang led to a record-setting non-stop flight from Hawaii to New York on February 27, 1947, when pilot Colonel Robert E Thacker flew a P-82B nicknamed *Betty Jo* 5,051 miles in 14hrs and 32mins at an average air speed of nearly 348mph. Nevertheless, the era of the propeller-drive fighter was on the wane and early P-82 airframes were placed in storage.

However, the American perspective changed with the revealing of the Soviet Tupolev Tu-4 bomber, a reverse-engineered copy of the B-29 Superfortress. At the dawn of the nuclear arms race, the USAAF establishment determined that the US might be vulnerable to attack by Soviet bombers carrying nuclear payloads. Therefore, the P-82 was thrust back into active service in something of a stop-gap plan until sufficient jet technology could be developed. Therefore, the first operational Twin Mustang, the F-82E, was deployed to the 27th Fighter Wing of Strategic Air Command (SAC) at Kearny Air Force Base, Nebraska, in the spring of 1948.

With the outbreak of the Korean War on June 25, 1950, three squadrons of F-82s were based in Japan. The North Korean Army struck south across the 38th parallel with significant armour and air support. Meanwhile, the South Korean military had little of either.

The suddenness of the communist onslaught brought the Twin Mustang to the fore. Escorting transport planes engaged in evacuation and delivery of supplies on June 27, just two days after the North Korean invasion, F-82 pilot Lieutenant William G Hudson and radio operator Lieutenant Carl Fraser spotted a flight of Soviet-built North Korean Yakovlev Yak-11 and Lavochkin La-7 fighters near Kimpo airfield northwest of the South Korean capital of Seoul. The Americans attacked, sending a Yak-11 spinning into the ground and becoming the first US fighter team to score an aerial victory in the Korean War.

While Hudson brought the enemy aircraft into range, Fraser tried to photograph the engagement with a 35mm camera, but it malfunctioned. At the same time, two other North Korean fighters, both La-7s, were shot down. Lieutenant Charles Moran blasted one after it had damaged his tail assembly, and Major James Little, who had been flying top cover, swooped in to dispatch the other.

F-82s remained active during the Korean War until withdrawn in 1952, when US North American F-86 Sabres and Soviet-built Mikoyan Gurevich MiG-15 fighters began duelling in the skies. The last F-82 was withdrawn from service and shipped to Alaska on March 28. According to US Air Force records, pilots of Twin Mustangs claimed 20 enemy aircraft destroyed in air-to-air combat and 16 on the ground during the Korean War. In turn, 22 F-82s were lost, 11 on combat missions and the remaining 11 in accidents or other non-combat circumstances.

The service life of the F-82 was only about seven years, from 1946 to 1953. Two years after it was deployed by SAC in 1948, it was replaced by the Republic F-84 Thunderjet in the escort fighter role. By April 1951, F-82s that had seen action during the Korean War were being supplanted by the Lockheed F-94 Starfire. The last operational Twin Mustang was retired from service at Elmendorf Air Force Base, Alaska, in November 1953.

LEFT: The F-82B nicknamed *Betty Jo* takes off on a historic flight from Hickam Field, Hawaii, in 1947.
Public Domain

LEFT: Airmen of the US 27th Fighter Wing stand before F-82Es and a B-29 Superfortress at Kearney Air Force Base, Nebraska.
Public Domain

LEFT: An F-82G Twin Mustang sits at an air base in Japan during the Korean War.
Public Domain

CARRIER-BASED MUSTANG

As US forces advanced closer to Japan during World War Two, the cities of the home islands became targets for bombing raids by Army Air Forces Boeing B-29 Superfortress heavy bombers based in the Marianas Islands. Soon after a sustained bombing effort got underway, it became clear that bomber losses might be curtailed with the presence of long-range fighter escort.

Although no land or aircraft carrier-based fighter in service with the US Navy possessed the range to accompany the big bombers on their missions over hostile airspace, where enemy pilots flying the nimble Mitsubishi A6M Zero and J2M Raiden fighters and other types took their toll, one potential solution did exist.

Naval staff officers had taken notice of the long-range capabilities of the Army Air Forces' P-51 Mustang, which provided escort for Allied bombing missions in the European theatre. The suggestion that the Mustang might be adapted as a carrier-based fighter escort gained momentum rapidly. Dubbed Project Seahorse, the feasibility study was allocated a single P-51D, and soon modifications were being explored that might add another dimension to the role of the already successful fighter.

The major alterations to the standard P-51 included a reinforced airframe to absorb the stresses of carrier landings – in essence controlled crashes – along with high pressure tyres, more robust shock absorbers, a catapult hook in the fuselage centre line just forward of the wing, an arrester tailhook, and a 'fin fillet extension' designed to improve operations at low air speeds.

Navy Lieutenant Robert Elder, a veteran airman and test pilot, supervised the testing that subsequently got underway at Mustin Field near Philadelphia, Pennsylvania, in September 1944. An area of landing strip at the airfield was marked with the dimensions of an aircraft carrier deck, and arrester cables were installed. Elder then personally made nearly 150 take-offs and landings with the modified Mustang, designated the ETF-51D.

Elder soon discovered that the laminar-flow wing construction of the Mustang reduced drag, but it also contributed to a tendency to stall at low speed under 82mph, while the arrester cables could not be successfully snared at speeds above 90mph. There was little room for error, and Elder remembered: "From the start, it was obvious to everyone that the margin between the stall speed and the speed imposed by the arrester gear was very limited." In addition, landing altitude had to be meticulously managed to avoid damage even to the reinforced airframe, while the pilot had difficulty with rudder control during high angle attack dispositions and at low speed.

With such challenges existing, the ETF-51D was ready for actual sea trials by October 1944, and transferred to the deck of the Essex-class aircraft carrier USS *Shangri-La*. Lieutenant Elder performed the first ETF-51D carrier landing off the Virginia Capes on November 15, 1944, and completed four successful take offs and landings that day. Elder wrote: "Made all carrier landings at the speed of 85mph. Luckily, the Mustang reacted well, even in the most delicate situations. One just had to use the throttle wisely."

A total of only 25 launches and landings were completed during the sea trials, and despite the apparent capability of the P-51, Elder remained concerned with its suitability for the complexities of carrier operations. Engineers at North American Aviation also produced carrier-based designs with the P-51H, the last Mustang production variant, designating it the NAA-133, but no progress was made beyond the drawings.

Regardless, by the spring of 1945, US Marines and Army troops had seized the islands of Iwo Jima and Okinawa, closer to the Japanese home islands, and within range of land-based fighter planes. Therefore, the window of opportunity was closed on Project Seahorse.

POST WORLD WAR TWO AND KOREA

Allied pilots flew P-51 Mustangs in 213,873 sorties during World War Two, and the type's tally of 4,950 enemy planes destroyed was second only to the famed Grumman F6F Hellcat carrier-based fighter that achieved mastery of the air in the Pacific.

The Mustang's deployment during the war had been an international affair. Flight Lieutenant Warren Peglar of the Royal Canadian Air Force was seconded to the US Army Air Forces' 354th Fighter Squadron and became Canada's most successful P-51 pilot, sometimes flying the Mustang nicknamed *Iowa Beaut*. He shot down two German Me-109s on September 11, 1944, and claimed two more German planes on August 3.

Polish ace Eugeniusz Horbaczewski shot down an Fw-190, an Me-109, and four V-1 Buzz Bombs flying the Mustang Mk III while leading Polish No 315 Squadron RAF. He landed his Mustang and borrowed a Jeep from some American troops nearby to rescue a downed squadron mate Warrant Officer T Tamowicz, flying back to base with the wounded pilot. With 16½ aerial victories, he was killed in action in August 1944 after shooting down three Fw-190s. Although the circumstance is not known, it is believed he was shot down by a German pilot of Jagdgeschwader (Fighter Wing) 26.

Norwegian ace Lieutenant Colonel Werner Christie flew a Mustang

LEFT: Squadron Leader Eugeniusz Horbaczewski of Polish No 315 Squadron RAF stands beside his Mustang Mk III. Public Domain

LEFT: Norwegian Mustang ace Werner Christie stands on the wing of a Spitfire fighter. He later flew the Mustang Mk IV during World War Two. Creative Commons Backer, Ole Friele via Wikipedia

Mk IV with a distinctive red spinner, yellow leading edges on his wings, and leader pennant streaming while commanding the Hunsdon Wing. His initials were emblazoned on the Mustang's fuselage, and he is believed to have scored the last RAF Mustang kill by an ace during World War Two, downing an Fw-190 in early 1945. He was shot down and captured on April 18, after flaming 11 German aircraft during his combat career.

There were others, however. The Mustang was rapidly growing obsolescent with the development of the jet fighter. Nevertheless, the fledgling nation of Israel, born in 1948, defended itself against a coalition of Arab countries »

LEFT: F-51 Mustangs fly low over North Korean territory during the summer of 1951. Public Domain

during its war for independence. The tiny Israeli Air Force acquired a few P-51s, and their pilots are believed to have scored at least a couple of aerial victories. During the Sinai incident in 1956, Israeli Mustangs attacked Egyptian ground forces, reportedly destroying at least a dozen tanks. But 10 Mustangs were lost to ground fire.

When the army of communist North Korea crossed the 38th parallel in June 1950, invading neighbouring South Korea, the juggernaut threatened to overrun the country. The United Nations authorised intervention on behalf of South Korea, but available air forces were initially limited. Five American F-82 Twin Mustangs based in Japan flew into action on June 27, 1950, two days after the communist invasion.

They engaged North Korean Yakovlev Yak -9 fighters and shot down three. Along with the F-82s were a few Lockheed F-80 Shooting Star fighters flying from Japan. Pilots of both types did their best in ground support and reconnaissance missions, but their numbers were few and distance limited time over targets and ordnance loads.

Capability and reliability

Meanwhile, as the US Air Force redesignated its fighters from P for 'pursuit' to F for 'fighter', most of its F-51 Mustangs had been turned over to National Guard and Air Force Reserve squadrons in the United States. Though fast becoming outmoded, the F-51 did possess long range capability and reliability that was needed at primitive airfields in South Korea. F-51s were gathered and shipped across the Pacific on the deck of the aircraft carrier USS *Boxer*.

When they arrived, the Mustangs flew many missions against North Korean ground troops and armoured formations. Thick dust threatened to clog the engines and fuel lines of the planes, and the heat was oppressive, but the F-51s stayed in the air, engaging Yak-9s in air-to-air combat. The United Nations pilots did encounter the Soviet-built Mikoyan Gurevich MiG-15 jet fighter, which mounted 23mm and 37mm cannon, and found themselves immediately at a distinct disadvantage. Still, they persevered and executed strafing and ground support missions, dropping bombs and napalm. Among the active US groups was the 51st Fighter Interceptor Wing, based at Okinawa, then airfields in both Japan and South Korea.

The Royal Australian, South African, and South Korean air forces flew the F-51 in action during the Korean War as well, and the type proved a capable stopgap as these airmen awaited the arrival of the

North American F-86 Sabre and Gloster Meteor jet fighters. The Australians lost 10 pilots flying the F-51 to enemy action between July 1950 and April 1951. South African air casualties amounted to 12 killed in action and 30 missing. One South Korean pilot made a heroic decision when he found that his F-51 was damaged too extensively to make the return flight to his base. He chose to crash his Mustang into a North Korean T-34/85 tank. Mustang ground attacks were highly effective, and on December 28, 1950, one intense aerial pasting caused a group of 100 Chinese soldiers to throw up their hands in surrender.

The Mustang was clearly more vulnerable in the skies over Korea than it had been anywhere else in its relatively short combat history. Edward Schmued, the F-51's chief designer at North American Aviation in the early 1940s, realised that it was difficult to expect Mustang airmen to do battle with the new jets. He commented on its use in Korea: "Unfortunately, the P-51 was a high-altitude fighter. It was used in ground support work, which is hopeless, because one .30-calibre bullet can rip a hole in the radiator, and you fly two more minutes before your engine freezes up. Flying a P-51 in ground support was almost a suicide mission. It is unfortunate that the airplane had to be used for ground support, but in the Korean conflict we were short of airplanes, and anything had to do. This was the reason for using the P-51 in low-level operations."

The first F-51 aerial victories of the Korean War were recorded on June 29, 1950, when Lieutenant Orrin Fox shot down two of four communist Yak-9s destroyed that day. Fox transitioned to the Lockheed F-80 Shooting Star with the 80th Fighter Bomber Squadron and died on September 2, 1950, when his jet failed to pull out of a dive during a

mission near Chinju, South Korea. The last air-to-air kill recorded by the F-51 occurred on June 20, 1951, when Lieutenant J G Harrison shot down an enemy Yak-9, but on that same day a MiG-15 shot down a Mustang.

One F-51 pilot received the Medal of Honor for heroism in Korea. Major Louis Sebille, commander of the 67th Fighter Bomber Squadron, was wounded seriously and his Mustang heavily damaged during a strafing run against an enemy column on August 5, 1950. Sebille, a veteran bomber pilot of World War Two, crashed his crippled plane into the enemy concentration on the ground. He had been advised to attempt an emergency landing at an airstrip at Taegu, but responded, "No, I'll never make it. I'm going back and get that bastard." Sebille fired his six remaining rockets, and as his machine guns chattered, he did not release his bomb, but struck an enemy armoured personnel carrier. The resulting blast did tremendous damage to the North Korean column, and two half-tracks were believed to also have been destroyed on impact.

Significant advantage

One significant advantage that veteran American pilots had in the Korean War was prior combat experience, much of it gained in the Mustang. One of the most proficient of these veteran pilots was Colonel William Whisner, who had flown as wingman to the Mustang ace of aces, Major George Preddy, in the European theatre with the 487th Fighter Squadron. Whisner had become an ace in a day on November 21, 1944, claiming six German Focke Wulf Fw-190 fighters destroyed in the air and a seventh damaged. On January 1, 1945, during the response to Luftwaffe Operation Bodenplatte, he shot down four more German planes in a single engagement. Whisner ended World War Two with

15½ confirmed air-to-air kills, 14½ of these while flying the P-51.

During the Korean War, Whisner deployed in September 1951 with the 334th Fighter Interceptor Squadron, 4th Fighter Interceptor Wing. Flying the F-86, Whisner shot down two MiG-15s. He transferred to the 25th Fighter Interceptor Squadron, 51st Fighter Interceptor Wing in November and shot down 4½ MiG-15s while damaging two others. He became the first Korean War ace of the 51st Fighter Wing with six kills and one of only seven American fighter pilots to achieve ace status in two different conflicts. Undoubtedly, his experience flying the P-51 in Europe had given him a competitive edge in the life and death contest of fighter combat.

Whisner received three Distinguished Service Crosses during his career, remained in the US Air Force until 1972, and commanded the 48th Tactical Fighter Wing. He retired after 30 years of active duty and died at the age of 65 on July 21, 1989, due to complications from an insect sting.

As more jet fighters arrived in Korea, the role of the F-51 was primarily ground attack. Those missions incurred significant losses at times and were discontinued in January 1953, months before the armistice ending the war was concluded. A total of 335 F-51D Mustangs were shot down during the Korean War, and 264 pilots were killed or listed as missing in action. Ten of the losses were due to enemy fighter action, while the vast majority – 172 – were lost to enemy anti-aircraft during those hazardous ground attack missions. The circumstances surrounding the loss of 44 Mustangs could not be reliably determined, and the rest were scrapped following accidents.

When the Americans discontinued F-51 combat missions in Korea, those aircraft that remained were passed to the South Korean Air Force. The South Koreans continued to operate them until 1957.

ABOVE: A youthful William Whisner sits in the cockpit of a P-47 Thunderbolt fighter during World War Two. He later flew the P-51 and became an ace in a day. Public Domain

FAR LEFT: William Whisner indicates multiple kills as he climbs from the cockpit of his P-51 Mustang. Public Domain

LEFT: Major Louis Sebille received a posthumous Medal of Honor for heroism while flying the F-51 during the Korean War. Public Domain

MODERN MUSTANG

After thundering across the skies of war-torn Europe and establishing itself as the premier propeller-driven fighter plane of World War Two, the P-51 Mustang continued in the service of air forces around the world. For some years, it became engaged in other conflicts, most notably the Korean War.

The Mustang served with the air forces of no fewer than 29 nations during and after World War Two. Many of these fighter planes were sold by the US government for nominal prices, although the wartime cost to produce a single P-51D and topped $51,000. The Royal Canadian Air Force operated the F-51 into the early 1960s in special duty roles, while the Philippine Air Force operated the type into the

1980s. The F-51 was the first aircraft of the Philippines' air demonstration team formed in 1953. The Dominican Republic was the last nation to maintain the F-51 in service. After acquiring six aircraft from the United States in 1948 and 44 planes from Sweden in the same year, the country discontinued its use in 1984 and sold the last of its 10 serviceable examples to American collectors by 1988.

The US government sold war surplus P-51s to individuals for as little as $1,500. Many of these were kept by collectors enamoured by the plane's combat record. Others were modified for air racing. Stunt pilot Paul Mantz purchased a P-51 and named it *Blaze of Noon*, modifying the wings to create large fuel tanks and capturing first place in the 1946 and 1947 Bendix Air Races, second place in 1948, and third place the following year. He also established a time record flying across the United States coast to coast in the plane in 1947.

Mantz sold the P51C to Charles F Blair Jr, who changed the plane's name to *Excalibur III* and set a New York to London time record of seven hours, 48 minutes in 1951. He also made a flight from Norway to Alaska, crossing the North Pole and covering 3,130 miles. He was awarded the Harmon Trophy as the world's outstanding aviator. *Excalibur III* is now on display at the Smithsonian's National Air and Space Museum in Washington, DC.

Many surviving P-51s were converted for post-war civilian use by Trans-Florida Aviation, which later became the Cavalier Aircraft Corporation. Modifications introduced included wingtip fuel tanks and a larger vertical stabiliser. Some conversions included a passenger seat that occupies the space where radio equipment and a fuselage fuel tank were placed in the military configuration.

By 2011, the US Federal Aviation Administration registry included 204 privately-owned P-51 Mustangs. Many of these are still airworthy and serve as frequent visitors to air shows or other special events, thrilling audiences with the roar of the engines and spirited flights. Today, the cost of a fully operational Mustang may reach more than $2.5 million. In the spring of 2013, a Mustang nicknamed *The Rebel* set an altitude record for piston-engine aircraft, reaching 42,500 feet, shattering the previous record of 36,902 feet that had stood since 1954.

The Mustang airframe last saw combat when Cavalier aircraft were retrofitted for military use and flew during the brief so-called Soccer War between Honduras and El Salvador in 1969.

The Mustang mystique is alive and well today, a testament to the enduring qualities of an iconic aircraft.

LEGEND OF THE MUSTANG

For the Allies, winning the air war in Europe in World War Two was a monumental task. The Luftwaffe was a formidable foe, its fighter pilots hardened by many months of unrelenting aerial combat. The 'experten', as some German pilots were known, flew outstanding fighter planes, the Messerschmitt Me-109 and Focke Wulf Fw-190 foremost among them. They had also flown countless hours of combat missions, and many had compiled aerial victory tolls of well over 100 Allied planes.

The days of reckoning, however, finally came. Allied fighter strength in the West steadily grew, while the Royal Air Force bombed Germany by night and the US Army Air Forces by day. Inevitably, Allied industrial might and the intrepidity of the pilots in their cockpits would prevail in a war of attrition in the skies over Europe. By late 1943, the aerial hammer that would nail the Luftwaffe coffin shut was arriving in quantity.

The North American P-51 Mustang was the epitome of propeller-driven fighter aircraft. Agile in the air, a swift and reliable gun platform in ground attack and strafing, a long-range escort fighter capable of shepherding bomber formations on raids deep inside Germany, and a superb air superiority fighter, the Mustang was lethal in the hands of a trained Allied pilot.

As the fortunes of war in the air turned against the Luftwaffe, many of its fighter squadrons were transferred from the Eastern Front to the west to combat the growing numbers of Allied bombers and fighters dropping tons of explosives on German cities and taking a heavy toll in German planes and pilots. Luftwaffe Lieutenant Colonel Kurt Bühligen, however, was a realist. He knew those air units and pilots relocating from east to west were in for an awakening.

With 174 air victories to his credit, Bühligen ended the war as a fighter wing commander, leading Jagdgeschwader 2 'Richthofen'. He said of the transfers: "I don't remember anyone who came to us from the east who survived. These fellows simply had no comprehension of what we were faced with in the air."

Another Luftwaffe ace, Lieutenant Colonel Heinz Bär, who shot down at least 208 Allied aircraft east and west, asserted that the Mustang was 'perhaps the most difficult of all Allied aircraft to meet in combat. It was fast, manoeuvrable, hard to ≫

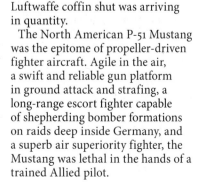

RIGHT: American soldiers inspect the wreckage of a German twin-engine Messerschmitt Me-110 fighter destroyed on the ground. Public Domain

ABOVE: Shot down in the Pacific, a Japanese Mitsubishi A6M Zero fighter lies derelict in the jungle. Public Domain

see, and difficult to identify because it resembled the 109'.

Not an easy flier

Although the Mustang was an outstanding performer, particularly in the types combined with the British Rolls-Royce Merlin engine that gave it superior performance at high altitude, the plane was not the easiest to fly, prone to instability with a centre of gravity that was influenced by the load of fuel it carried. A full fuel load made the aircraft somewhat slow and sluggish. Then, for all its power the Merlin engine was liquid cooled, which made it more vulnerable to damage than contemporary air-cooled engines. A single hit from a German cannon shell or bullet was likely to cause coolant lines or radiators to rupture. When that happened, the pilot had only moments left in the air.

Some analysts also argue that the P-51 was under gunned with four .50-calibre wing mounted machine guns, later increased to six with 1,880 rounds of ammunition in the D variant. Still, the ammunition supply could be depleted in as little as 21 seconds of firing. Further, early Mustangs were criticised for their lack of pilot visibility as the cockpit canopy created blind spots. Nevertheless, the introduction of the P-51 B and C models changed the course of World War Two. The modifications of the P-51D addressed firepower with more

RIGHT: Gear down, a P-51 Mustang comes in for a landing during the 2022 Royal International Air Tattoo. Creative Commons Airwolfhound via Wikipedia

machine guns and the visibility deficit with the bubble canopy.

Still, when the Mustang was readied for battle and the pilot took the plane aloft, he was continually aware that he was flying a thoroughbred with control and balance that were so smooth that flying the plane became second nature. One P-51 pilot explained: "You don't fly this plane. You wear it." In its first eight weeks of combat, pilots flying the P-51B shot down just over 13.1 German planes for every 100 sorties, a kill rate nearly three times higher than the Lockheed P-38 Lightning and nearly five times that of the Republic P-47 Thunderbolt.

An early report on the Mustang's performance praised its airworthiness. "Below 22,000ft the P-51 has the best all-around fighting qualities of any fighter." Such a statement was indeed noteworthy given the performance of other legendary Allied fighters, including the Supermarine Spitfire, the P-38, and the P-47. When the P-51D was introduced in mid-1944, it made a lethal fighter that much more deadly. Top speed was increased from roughly 386mph to 440mph and the service ceiling extended from 34,000ft to more than 43,000ft.

The Mustang made its impact in virtually every aspect of aerial warfare, ground attack, reconnaissance, high altitude escort, and air superiority. Its presence in company with heavy bombers of

the Eighth Air Force over Germany compelled the Nazis to face the stark reality that the war was lost.

After Reichsmarschall Hermann Göring, chief of the Luftwaffe, was taken into Allied custody in 1945, he was questioned by General Carl Spaatz, commander of US Strategic Air Forces in Europe. "When did you realise that the Luftwaffe was losing control of the air?" Spaatz asked.

"When the American long-range fighters were able to escort the bombers as far as Hanover. It was not long before they got to Berlin," replied Göring. "The reason for the failure of the Luftwaffe against the Allied air forces was the success of the American air forces in putting out a long-range escort fighter plane which enabled the bombers to penetrate deep into Reich territory and still have a constant and strong fighter cover. Without this escort, the air offensive would never have succeeded."

Göring's statement is borne out by the facts. Not only was the P-51 a war-winning escort fighter, but also a destroyer of the Luftwaffe air defence. On April 24, 1944, in the skies over Germany and occupied Europe, Mustangs shot down 64 German planes and destroyed 21 on the ground while 12 P-51s were lost. On May 12, three Mustangs were lost in exchange for 33 German fighters blown out of the sky and five destroyed on the ground. A week later, P-51 pilots shot down 41 enemy planes and destroyed four on the ground as 11 Mustangs were shot down.

Clearly, the Germans could not sustain such heavy losses in planes and experienced pilots. The air war was lost when Nazi pilots were slaughtered in the skies by Allied airmen flying the P-51 Mustang.

The legend of the Mustang, therefore, was earned in the crucible of battle. The fighter simply became synonymous with victory. In flight, the roar of its Merlin engine and the sleek silhouette of its aerodynamic frame were sights and sounds to behold.

The North American P-51 Mustang, then, has flown into history with an unmatched and terrible beauty.